The Constitution
and American Political
Development

The Constitution and American Political Development

★

An Institutional Perspective

EDITED BY

PETER F. NARDULLI

★

UNIVERSITY OF ILLINOIS PRESS

Urbana and Chicago

Publication of this book was supported in part by a grant from the College of Liberal Arts and Sciences at the University of Illinois at Urbana-Champaign.

© 1992 by the Board of Trustees of the University of Illinois
Manufactured in the United States of America
1 2 3 4 5 C P 5 4 3 2 1

This book is printed on acid-free paper.

Library of Congress Cataloging-in-Publication Data

The Constitution and American political development : an institutional
perspective / edited by Peter F. Nardulli.
    p. cm.
    Revisions of papers originally presented at a conference sponsored
by the University of Illinois in December 1987.
    Includes bibliographical references and index.
    ISBN 0-252-01787-0 (cl. : alk. paper).—ISBN 0-252-06174-8 (pb. :
alk. paper)
    1. United States—Constitutional history.   I. Nardulli, Peter F.
II. University of Illinois at Urbana-Champaign.
JK21.C72 1992
320.973—dc20   90-25602
                                                                CIP

Contents

Preface

This book is a collection of original essays on the role of the U.S. Constitution in the development of American political institutions. It represents a marriage between neo-institutionalism and the renewed interest in the U.S. Constitution spurred by the bicentennial. A fundamental issue that needs to be addressed within the new institutionalism is the role of the Constitution in American politics. The Constitution embodies the structural design for American political institutions. To understand these institutions fully, one must begin with their constitutional roots and examine the Constitution's impact on their development.

By viewing the Constitution as an independent force in American politics and integrating it with the renewed interest in institutionalism, this book differs significantly from much of the scholarship on the Constitution that proliferated in the bicentennial period. Much of this literature has an historical-legalistic hue. There is a marked tendency to view the Constitution as an organic whole upon which external forces act. As such these works follow the traditional paradigm in constitutional studies. This body of literature has long been concerned with the evolution of the Constitution (or parts thereof) and the impact of social, economic, and political factors on its development. Was a constitutional provision interpreted in a particular case in a manner consistent with the text of the Constitution? With the intent of the framers? Does a line of precedent constitute a constitutional doctrine or change in a doctrine? What are the factors that led to the establishment and evolution of that doctrine?

No one could deny the importance of these traditional concerns. The smooth functioning of the American political system depends on the continued evolution of constitutional doctrine; the legitimacy of that system depends on the nature of the evolutionary process. But scholars' preoccupation with constitutional development has led them to ignore its role in structuring American political development. This is unfortunate because fundamental issues exist in this field of inquiry. Despite the relative constancy of its constitutional framework, no political scholar would claim the American political system has remained unchanged over the course of its history. Does this mean that the American political system is unbounded, that the Constitution has exerted no significant force on political development? If the Constitution can be said to have exerted some independent developmental force, has it channeled institutional development in a manner consistent with the broad aims of the framers? If so, how? Have unrecognized subtleties of its complex structure led to unintended and unforeseen developments? How have historical developments interacted with constitutional factors to mold political development?

The immensity of these questions makes it impossible to answer them definitively; their importance requires that we begin. To do this a conference was sponsored by the University of Illinois in December, 1987, to which recognized American politics scholars, not constitutional experts, were invited. We were most concerned with the impact of constitutional factors on the development of national political institutions (Congress, the presidency, the bureaucracy, and the Supreme Court), political institutions in the penumbra of the Constitution (political parties and interest groups), and federalism. Scholars in each of these areas were asked to address the issues raised here using whatever perspective and methodology they thought most appropriate. The result was a set of original essays that blended historical and comparative approaches with explicitly political perspectives into an analysis of their respective domains.

This volume contains highly refined versions of the papers presented at this conference. As a whole they represent a unique perspective on constitutionalism in American politics and its impact on American political development. They should stimulate new thinking on the role and importance of the Constitution in American politics and reintegrate it into mainstream political research.

Acknowledgments

A number of individuals made important contributions to the conference from which this volume emerged and to the volume itself. William Prokasy, former dean of the College of Liberal Arts and Sciences at the University of Illinois, supported the conference and the publication of this volume. Roger Kanet, former head of the Department of Political Science, played a crucial role in appointing a committee to organize the conference and in both prodding and supporting the committee in its efforts to complete its tasks. The planning committee consisted of Ira Carmen, Peter Nardulli, and Frederick Wirt. While Nardulli and Wirt assumed the primary organizational responsibilities for the conference, they were greatly assisted by Susan Hanson, Merrily Shaw, and Janie Carroll of the Department of Political Science. Others helpful in planning and organizing the conference included Winton Solberg, Robert Sutton, and William Widenor of the Department of History, Gerhard Casper of the University of Chicago, and John Hope Franklin of Duke University.

A variety of other individuals contributed to the execution of the conference. Walter Murphy of Princeton University presented a thought-provoking keynote address to initiate the conference; Robert Weissberg, Frederick Wirt, and Samuel Gove served as panel chairs; Winton Solberg, Rein Staal, Wallace Farnham, Dianne Pinderhughes, and Carol Mock served as paper discussants. The paper givers dutifully integrated the comments from these discussants, one another, and various anonymous reviewers into the essays presented in this volume.

Shirley Burnette and Lorena McClain performed admirably, as usual, in the preparation of various drafts of the manuscript. The efforts of Larry Malley, now at Duke University Press, and Richard Wentworth of the University of Illinois Press in seeing this project to completion should also be acknowledged, as well as the admirable efforts of Jane Mohraz, who edited the manuscript and shepherded it through the publication process.

Introduction

CHAPTER

★ 1 ★

The Constitution and American Politics: A Developmental Perspective

PETER F. NARDULLI

An important but much neglected concern in the study of the Constitution is its effect on the development of the American political system. A fundamental tenet of American constitutionalism is that its founding document both empowers and limits government. It defines the social contract, provides public activity with its unique flavor and character, and controls the latent potential for abuse. The Constitution is so fundamental to the structure of the American political system that its developmental significance seems axiomatic. Indeed, constitutional scholars' more traditional concern with the forces that affect constitutional evolution and interpretation can be viewed as a testament to the ascribed importance of the Constitution for American political development.

Viewed differently, however, constitutional evolution can be seen as undermining the developmental significance of the Constitution. How can an instrument that is continually unfolding be an independent force in the development of other political institutions? To the extent that both the Constitution and its institutional creations are continually unfolding, would not it be more appropriate to attribute political change to the more fundamental forces shaping constitutional evolution? Questions such as these have made it fashionable over the past several decades to discount the political significance of such institutional factors as the Constitution. Political scientists often view the field of public law as being outside the ambit of American politics; the Constitution is usually relegated to the "black box" of the political system. That black box too frequently becomes a black hole, as scholars fixate on the actors and forces that swirl around it before being sucked into its vortex.

As political scholars become more aware of the institutional context of politics, the costs of relegating the Constitution to this black
hole become more obvious. This is especially true with respect to
its developmental consequences. Political institutions must adapt
to changing social and economic conditions. Yet change is difficult
even within the simplest of political settings; powerful groups with
a vested interest in the political status quo have existed throughout
history. Political change is even more difficult to achieve in a constitutional government, especially when constitutionalism is a fundamental political value. The government's founding document
defines the relationship between the citizens and the government
and limits the sphere and structure of governmental activities.
Once a government is constitutionally defined, modifications in formal institutions and structures are constrained—regardless of the
level of societal consensus for political change. While a failure to
adapt could be destabilizing, unconstrained changes would undermine the system's legitimacy and could erode the moral force of
the Constitution.

In a political system such as that in the United States, the relationship between the Constitution and political development is
thus important and complex. The following essays address some of
the issues in this relationship and provide important insights into
the Constitution's various roles in American political development.
They employ historical and comparative approaches to examine the
impact of the Constitution. This essay simply addresses some preliminary issues involved in assessing the Constitution's roles in the
developmental process. It begins with an analysis of the factors
clouding the formative roles of the Constitution. Next, it under-
takes a reassessment of the Constitution's developmental roles and
extends that reassessment to some broad developmental questions.
Finally, a conceptual overview of constitutional influences on institutional development is provided, with illustrations drawn from the
essays in this volume.

Ambiguity in the Developmental Role
of the Constitution

To question the impact of the Constitution on American political
development appears heretical, particularly considering the situation
that existed in Europe at the time the U.S. Constitution was adopted.
In many eighteenth-century European nations, governmental insti-

tutions and procedures had evolved, fitfully at times, out of the needs and structure of feudal society. They seem to have existed for as long as most could recall, and therein lay the source of their legitimacy. In contrast, the U.S. government resulted from a conscious effort by an assembly of distinguished statesmen to create a workable political system that met the needs of American society, as Madison noted in *Federalist No. 38*. The U.S. Constitution was the product of that effort. Since political legitimacy depends on conformity with constitutional principles and provisions, that document's role in American political development would seem self-evident. Reinforcing this perspective is the fact that the federal judiciary has exercised—for the better part of two centuries—the power to invalidate activities and developments it deems unconstitutional.

Despite the seminal role of the Constitution in the creation of the American governmental system, an examination of the current political landscape gives rise to considerable skepticism concerning its developmental impact. Such an examination reveals few parallels between the government of the late eighteenth century and the late twentieth century, except those of a very superficial nature. How can such historical differences exist in the face of a largely unchanged constitutional framework, if that framework constrains institutional change? Two explanations are plausible here, both of which undermine the developmental significance of the Constitution. The first concerns constitutional ambiguity and the evolutionary process by which those ambiguities are resolved. The second involves the implications of what some would contend was a very limited political presence of the Constitution during the formative years of the Republic.

Constitutional Ambiguity and Evolution

A certain level of ambiguity in a document such as a constitution is unavoidable and to some extent desirable. The ambiguity of key provisions of the U.S. Constitution has permitted it to breathe with history and undoubtedly accounts for its longevity, but it is the same ambiguity that obscures the Constitution's role in American political development. Exacerbating the impact of unavoidable textual ambiguity were the behavior and views of political leaders in the formative years of the Republic. Instead of creating a tradition of strict constructionism, they created precedents for taking license with the constitutional text. Constitutionalism yielded to pragmatism as Thomas Jefferson, John Marshall, James Monroe, and Andrew Jackson tried to deal with such issues as the Louisiana Purchase, judicial review, federally supported internal improvements, and the controversy over a national bank. In addition, James Madison's constitutional judgments on the relationship between the nation and the states underwent several changes in the four decades following the Convention.

The ambiguity that has obscured the Constitution's role in American political development also can be seen in the changing metaphors that have been used to characterize the Constitution and its relation to society (Kammen, 1986:16–22). These metaphorical changes reveal how constitutional malleability has enabled perceptions of it to evolve, thus allowing it to accommodate new demands on government. This malleability, of course, further contributes to questions concerning the independence of its developmental role.

The earliest of these metaphors, routinely invoked around the time of the Convention by such luminaries as Benjamin Franklin and John Marshall and later by Daniel Webster, was that of an "instrument" of government. Thomas Jefferson, in his inaugural address, invoked the image of the Constitution as the sheet anchor of the ship of state, a device that could be used to stabilize the ship and rein it in during stormy times. The sheet anchor analogy did not become common until after the Civil War, partly in rebuttal to Thomas Babington Macaulay's 1857 diatribe that the American Constitution was "all sail and no anchor." Like the instrumental conception, it stressed the restrictive facets of the constitutional text. A Newtonian conception of the Constitution based on David Hume's view of the world as a great machine replaced the anchor metaphor within a quarter of a century. Michael Kammen quotes an 1888 address by James Russell Lowell that captures this notion with vivid imagery: "After our Constitution got fairly into working order it really seemed as if we had invented a machine that would go of itself, and this begot a faith in our luck which even the civil war itself but momentarily disturbed. Circumstances continued favorable, and our prosperity went on increasing. I admire the splendid complacency of my countrymen, and find something exhilarating and inspiring in it. We are a nation which has *struck il* [sic], but we are also a nation that is sure the well will never run dry" (1986:18). The next constitutional metaphor emerged in the early twentieth century. It was an organic conception with Darwinian overtones that emerged in the writings of such juristic giants as Oliver Wendell Holmes, Benjamin Cardozo, and Felix Frankfurter and such political leaders as Theodore Roosevelt and Woodrow Wilson. It viewed the Constitution as an integrated organic whole that slowly grew to meet the needs of an ever-changing nation.

The implications of the Newtonian and Darwinian metaphors for understanding the Constitution's role in American political development are significant. If the Constitution were "a machine that would go of itself," constitutional ambiguity and interpretation would be less of a problem. The Newtonian conception suggests an internal logic that clarifies ambiguities and determines the course of constitutional development. These principles of operation dictate how the machine of government should work. They can be used by jurists and other political leaders to determine the constitutionally appropriate response to issues as they arise. The constitutional path of political development can be made clear and its independent effect can be determined.

An organic, Darwinian view, however, suggests a different process of constitutional evolution that contributes to the ambiguity of the Constitution's developmental role. Justice Holmes in *Missouri v. Holland* nicely illustrates these difficulties:

> When we are dealing with words that also are a constituent act, like the Constitution of the United States, we must realize that they have called into life a being the development of which could not have been foreseen completely by the most gifted of its begetters. It was enough for them to realize or to hope that they had created an organism; it has taken a century and has cost their successors much sweat and blood to prove that they created a nation. The case before us must be considered in the light of our whole experience and not merely in that of what was said a hundred years ago [1920:421].

If constitutional issues are examined in light of our entire experience, then purely mechanical principles do not dictate constitutional evolution. Rather, the possibility exists that political, economic, and social considerations play an important part in such matters. This possibility, of course, obscures the role of purely constitutional factors in the formation and operation of the political process; it suggests that, in at least some instances, environmental forces may overwhelm constitutional constraints and dictates.

What makes these possibilities troubling is that few today view the Constitution as "a machine that would go of itself." If mechanical principles of operation and interpretation exist for the Constitution, the most learned jurists and legal scholars have yet to discover them. Moreover, few who have traced the evolution of constitutional doctrines would deny the relevance of social, political, and economic influences. Thus, instead of the Constitution's being driven by its own internal logic and principles, the pulls and pressures of external forces have played a part in doctrinal growth.

Early Constitutional Presence

What reinforces the importance of arguments based on ambiguity and the nature of evolutionary process is historical evidence suggesting that the political presence of the Constitution on the American scene was slow in developing. The political institutions it created had to struggle with preexisting centers of public authority—state political systems—that were loathe to cede power to their fledgling competitor, or at least no more than was incumbent after a strict reading of the document. Upon ratification, the Constitution did not immediately enjoy the type of moral authority it has today. Its theories, concepts, and institutions could not be turned to as binding authority in the resolution of disputes and political crises.

The slow emergence of a strong constitutional presence left a political vacuum that permitted greater play for extraconstitutional forces, enhancing their role in shaping our notions of American constitutional government. The absence of a strong constitutional presence in the early years of the Republic can be seen in the smoldering controversy over the nature of the Union, in the reach of national lawmaking authority, and in the low regard with which the federal judiciary was held.[1]

The slow emergence of a constitutional presence on the national political landscape is reflected not only in the early resistance to its institutions but also in the slow acceptance of the Constitution as a national symbol. Kammen's (1986) cultural history underscores the ambivalence surrounding the Constitution during the early years of the Republic. But, although there was some initial opposition to the Constitution, as well as some uncertainty and apprehension, it was soon viewed as a document that was well suited to American needs. As the Constitution became associated with political stability and economic prosperity in the post–Civil War era, it came to be viewed as "a masterpiece, applicable to every country" (Kammen, 1986:22). The "cult of the Constitution" probably reached its early apex at the time of the centennial and, since then, has enjoyed immense stature as the symbolic representation of

American democracy and politics. It is difficult however, to discount the impact of external influences on American government during this century-long gestation period, which contributes to the problematic nature of the Constitution's developmental role.

The Constitution and American Politics: A Reconceptualization

Taken at face value, the implications emerging from constitutional ambiguity, evolution, and presence are profound. They suggest that the governmental framework embodied in the Constitution exerted little independent influence on the structure and evolution of American politics. According to this view, the Constitution's ambiguity and adaptability make it little more than an integrated set of conduits through which more fundamental forces exert their influence on American politics, encountering little resistance along the way. Before embracing this view, however, we should be aware that it rests on a certain conceptualization of politics and the Constitution. Neither conceptualization is beyond criticism, and alternatives exist. An assessment of these critiques and alternatives can shed new light on the Constitution in American political development.

Politics, Political Values, and Neo-institutionalism

The conception of politics underlying the analysis presented above stresses the importance of individual actors and the role of social and economic factors as they are manifested in the activities of groups outside the government. That analysis thus falls prey to an emerging set of criticisms aimed at prevailing approaches to political research. The essence of these critiques is that politics cannot be reduced to a set of interactions among competing groups that pressure governmental actors. Equally important are political ideals and moral values, as well as the force of governmental institutions. These institutions embody value commitments, and their structures and mechanisms represent vested interests of important political actors. Political institutions can therefore mold external influences and constrain individual actors.

Samuel P. Huntington has written eloquently and persuasively on the importance of ideals and values in American politics: "To see American politics purely as a reflection of social structure is to miss the teleological—as distinguished from the mechanistic—dimension of that politics" (1981:11). In critiquing the inadequacy of what he terms "structural paradigms," he noted:

> They omit almost entirely the role that political ideas and idealism, moral causes, and creedal passions have played in American politics. Almost everyone agrees that the United States was conceived in terms of certain political ideals and inspired by the promise or dream of liberty and equality. These political ideals are central to American national identity and have played a critical role in shaping American political evolution and development. . . . The structural paradigms portray an American politics without purpose, without moral conflict, without passion, without promise, and most importantly, without guilt [1981:10].

In a complementary vein, James G. March and Johan P. Olsen have noted:

> From a behavioral point of view, formally organized social institutions have come to be portrayed simply as arenas within which political behavior, driven by more fundamental factors, occurs. From a normative point of view, ideas that embedded morality in institutions, such as law or bureaucracy, and that emphasized citizenship as a foundation for personal identity, have given way to ideas of moral individualism and an emphasis on conflicting interests. . . . Without denying the importance of both the social context of politics and the motives of individual actors, the new institutionalism insists on a more autonomous role for political institutions. The state is not only affected by society but also affects it. . . . Political democracy depends not only on economic and social conditions *but also on the design of political institutions* [1984:734,738, emphasis added].

It should be clear that these views on the nature of politics are not necessarily new. Indeed, Huntington (1981:11) asserts that "patriotic" historians stressed the role of political ideas and values throughout much of the nineteenth century; it was their misunderstanding of the role of ideas and values that discredited their work. Likewise, not everyone accepts the neo-institutionalists' assertions that mainstream political science has entirely neglected the role of the state (Almond, 1988; Lowi, 1988). Nonetheless, few would deny that these developments reflect a current uneasiness with political paradigms that ignore or underplay the significance of the governmental fabric integrating political systems.

The Organic Constitution and a Marketplace Metaphor

In addition to the dangers of overemphasizing the effect of external forces in our view of politics, we should be sensitive to the implications of uncritically adopting the organic, Darwinian conceptions that have dominated our thinking about the Constitution for the better part of a century. They reinforce a bias in our views of the Constitution's developmental roles similar to that of group-oriented and individually oriented conceptions of politics. Underlying the organic conception is the notion that the Constitution breathed life into a viable, fully integrated organic structure, complete with an ascertainable gene structure. It also gives rise to visions of a virginal, idyllic governmental organism forced to adapt to the ravages of time and environment. The result is a genetic mutation bearing little resemblance to its original embodiment. This perspective focuses scholarly attention on those elements of the environment that led to the mutation; there is seldom much interest in explaining what is constant. Although this view of the Constitution facilitates the explanation of doctrinal evolution, it is less useful in understanding the role of the Constitution as an independent force in American politics. Simply stated, it understates the significance of constitutive factors in the developmental process.

Alternatively, we can think of the founders as having created a mechanism, rather than an organism, for dealing with the public and its problems in a balanced way. Here the Constitution is seen as having established an institutional network composed of competing power centers as a means of providing governmental capacity while minimizing the threat of tyranny. The development of this integrated network, however, is guided not by mechanistic, Newtonian principles inherent in the constitutional text but, as Bert A. Rockman (herein) suggests, by principles analogous to those governing the marketplace. The marketplace created by the interactions within this institutional network is by no means a purely competitive one in which alternative providers rationally pursue strategies aimed at maximizing institutional and personal goals. Using limited cognitive abilities and minimal information, institutional actors within this marketplace select their choices from a fairly narrow range of politically acceptable alternatives. More important, marketplace strategies are profoundly affected by a variety of constitutional provisions, structures, and values.

The Constitution endows alternative policy providers (Congress, the president, the courts, the states) with different roles, characteristics, and powers. These institutional traits interact with historical and political needs to determine a policy provider's role in the marketplace at a given time. Participation in the policy marketplace is also affected by the constitutional scheme (selection procedures, interinstitutional checks, and value commitments) used to ensure institutional compliance with constitutional roles. Over time, these marketplace activities become integral parts of a provider's operations, thereby affecting institutional development. Moreover, within the marketplace metaphor, we can view the resulting developments as part of the normal functioning of the constitutional framework, not as genetic mutations.[2]

The Constitution and Political Development Reconsidered: Some Brief Illustrations

Our primary concern here is to explore the implications of our reconceptualization of politics and the Constitution for *institutional* development, but it is clear that the perspective just laid out has implications for broader developmental concerns. A brief discussion of two such concerns will help illustrate the insights that can be generated by our reconceptualizations and will lay the groundwork for the discussion of institutional development. We will first examine the Constitution's impact on the development of cohesiveness within the early Republic and then consider its ongoing influence in stimulating political activity, shaping political inputs, and structuring outcomes.

Cohesiveness, Capacity, and the Constitution

In the marketplace metaphor, the slow acceptance of the Constitution, as well as the relatively minor role initially played by the central government, does not mean that the constitutional scheme was insignificant for early American political development. The fact that the policy marketplace was, for the most part, dominated by preexisting state providers only means that the institutional traits and resources they had to offer were more appropriate for the political demands and preferences of the time. An effort to establish a dominant, central provider would never have been acceptable to the existing providers. If one had somehow been imposed on them, interminable wars over political turf would undoubtedly have ensued, sapping the nation's energies and crippling, if not destroying, the Union.

The genius of the Constitution is that it created a network of providers, whose role in the marketplace would rise and fall with the needs and demands of the nation. These market principles made possible political development that minimized political discord, thereby promoting cohesiveness. This cohesiveness enhanced the economic capacity of the emerging nation, unleashing its burgeoning potential and channeling its energies and resources toward productive ends. The ensuing prosperity fostered the relative stability the nation enjoyed and reinforced in people's minds the benefits of the Union, at least until the ordeal of secession. Perhaps the most important insight from this ordeal for our purposes, however, is that enough people placed so much value on the Union that they fought a civil war to preserve it.

After that, the Constitution and the central government it had created emerged as greatly strengthened political entities. Central policy providers slowly began to dominate selected policy arenas and continued to broaden their market activities throughout the next century (Skowronek, 1982). This tremendous growth in the federal government, especially after 1932, is usually offered as evidence of the relative importance of social and economic factors in American political development. Although the role of these factors is undeniable, the general failure to recognize the independent significance of constitutional factors can be attributable to the prevalence of the organic metaphor. The monstrous federal monolith that is perceived to have emerged was viewed as a mutant form of the pristine creature that was brought to life by the Grand Convention. Unfortunately, this view ignores how the centralization of American government took place (a principal focus of the analysis of institutional development that follows) and the fact that it took place at all (the principal concern here). The Constitution played a profound role in both.

To appreciate its facilitating role, one need only contrast the American political experience with what might have been if the Constitution had failed. A more rigid governmental framework could well have made political relations between the central government and the states insufferable and impeded the provision of needed public policies. In that case, the costs of ongoing federal relations might well have outweighed the benefits of the Union. What is now the United States might well have developed as two or three independent nations. Would the continental economy have prospered as much if national markets were encumbered by the barriers of sovereignty? How different would the frontier experience have been if three nations had competed for the frontier? Would the experiment in liberal government have long survived in such a potentially hostile setting? The national experience would have been much different without the cohesiveness, stability, and prosperity the early nation enjoyed. To the extent that the Constitution contributed to this state of affairs, it has had a profound effect on the American political experience.[3]

The Constitution as Stimulator and Shaper

To understand the Constitution's role in stimulating political issues and shaping their resolution, it is necessary to turn again to Huntington's ideas on the importance of the American creed, the high level of consensus on important moral values and political ideals in the United States:

In the United States, ideological consensus is the source of political conflict, polarization occurs over moral issues rather than economic ones, and the politics of interest groups is supplemented and at times supplanted by the politics of moralistic reform. America has been spared class conflicts in order to have moral convulsions. . . . It is precisely the central role of moral passion that distinguishes American politics from the politics of most other societies, and it is this characteristic that is most difficult for foreigners to understand. . . . American history is the history of the efforts of groups to promote their interests by realizing American ideals. What is important, however, is not that they succeed but that they fail, not that the dream is realized but that it is not and never can be realized completely or satisfactorily [1981:11].

The components of the American creed are defined by Huntington as constitutionalism, individualism, liberty, equality, and democracy (1981:14). These values and ideals are important to American politics because in a very real sense they define what it is to be an American. Huntington recalls Carl Freidrich's observation:

" 'To be an American is an ideal, to be a Frenchman is a fact' " (1981:30). This view of Americanism suggests, of course, that there is an external standard of conduct against which Americans' behavior can be judged. These standards have important political implications because they are never met. The gap between ideals and realities evokes different reactions from different groups during different eras in American history, and these "moral convulsions" lend a unique flavor to American politics.

The role of the Constitution here is clear: it is the formal embodiment of the external standards that define American ideals. These ideals and values did not originate with the Constitution, to be sure, but they receive legal standing and definition in it (Devine, 1972:139). Although the Constitution reflects Lockean values, it also has affected their evolution and extension. This effect is clear with respect to the political liberties which are defined in the Constitution but which have also evolved within the constitutional framework. The impact of that framework on American notions of what constitutes "democracy" is also formidable. It can be seen in the political systems adopted by new states as they were admitted to the Union, as well as in the history of state constitutional conventions. Our ideas of what constitutes individualism and equalitarianism, as well as what limits them, have also been couched in constitutional terms and theories and thereby influenced by them.

American constitutionalism enhanced the significance of the Constitution for the cycles of moral convulsions Huntington described. It would be much more difficult for Americans to work up a moral fervor if the unfulfilled ideals were not embodied in the Constitution or if they did not take that document seriously. The Constitution's significance, however, is not limited to generating issues that at times dominate American politics. It also shapes how groups define the issues they raise. Constitutional historians have contended:

> Groups and individuals choose courses of action that are consistent with or sanctioned by the Constitution. They do so not because they are in each instance irrevocably committed to the constitutional rule or principle at issue; on the contrary, in different circumstances they may employ a conflicting principle or rule. Rather, political actors adhere to constitutional principles and doctrines because they know that the public takes the Constitution seriously. The American people believe that it embodies fundamental values and prescribes procedures that are the

touchstone of governmental legitimacy [Kelly, Harbison, and Belz, 1983:xviii].

Constitutionalism was an important influence even during the period before the apotheosis of the Constitution. Actors offered different interpretations, but the controversies involving the Alien and Sedition Acts, the bank, and internal improvements were formulated in constitutional terms. With the exception of abolitionists such as William Lloyd Garrison, much the same can be said about those arguing over slavery, at least until *Dred Scott* (1857). After the Civil War, the struggle over how industrialization was to proceed generated innovative constitutional theories and decisions, but the battle was waged on constitutional terrain, which constrained the debate. Much the same can be said about the controversy over the New Deal and the civil rights movement.

In commenting on the role of the Constitution in resolving issues with profound social or political overtones, C. Herman Pritchett (1977) cautions against expecting the Constitution to provide or permit just one resolution. At the same time he notes:

> It is a profound mistake, however, to think that the range of choice is left unlimited by this freedom. Not everything that the public may currently want to do is necessarily constitutional. The distinctive feature of the experiential approach is that decisions on constitutional allowability are made with full recognition of the need for the adjustments and expansions inevitable in a dynamic society. The constitutional system is not regarded as separate from the political system, but a necessary part of it, performing the vital function of giving order and structure to the inevitable processes of change [35–36].

Thus, to deny that the Constitution has had a profound impact on the outcome of controversies generated by social and political conflict and change would be as misleading as to deny the role these forces have had in the evolution of constitutional doctrine.

The Constitution and Institutional Development

The development of American political institutions provides us with a concrete arena within which we can further explore the Constitution's developmental role. To understand this role, however, we must look beyond isolated textual treatments of specific institutions. We must continue to look at the institutional network created by the Constitution in light of the marketplace metaphor. To facilitate this analysis, we first review the institutional traits relevant to understanding the role of various providers in the policy marketplace. We then discuss those components of the constitutional scheme with developmental implications. Finally, we draw examples from the essays in this volume to illustrate how institutional traits mesh with the constitutional scheme and historical circumstances to affect institutional development.

Institutional Traits: Constitutional Roles, Internal Design, and Powers

Institutional roles are fairly clear from a reading of the text of the Constitution and the commentary that has surrounded it. The federal government, centralized and removed from the people, was a necessary evil. If properly controlled, however, it could do much to enhance the prosperity and security of the new nation. It was to have broad powers, but only those delegated to it by the Constitution. The remaining powers were reserved for the state governments and the people. The legislative power of the central government was to be vested in two branches with different constituencies. The House was to be the people's branch that would act as a conduit for their desires and needs within the new government. The Senate was to represent the interests of the states and the more conservative elements of American society. It was once removed from the people and was to share some executive responsibilities with the president.

The president was to be, broadly defined, the chief executive officer of the new government. This involved enforcing the laws enacted by Congress, appointing officials to government posts, and heading the armed forces. As titular head, the president was also to take the lead in foreign affairs and agenda setting. The Supreme Court was the only judicial body created by the Constitution, although Congress could provide for more. Setting aside the irresolvable question of whether the framers intended to give the Supreme Court the power to invalidate congressional enactments, it is clear that the Court was the "keeper of the Constitution." The Court was to resolve constitutional questions, which necessarily entailed interpreting and extending the Constitution.

In constructing this institutional network, the framers could have used a number of different techniques to ensure that constitutional roles were fulfilled and institutional boundaries maintained.

They could have specified in some detail the internal, structural design of the institutions, thereby limiting and molding their participation in the policy marketplace. Evidence for the effectiveness of this technique can be found in the experience of many state constitutions. But the framers were not micromanagers, and the Constitution is largely devoid of structural detail.[4] It is beyond the scope of this essay to consider why the framers neglected this very powerful control technique, but it is important to note the implications for institutional development. The framers' decision not to specify structural details permitted infrastructures and procedures to emerge that reflected and served internal, institutional needs. It also provided the flexibility needed to mold and reshape infrastructures to meet changing societal needs and desires.

Despite the overall lack of structural detail, some institutional features are inherent in a body's constitutional origins and roles. These inherent traits are not easily modified and have had a profound effect on marketplace activities and institutional development. Consider the Congress. Its size and ties to local constituencies imbue it with a certain institutional clumsiness that make quick, bold actions in the policy marketplace difficult. The need for agreement across both houses makes such actions all the more problematic. At the same time, Congress's constitutional role gives it an absolutely pivotal position in many policy arenas. Thus, a formal organizational structure, informal norms and relationships, and extraconstitutional mechanisms have developed to shore up Congress's market position and maneuverability.

The situation is quite different with respect to the presidency. The ability to act decisively and quickly, to speak with one voice, to initiate actions and set agendas, and to claim the only national constituency all derive from the president's constitutional origin and roles. These traits provide the presidency with special endowments that can give it a competitive edge within certain policy fields and, during certain eras, across policy arenas. Presidential initiatives often become institutionalized and condition expectations for future actions, thereby affecting the development of the presidency.

Much the same can be said about the Supreme Court. That body cannot directly initiate the conflicts with which it becomes involved, and it is wholly dependent on the support of the other branches and the goodwill of the public to operate effectively in the policy marketplace. Although it is insulated from many pressures, it must be cautious in dealing with problems that others place on its agenda. While it has developed a number of techniques to avoid becoming drawn into certain disputes, its role as the "keeper of the Constitution" necessarily involves it in some disputes that could endanger its institutional standing. Many of these disputes involve issues with which the popular branches have been unable or unwilling to deal. The Court's involvement in them has increased people's expectations about it and has institutionalized its position in selected policy arenas.

The place of the states in the institutional network created by the Constitution vests them with a unique set of resources. Perhaps the most important—in a nation that has feared centralized governmental power since its inception—is their proximity to the people. It led the framers to be concerned less with restricting state power than with restricting national power. The framers believed this proximity put the states in a better position to understand the needs and desires of the people and made them more responsive to people's needs. Proximity may also make the states more efficient than the central government because they can tailor programs to the special conditions in their locales. They also are useful as "laboratories of democracy." These traits ensure the states a prominent, but not necessarily dominant, role in most policy arenas, irrespective of the forces and trends favoring centralization.

The framers' approach to empowerment in the new government evidenced a blend of strategies. The Constitution assigned broad powers corresponding to institutional roles and distributed various tasks and duties to the different branches (roles in the impeachment process; maintaining a record of congressional proceedings, reporting on the state of the union, and so forth). It also placed very specific limitations on both levels of government (Article I, sections 9 and 10; Article IV) and provided certain protections (legislative immunity from prosecution, prohibition against diminution in pay). The designation of broad powers to various branches of the federal government (legislative, executive, judicial) was limited by the powers delegated to the federal government. Moreover, the scope of those powers was spelled out with some specificity, especially with respect to Congress (Article I, Section 8). The primary limitations on the federal judicial power are embodied in the "case or controversy" requirement, its constitutionally specified jurisdictional scope, and its inherently weak institutional structure. The scope of presidential activity is far less encumbered by specific constitutional provisions, other than those inherent in the office and those embodied in the Constitution's set of interinstitutional checks.

Despite these attempts to delimit federal powers, the most important consequence of the framers' empowerment efforts—from a developmental perspective—is the Constitution's adaptability, its ability to respond to changing needs and tastes. This attribute is all the more apparent if we compare the federal document with state constitutions. We should not, however, equate the Constitution's adaptability with a failure to limit and channel government. Political actors have not been able to trample over constitutional provisions in order to respond to the force of prevailing political winds. Rather, the institutional network created by the Constitution has normally been able to make adjustments within the constitutional framework. Although some failures have occurred during various crises in U.S. history, most specific constitutional proscriptions have been observed. When violations occurred, they were not institutionalized but stand out as historical aberrations.

Institutional adaptability is actually the result of constitutional ambiguity, particularly in the "necessary and proper" clause, the power to regulate commerce "among the several states," the supremacy clause, and the general grants of executive and judicial power. We can trace other developments to various empowering amendments to the Constitution, such as the Fourteenth and the Sixteenth. The point is that various policy providers can respond to crises within the context of the constitutional marketplace. Schematic features are more important in restricting their efforts than are specific limitations in constitutional empowerments.

The Constitutional Scheme

Although the framers did not use highly detailed institutional architecture or specific, unambiguous grants of power, they did design schematic features to enforce constitutional roles and limits. These schematic features have had important, but not always predictable, implications for institutional development. The most important of these features are the selection procedures tying institutions to their constitutional roles, power-sharing arrangements and interinstitutional checks to limit the power of constitutional organs, and the value commitments embodied in the Constitution.

Provisions for the selection of personnel were among the first points covered in the creation of the key organs of the central government, second only to the broad grant of power given each branch. In every case the selection procedures were specified in great detail;

they were far less ambiguous than the description of many delegated powers. Moreover, these selection provisions reinforced constitutional roles. The people directly elected representatives for short terms, while state legislatures were to select senators for longer terms, making them considerably more insulated from the vagaries of public opinion. The president was to be selected for an intermediate term by an indirect, national scheme that could accommodate the interests of both the states and the people. The selection process for Supreme Court members was the most insulated from popular influences to ensure their fidelity to the Constitution. Their term of office was also the most indefinite, depending only on their "good behavior."

Another schematic feature that has significant developmental consequences is the system of interinstitutional checks built into the constitutional framework. While the framers eschewed institutional design at the micro level (within institutions), their use of it at the macro level was masterful. Such devices as vetoes, override provisions, and power sharing have proven effective in checking the growth of institutional power. It has proven extremely difficult for any participant in the constitutional marketplace to establish a monopoly in any policy arena, if others wanted to supply policy. Moreover, these interinstitutional checks affect relations among policy providers. Policy providers are so interdependent that long-term strategies to exclude or ignore them are largely infeasible.

As the structure of delegated power sharing and institutional checks affect market shares and provider relations, so the value commitments evidenced in the Constitution affect the types of products marketed. More important for our developmental concerns, however, these commitments also shape the production infrastructure. The Constitution embodies a set of value commitments we might characterize as democratic constitutionalism (Rosenbloom, herein). It stresses the importance of such values as constitutionalism, representation, accountability, and due process in the structure and operation of public bodies. These commitments define the government's role in American society. Their outward manifestation makes it difficult for government to play more than a minimal role and circumscribes government activities in many areas. Constitutional values also create expectations that affect how government does what it does. The framers shied away from explicit value commitments, except in the preamble, but their framework reflected implicit value commitments that have had important developmental implications for public infrastructures.

Institutional Development

These constitutional features have undeniably left their imprint on American institutional development, as is evident in the essays in this volume. It is equally evident that their developmental impact has not been simple but depends on how the constitutional scheme meshes with institutional traits in different historical settings. David Brady's analysis of incrementalism in the House of Representatives illustrates this point nicely. Incrementalism cannot be understood if we focus only on the House's role as the populist branch of the federal government or on the electoral controls designed to reinforce that role. That focus would have led to an expectation of sweeping policy initiatives that were thwarted by other branches of the government. Incrementalism is much more understandable in light of the framers' reluctance to engage in detailed infrastructural design. Had the Constitution provided the Speaker of the House with sufficient legal powers to mobilize and control majorities and effectively manage the business of the House, its operation might well have been more in line with populistic expectations consistent with its role as the people's voice in the new government. As it was, the difficulties of managing the House mushroomed as it grew in size and diversity. Moreover, constitutional value commitments made it difficult for a hierarchically organized infrastructure to emerge and persist. The basic political drive of House members for reelection, which became more relevant with the emergence of career legislators, combined with the demands of sectional diversity to undermine the development of a strong congressional party system capable of integrating and mobilizing diverse interests. Instead of a strong Speaker or a strong party system, what arose, especially after the Civil War, was a decentralized committee system. The local interests of a member's district affected committee membership, and this contributed to the difficulties in mobilizing the House to enact sweeping, innovative change—at least during normal times.

The electoral scheme used by the framers to reinforce the Senate's constitutional role was as ineffective as that designed for the House. Charles Stewart III provides convincing evidence that the differences between the House and the Senate in terms of political insularity began to disappear long before the enactment of the Seventeenth Amendment. The framers clearly underestimated the effects of the growing democratic ethos on the process by which senators were selected, and the electoral careers of senators and representatives began to resemble one another at an early point in U.S.

history. This is not to say that the Senate failed to perform its role as a political buffer between hasty shifts in public opinion and public policy. More effective in reinforcing these role expectations, however, were the unanticipated effects of certain constitutionally determined traits (small size, lack of a strong leader). These features meshed with constitutional value commitments to create an infrastructure in the Senate that moderated the impact of ideological extremes and shifts in policy preferences.

The relatively small size of the Senate allowed it to evolve as a more collegial body than the House, one that developed less formal structures and rules and was more apt to defer to the prerogatives of individual senators. The fact that the Senate's presiding officer is not one of its members makes that office far weaker than the Speaker of the House, who, as just noted, was not constitutionally endowed with strong powers. These factors combined to make it relatively easy for a small cadre of senators to frustrate the preferences of a majority, thereby impeding the passage of sweeping, innovative policy initiatives. The irony of this situation, of course, is that the failure of the framers' attempt to create a politically insulated upper chamber is what accounts for the Senate's continued viability. While parallel institutions in Western democracies have lost their legitimacy as policy-making organs, the Senate thrives in its original role.

The recent emergence of the president as a powerful actor in the policy marketplace is somewhat difficult to reconcile with the framers' conception of the government they were creating. They rejected a hierarchical, command-oriented model of government with a strong central locus. The role of the Constitution in the emergence of the presidency is clearer, however, if we contrast the president's constitutionally endowed powers with those of other providers and examine the implications of those differences for market positions, as Bert A. Rockman notes. As the structure of demand for public policies changed (international versus domestic, mixes of domestic policies) and the overall level of demand for public action increased, the president was in a better position to respond than were other providers. He was able to act decisively, expeditiously, and with a unified voice. He was able to set agendas and speak to a national constituency. These abilities enhanced his market position vis-à-vis Congress, the Supreme Court, and the states, each of which suffered from different handicaps.

These market activities became institutionalized, and heightened expectations of presidential leadership were created. Yet despite these advantages and their consequences, the president has never been able to assume a monopolist's position across policy arenas for any extended period of time. The constitutional framework simply endowed competing institutions with too many other resources for any single organ to monopolize the policy marketplace. This diffuse power structure tempered the relations among competing providers and moderated the strategies used by each in a manner that would have pleased the framers.

The emergence of the bureaucratic state, even more than the increasing dominance of the president, seems to provide irrefutable evidence of the failure of U.S. constitutionalism. In a framework characterized by separate centers of power, electoral controls, and interinstitutional checks and balances, a politically insulated executive organ stressing the primacy of professional expertise and hierarchy and vested with both legislative and judicial powers seems an anomaly, to say the least. Attempts to rein in the bureaucracy by other bodies only seemed to distort further the constitutional scheme.

Nonetheless, it is clear from David H. Rosenbloom's essay that the bureaucratic state emerged as part of the normal functioning of the policy marketplace. It provided the policy suppliers with the badly needed capacity to meet the demands of an advanced industrial society, facilitating both horizontal and vertical integration of the complex constitutional system. Moreover, the tension between constitutional values and bureaucratic operating norms has been resolved by the ongoing "constitutionalization" of the U.S. administrative state. Rosenbloom points to the increasing attention bureaucracies pay to such values as due process, representation of diverse interests, citizen participation, and accountability. These administrative trends are, of course, further evidence of the importance of constitutional values in the development of public infrastructures.

It was not at all clear from the text of the Constitution that the Supreme Court would emerge as an important participant in the policy marketplace. But, as Lawrence Baum's essay suggests, the Court's constitutional role and traits, combined with the market activity of other providers, made it an important player in at least some policy arenas. The immobility and shirking behavior of other providers created a market for its services. The Court was uniquely able to fill those voids, even though it had to tread carefully on the turf of other providers. The Court's activities, like the president's, eventually created expectations concerning its market participation. These expectations, of course, increased the demand for the Court's participation, if for no other reason than the Court was the only viable recourse available. The Court's attractiveness to certain publics and limited control over its agenda make it unlikely that it will be able to relinquish its market participation in the foreseeable future, even if the justices desired to do so.

It is not possible to explore here the significance of constitutional roles, powers, traits, and selection mechanisms in the development of such political institutions as political parties and interest groups. Nonetheless, the Constitution has not been unimportant in the development of these institutions, as the essays by Kenneth Janda and Graham K. Wilson illustrate. Of most obvious relevance, again, are the value commitments embodied in the Constitution. It is hard to overestimate the direct significance of such guarantees as freedom of assembly, speech, and press in the structure and operation of these groups. Less evident is the indirect impact of such democratic values as representation and accountability on the infrastructure of these ostensibly private institutions.

Despite the importance of these values, both Janda and Wilson are most concerned with the influence of a less obvious component of the constitutional scheme—its system of interinstitutional checks. Janda uses data from a large comparative study of political parties to examine the impact of a federal system of government and a formal separation of powers on party structure. He concludes that these constitutional features account for the weak, decentralized nature of U.S. parties. This decentralized structure, of course, inhibits their ability to integrate the unwieldy system of government and foster innovative policy initiatives. Wilson's essay challenges the conventional notion that the constitutional structure strengthens U.S. interest groups vis-à-vis those in other countries. He acknowledges that such features as constitutional guarantees, more open government, multiple access points, and weak political parties are advantageous for the operation of interest groups. But if we consider the advantages for interest groups in corporatist and neocorporatist states, as well as the relative immobility of the U.S. government, the advantages for American interest groups may be comparatively minimal.

The developmental impact of the Constitution on interest groups can be seen more clearly in their structure and organization than in their strength, according to Wilson's analysis. The separation of powers and the federal system provide multiple points of access and permit more diversity within functional areas. Groups lacking influence with one policy provider need not yield to those groups influencing that provider. Instead, the disenfranchised groups may simply turn their efforts to another policy provider, resulting in an untidy, disorganized interest group structure. The establishment of the legislature as an important provider in the policy market requires that U.S. interest groups pay more attention to legislators than do their counterparts in some other Western democracies, which tend to focus their energies on the executive. This means that U.S. interest groups must use more political, less technical appeals and must engage in more coalition building than do their counterparts in countries where interest groups deal mainly with bureaucrats.

Another development, just as significant as the emergence of the president as a dominant participant in the policy market, is the relative decline of the states. Kermit L. Hall's essay sheds light on this development. He notes that although the U.S. Constitution did affect state constitutions, it was largely silent on the organization of state governments, just as it was on the infrastructures within the central government. The organization of state governments was not a concern to the framers because those governments were closer to the people and could be better controlled by them. As Hall's essay documents, the people were too effective in controlling state governments. That control, combined with widespread antigovernmental sentiments, turned state constitutions into detailed codes that often hampered the political responsiveness of state governments. As other providers in the policy marketplace were able to respond, the structure of the market changed dramatically.

Despite the significance of state constitutional constraints in the evolution of the policy market's structure, John Chubb asserts that incapacity at the state level was only one factor fostering centralization. The political interests of officials throughout the federal system were also involved. A centralized system of categorical grants served those interests nicely, and in a way that illustrates the workings of the constitutional marketplace. These grant programs satisfied demands the states could not meet, they provided tangible benefits to the constituents of congressional representatives, and they involved the state bureaucracies in the administration of services. In a very real sense, these grant programs coopted those with control over the interinstitutional checks that prevented forceful federal action in addressing social problems. Moreover, once refined and institutionalized, these vertical networks became difficult to eliminate. Participants across the federal spectrum had vested interests in the status quo.

Despite the marked changes in the policy marketplace introduced by the emergence of the federal grant system, it is not without significance that the constitutional framework did not permit the states to be excluded from participation, any more than the rise of the president during the middle of the twentieth century led to the total eclipse of Congress. These changes are a testament to the adaptability of the marketplace, but they also evidence the continuing impact of the institutional network created by the Constitution in shaping the evolution of the federal system.

Conclusion

Political change is inevitable, and the Constitution's relationship to the developmental process is an important one to understand. To assert that the Constitution has had no enduring impact would suggest that, in the long run, the U.S. government is unbounded, which is contrary to the very notion of constitutionalism. If widely espoused, it would undermine the legitimacy of U.S. political institutions. The intellectual foundations for this view, while seldom articulated, lie in the decided ambiguity of key provisions in the Constitution, the undeniable evolution of constitutional organs and doctrine, and the long delay in the apotheosis of the Constitution. These intellectual footings notwithstanding, the position they support is based on a faulty view of politics and a narrow view of the Constitution. Politics is not simply the summing and balancing of prevailing social and economic forces. Political and moral values make a difference, as does the design of political institutions and institutional networks. The Constitution is an important source of these influences, and therein lies its continued ability to affect the developmental process.

To view the Constitution as having given birth to a virginal organism that time and environment have ravaged is to misconstrue its nature. The framers set up a mechanism, one that operates, in part, according to market principles. The flexibility of that mechanism permitted the nation to cohere and persist in its earliest days, and its values have played an important role in determining the tenor of American politics. An important part of that governmental mechanism is an institutional network that created competing power centers with different roles, constituencies, and powers. Equally important is the scheme created to enforce constitutional roles, limits, and values. The real force and limits of U.S. constitutionalism lie not in the Constitution's literal text but in the interactions among these competing power centers within the context of a constitutional scheme that reflects widely shared societal values.

The framers' choice of strategies to ensure institutional compliance with their scheme of government had profound implications for the development of U.S. political institutions. Efforts to control intrainstitutional behavior and reinforce constitutional roles through the use of carefully calibrated selection procedures were largely ineffective. These selection-oriented controls presumed much about the cognitive abilities and inclinations of the selectors. They also could not deal with changes in the preferences of those selected or with institutional constraints on the realization of those preferences. The use of interinstitutional checks has proven effective in curbing institutional excesses, but at a significant cost in terms of political responsiveness and efficiency.

The void left by the framers' failure to engage in intrainstitutional architectural design has been filled, in part, by the diffusion of values implicit in the Constitution. These value commitments have delegitimized various structures and practices and have channeled institutionalization in various directions. This architectural vacuum has not always been filled by structures promoting responsive, popular government. This is, of course, consistent with the structure of the Constitution; it was not designed to maximize those values. Indeed, had the framers engaged in micromanagement, their proposed infrastructure would not have maximized responsive, populistic government. Worse yet, one can only imagine how well a detailed infrastructure designed in the late eighteenth century would have fared in the twentieth century, if it had lasted that long. Herein lies the real genius of the Constitution; it relies on a structured system of institutional dynamics that reflects fundamental societal values, rather than on staid organizational charts, to control and channel government. The key to charting the Constitution's role in U.S. political development lies in understanding those institutional dynamics.

NOTES

I would like to acknowledge the insightful comments of Ira Carmen, Walter Murphy, Bert Rockman, and Frederick Wirt on earlier drafts of this essay. I bear total responsibility for not having responded to all of their comments.

1. A series of familiar controversies illustrates the problems encountered by the newly created national government as it struggled with established power centers located in the various states—the Kentucky and Virginia resolutions and the doctrine of interposition, the convening of the Hartford Convention, John Calhoun's nullification doctrine, and finally the attempt by the Southern states to secede from the Union. These controversies all involved fundamental questions concerning some of the most important changes in the existing political landscape introduced by the ratification of the Constitution. What was the scope of national legislative authority? Who was to be the final arbiter of constitutional disputes? What was the nature of the Union?

The same type of resistance from established power centers was encountered by the newly created federal judiciary. Although a national judiciary was considered essential for the success of the new Union, the body that initially emerged was hardly the revered, prestigious national institution that exists today. George Washington had a difficult time convincing John Jay that an appointment as chief justice was worthy of his consideration (Pritchett, 1977:37). The Supreme Court was rebuked severely in 1793, when in *Chisholm v. Georgia* it held that citizens of one state could sue another state in federal court, a serious blow to state sovereignty. The ruling was nullified by the adoption of the Eleventh Amendment. The early prestige of the federal judiciary was also damaged by Federalist attempts to politicize the bench and the Republicans' counterattack led by Thomas Jefferson (Kelly, Harbison, and Belz, 1983:173–75).

2. Nowhere is the interinstitutional competition among policy providers clearer than in Skowronek's (1982) already classic analysis of the nationalization of administrative functions in the post–Civil War era, especially in the area of civil and military administration. He describes in great detail how vested interests in the "party" state resisted pressures to rationalize and nationalize administrative authority. The constitutional empowerment of state and local forces enabled them to resist international trends and national campaigns to restructure administrative authority until well into the twentieth century. Moreover, even when nationalization become inevitable, its structure was the result of institutional give-and-take between the executive and legislative branches. Neither could dominate the other, and each attempted to capitalize on its unique institutional traits and historical circumstance to maximize its role in the formation of the new administrative state. The contributors to this volume will further illustrate the insights this theoretical perspective yields and will deal more explicitly with the Constitution's role in structuring marketplace interaction and outcomes.

3. Can we fairly attribute the persistence and prosperity of the early nation to the Constitution? Others have pointed to a variety of other factors. Alexis de Tocqueville emphasized the cultural homogeneity of the populace and the economic benefits of the Union ([1835]1981:256–57). Seymour Martin Lipset, in a more recent review, stresses the experiences the young

United States shared with the emerging nations of today. For example, he points to the emergence of a charismatic leader (George Washington) who provided stability to the nation and set a precedent for the peaceful transfer of power (1979:18–23). He also cites the existence of an intellectual elite committed to nationalism (1979:27–30), which was influential even though it had to compete against another group of elites, led by Thomas Jefferson, that favored localism. Also important was the emergence of a national system of political parties that quickly devolved into a one-party system (Lipset, 1979:30–33, 41). Finally, Lipset stresses the shared cultural heritage of the American people, along with the content of those values (such as belief in the rule of law), as contributing to the stability of the federal union.

No one could deny the significance of these factors, but they are also representative of the bias that the neo-institutionalists have identified. These analyses tend to emphasize the importance of political actors and social and economic conditions. When viewed from the perspective of the marketplace metaphor, the exclusion of the Constitution from the array of factors accounting for the stability of the fledgling Union seems inexplicable. It had a profound effect on early American political development, if only because of what its failure would have portended.

4. The Constitution says nothing about the administrative infrastructure of the executive or the organization of the courts. The states must have a "republican form of government." The most detail is provided for Congress. The Constitution specifies that it must convene once a year, provides for the selection of the leadership, dictates the origin of revenue bills, requires a written record of its proceedings, and outlines the process by which a bill becomes a law. Even here, however, the Constitution gives each house the power to specify its own procedural rules.

REFERENCES

Almond, Gabriel A. 1988. "The Return to the State." *American Political Science Review* 82:853–74.

Chisholm v. Georgia. 1793. 2 U.S. 419.

Devine, Donald J. 1972. *The Political Culture of the United States.* Boston: Little, Brown.

Huntington, Samuel P. 1981. *American Politics: The Promise of Disharmony.* Cambridge, Mass.: Harvard University Press.

Kammen, Michael. 1986. *A Machine that Would Go of Itself.* New York: Alfred A. Knopf.

Kelly, Alfred H., Winfred A. Harbison, and Herman Belz. 1983. *The American Constitution: Its Origins and Development.* New York: W. W. Norton.

Lipset, Seymour Martin. 1979. *The First New Nation: The United States in Historical and Comparative Perspective.* New York: W. W. Norton.

Lowi, Theodore J. 1988. "The Return to the State: Critique." *American Political Science Review* 82:885–91.

March, James G., and Johan P. Olsen. 1984. "The New Institutionalism: Organizational Factors in Political Life." *American Political Science Review* 78:734–49.

Missouri v. Holland. 1920. 352 U.S. 416.

Pritchett, C. Herman. 1977. *The American Constitution.* New York: McGraw-Hill.

Scott v. Sanford [Dred Scott case]. 1857. 60 U.S. 393.

Skowronek, Stephen. 1982. *Building a New American State: The Expansion of National Administrative Capacities, 1877–1920.* Cambridge: Cambridge University Press.

Tocqueville, Alexis de. [1835] 1981. *Democracy in America.* New York: Random House.

★ II ★

The Constitution and the Development of National Political Institutions

★ 2 ★

Incrementalism in the People's Branch: The Constitution and the Development of the Policy-making Process

DAVID BRADY

The American constitutional system was designed to keep majorities from hastily enacting public policy of a broad, decisive nature. Almost two hundred years later, it is clear it has succeeded: scholars and observers of the U.S. Congress attest to Congress's inability to legislate major policy changes. Although the founders might well be pleased with the overall results of their efforts in this regard, they would be puzzled by the House's role in a policy process characterized by its continuity, stability, and incrementalism. The House of Representatives was created as *the* democratic institution. The authors of the Constitution were so concerned the House would act quickly and chaotically that they created an indirectly elected upper chamber, one they hoped would use reason and judgment to temper the House's passions, and they embedded the Congress in an elaborate system of checks and balances.

Although the House's role in the policy incrementalism that has characterized Congress through much of its history would have surprised and pleased the framers, this incrementalism has contributed significantly to popular dissatisfaction with Congress. Samuel Huntington has argued that the intensity of criticism of Congress varies inversely with the degree and speed that Congress approves the President's program (Huntington, 1965). Partial proof of Huntington's assertions is that as recently as 1966 the Eighty-ninth Congress was hailed as "the most productive congressional session ever held," "the Congress of realized dreams," and "fully 71 percent of the American electorate gives a favorable rating to the job done by the Congress in 1965" (*Washington Post*, January 9, 1966).

Given the role of the House of Representatives in the constitutional scheme and the external pressures on it to conform to its populist role, its emergence as an incrementalist body becomes important in studying American political development. Equally important are the implications of this development for the functioning of American democracy. The essay thus begins with an analysis of the emergence of incrementalism in the House that builds on two fundamental forces in American politics. It outlines how the driving desire for reelection and the grim realities of sectionalism are manifested in constitutional and structural factors. The role of the basic constitutional design is integrated with the structure of political parties and the operation of the House committee system to show how incrementalism is fostered. Some thoughts on nonincremental change are then presented and examined across three different periods of political realignment in American history. The conclusion comments on the future of nonincremental change in American politics.

The Development of Incrementalism in the House of Representatives

To understand the development of a deliberate, incremental policy process in what was envisioned as a populistic body, one must look to the complex historical interactions between the basic desire for reelection and the primacy of sectionalism, since that sectionalism is manifested in the Constitution and other basic political institutions. Sectional animosities contributed much to the fear of a powerful central government, and that fear had a profound impact on the design of the constitutional scheme. That cumbersome scheme contributed to the development of national political parties, but it also prevented those parties from exerting strong pressures on House members, who had to remain responsive to the local constituencies that elected them. As the increasing complexity of the nation's business created the need for standing committees in Congress, these same local pressures drove the demand for committee assignments and the policy preferences of the committees. The effect of these developments on the policy processes of the House meshed well with other facets of the constitutional scheme that promoted incrementalism.

The Constitutional Context

The U.S. Constitution was to a large extent a response to problems the Articles of Confederation proved unable to solve. Any viable government must be organized to deal with extant problems in the society, but the Articles had proven ineffective in harnessing and controlling the diverse state and sectional interests.[1] A major problem confronting the framers was to create a more effective centralized government that was not so centralized it would be repudiated by the various sectional interests. There was never any serious question of creating a unified national government. Not only would the idea have been repugnant to many of those gathered in Philadelphia, but there was no possibility that such a government would be adopted. Delegates to the Constitutional Convention were selected by each state, voting was by state, various governmental proposals, such as the Virginia and New Jersey plans, were proposed by and named after states, and ratification was by state. Before, during, and after the Constitutional Convention, state and sectional interests were an accepted fact of political life.

The federal nature of the constitutional system was a primary manifestation of the founders' concern with sectional sensitivities and interests. Federalism permitted latitude in the political process for the social, economic, and religious differences between states and sections (Elazar, 1966). Indeed, many have argued that sectionalism has been and remains the mainspring in understanding American history (Turner, 1910, 1932). Whether or not that thesis is correct, sectionalism has had a profound impact on the congressional policy-making process. That impact has been enhanced by the manner in which sectionalism was institutionalized in the Constitution. The disjoined federal system provides many opportunities for diverse, localistic interests to affect Congressional deliberations, and this fosters slow, deliberate, incremental processes.

This was, of course, no surprise to those who designed the Constitution. James Madison argued that diversity constituted a real check on the formation of a majority capable of acting in haste. From Alexander Hamilton's use of the Treasury Department to boost industrial and monied interests to the present sunbelt-snowbelt controversy, different sectional interests have pressured

Congress to pass legislation viewed as beneficial to one and inimical to others (Bensel, 1984; Reed, 1983). The Civil War, the 1896 realignments, and countless other events in American history all testify to the effects of sectional diversity on the U.S. system of government. As a focal point for those differences, the Congress has had not only to deal with issues in a political sense but also to temper sectional demands by integrating sectional divisiveness. As Madison anticipated, such diversity made it difficult to form "hasty" majorities— majorities capable of enacting significant policy changes.

While it is true that sectional diversity has been the root cause of much policy disagreement in American political history, it is also true that the drafters of the Constitution did not think a federal government would sufficiently guard against potential governmental abuse. Concerned that the concentration of legislative, executive, and judicial powers in the same hands would invite tyranny (Dahl, 1965), they institutionalized the doctrines of separation of powers and checks and balances. These doctrines have resulted in a U.S. system of government that is characterized by "separate powers sharing functions" (Huntington, 1965), in contradistinction to other Western democracies, where power is centralized and functions are more specific. The U.S. Congress, unlike the British House of Commons, shares power with the president, the courts, and the bureaucracy.

The most immediate effect of separation of powers and checks and balances on the Congress is that even when Congress can build majorities for innovative policies, the president or the courts may thwart it. In the contemporary period, control of the House and Senate has been split, thus increasing the difficulty of passing broad, purposeful legislation. Richard Neustadt and others have shown that each of these institutions has different constituencies to please and therefore different policy solutions, even when they agree on where the problem lies (Neustadt, 1976; Lowi, 1979). Policy makers in both the House and the Senate are likely to compromise or dilute strong policy proposals by the other branches of government (Anderson, 1979). Moreover, opponents of policy changes have access to a large number of power points, where a defeat for their majority position spells defeat until the next Congress.[2] Thus, in the U.S. system, having a policy majority does not readily translate into significant policy change. Those who seek to preserve the status quo always have a decided advantage, which contrasts with the way most other Western democracies function (Lowi, 1979; McConnell, 1966; Redford, 1966; Davidson, 1981).

Political Parties in Context

Although the doctrines of federalism, separation of powers, and checks and balances have been modified to make the constitutional system more democratic and centralized, the U.S. system of government remains fragmented and cumbersome (Huntington, 1965). Shortly after the Constitution took effect, the inherent difficulties of governing within its framework became apparent. In response, Hamilton crossed executive boundaries and led pronational factions in the Congress (Holcombe, 1950; Miller, 1969). Over time these factions developed into political parties. Although American parties were founded because of systemic cumbersomeness, the same system inhibited full development of the parties. To ensure reelection in single-member districts in which the winner is determined by a plurality of votes, candidates stress local issues (Key, 1966). The diversity of those interests inhibited the emergence of strong national parties that could control nominations and secure elections. In time candidates developed their own organizations and conducted their own election campaign. U.S. representatives are much more independent in their voting behavior than their Western European counterparts, who are very dependent on their party for their electoral success (Brady and Bullock, 1985; Epstein, 1980).

The most basic effect of federalism on the American party system is that its two-party system is, in reality, a fifty-state system (Key, 1966). Each state's party system has demographic, ideological, structural, and electoral peculiarities. Thus, the Democratic party in the electorate and as an organization in New York has been distinct from the Democratic party in the electorate and as an organization in Georgia. The same applies to the components of the Republican party in these states. The heterogeneity of the state party systems means that at the level of party as government, unlike-minded individuals bearing the same party label will come together in the U. S. Congress. Put another way, the federal system brings to the Congress built-in differences between states and regions.

Although this system may be useful in maintaining system equilibrium, it has most often been an extremely poor basis for building coherent congressional parties. The New Deal coalition of rural southern agricultural interests and urban northern industrial interests is a case in point. Long after this coalition had passed its major policy changes, it served as an electoral base for the Democratic party (Neustadt, 1976). Such successful electoral coalitions, however, often were divided on major policy issues.[3] In fact, on a number of such major policy issues as civil rights and social welfare, the components of the New Deal coalition were poles apart (Sinclair, 1977). American political history abounds with examples of successful electoral coalitions that could not make major policy changes because of ideological differences. It is not difficult to surmise how such coalitions led to static or incremental policy.

The separation of powers and checks and balances also enhance the fragmentary, disjointed status of American parties, which undermines their influence at the policy-making level. Parties formed out of numerous and diverse state party systems emphasize electoral success and minimize policy cohesion (and thus policy success). National parties formed on a sectional, coalition basis become further factionalized when appointive and electoral offices become available in the various branches. Thus, for example, one faction of the party may be dominant in presidential politics, another in congressional politics. Since both have powers over the courts, an equal division of court appointments may result (Burns, 1963; Key, 1966). The Democratic party from 1876 to at least 1976 was characterized by just such an arrangement. The northern wing dominated presidential politics and elections, the southern wing controlled congressional leadership posts, and both wings influenced court appointments. Such a system may enhance representation of differences, but it does little to elect congressional majorities capable of legislating public policy changes.

The constitutional arrangement of single-member-district, plurality elections also aids in fragmenting the party system. House members elected on local issues by a localized party in the electorate build local party (or personal) organizations (Mann, 1978; Mayhew, 1974). Once elected, owing little to national party leaders, representatives can behave in nonpartisan ways with little consequence for themselves. Throughout most of Congress's history, party leaders have been able only to persuade, not force, members to vote "correctly." The inability to impose sanctions means party leadership has difficulty building consistent partisan majorities. It should not be surprising that the highest levels of voting along party lines in the history of Congress occurred when the Speaker's sanctions over members were greatest and the Senate was run by a hierarchy that had powerful sanctions. Regardless of the national party position, representatives elected by local majorities can work and vote on behalf of those interests. Congressional leaders do not "persuade" from a position of power.

The U.S. constitutional framework allows local and state diversity to work its way up from party in the electorate through party organizations to the congressional parties almost unchanged. At the top as well as at the bottom, the American party system thus reflects the cumbersomeness and fractionalism of the American system of government. Whatever policy the parties are able to enact under these conditions is bound to be incremental in nature, and changes in the status quo will be hard to come by. This cumbersomeness is also reflected in the organization of the U.S. Congress.

House Organization

Like all organizations, the House of Representatives adapted to social changes by creating internal structures designed to meet pressures from its various constituencies and to perform its policy-making function.[4] Given the enormous range of interests in the United States and the concomitant pressures they generate, the House responded by erecting a division of labor in the form of a highly complicated committee system. When the country was in its infancy and government was limited, the House formed ad hoc committees; however, by the Jacksonian era, a standing committee system was in place (Cooper, 1970). As the country grew more industrial and complex, the House reacted by expanding and enlarging the committee system. Early in this process, committees were established to deal with such policy domains as war, post offices and roads, and ways and means to raise revenues to support the government. These committees, in George Goodwin's 1970 words "little legislatures," were organized around governmental policy functions; they were and are decentralized decision-making structures. The making of reconstruction policy after the Civil War and Woodrow Wilson's claim that congressional government is committee government testify to the power of committees relatively early in the nation's history (Benedict, 1974; Wilson, 1985).

Decentralizing power to committees was a necessary response to pressures for government action in certain policy areas. It means, however, that to the extent the committees decide policy, party leaders are limited. As decentralized decision-making mechanisms, committees are dominated by members elected to represent local interests (Huitt, 1954, 1957, 1961). The fact that within limits members can choose the committees they serve on determines to a large extent the direction the committees' policy choices will take (Riker,

1982; Fenno, 1973). Representatives choose committees that will enhance their reelection probabilities (Eulau, 1985; Bullock, 1972; Fenno, 1973). Members from agricultural districts serve on the relevant committees and subcommittees; members from other types of districts serve on committees and subcommittees relevant to their constituencies. The domination of committees and policy outputs by local interests is essentially what William Riker (1982) means by congealed preferences.[5]

The decentralized committee system that allows members to represent local interests has become a powerful force for policy stability. In the modern House, Ralph Huitt (1954, 1957, 1961) and others have shown that committees are entities unto themselves—they are stable, having little membership turnover, and new members are socialized to committee norms that affect policy decisions. Since turnover is slow and decision norms remain stable, committee leaders are often able to prevent House majorities from enacting major policy changes. The norms of specialization and expertise as bases of power take years for new members to acquire, thus enhancing both the committees' power and policy stability (Ferejohn, 1974; Shepsle, 1978; Riker, 1982). For example, even though from the late 1930s on a majority of both the American people and the House favored such policies as medical aid for the aged and federal aid to schools, committee leaders were able to obstruct enactment until the mid-1960s. Almost thirty years of obstructing majorities underscores both the independence and the power of the committee system. It is reasonable to conclude that the decentralized House committee system constitutes an effective deterrent to building majorities capable of enacting major policy changes.

What the division of labor pulls apart in organizations, integrative mechanisms have to pull together (Cooper, 1975, 1977). In the House the major integrative mechanism is the majority congressional party. As we have seen, congressional parties are limited by the governmental structure established by the Constitution and by the fact that members are elected by local parties (or groups) on the basis of local issues. Members responsible to, and punishable by, local electorates tend to be responsive to constituents, not parties. Under such conditions, party strength tends to be low. Even when party voting was at its peak in the U.S. House of Representatives, it was low when compared with that of other Western democracies (Lowell, 1909; Brady, Cooper, and Hurley, 1979). Even under ideal conditions the congressional parties in the House have limited integrative capacity (Cooper, 1977; Cooper and Brady, 1981). This means that under normal conditions policy decisions are likely to reflect localized committee interests, thereby limiting the national party leaders' attempts to lead majorities toward forceful policy solutions to pressing problems. House voting patterns show different coalitions active on different policy issues (Clausen, 1973; Sinclair, 1982). Coalitions cut across regional party and social and economic lines, making party leaders' jobs a "ceaseless maneuvering to find coalitions capable of governing" in specific policy areas (Key, 1966).

A third factor also affects the House's ability to legislate quickly. As a collegial body, the House has a limited capacity to organize itself hierarchically (Cooper, 1977; Polsby, 1964, 1968). The American constitutional and cultural emphasis on equality has affected the operation of the House. Because each member represents a separate and equal constituency, members receive the same pay and have the same rights to introduce bills, serve on committees, and so on. Equality in this sense limits the House's ability to organize on a hierarchical basis. Since hierarchy is limited, the House has established elaborate procedural rules and precedents to control the passage of legislation from Speaker to committee to floor (Cooper, 1977). This procedural elaboration emphasizes individual members' rights to affect legislation at various decision points in the policy process. The effect is to slow down the policy process and to encourage compromise to avoid parliamentary snafus. Both slowness and compromise favor incremental solutions to policy problems.

The House, then, is organized as a relatively nonhierarchical body, with power decentralized in committees and elaborate rules and procedures for passing legislation. The weakness of the congressional parties is partly the result of factors external to the House (local elections, cultural stress on equality, separation of powers, and the like) and partly the result of the way the House is organized (members' preference for decentralized power and the lack of leadership sanctions). Although the relationship between committee power and party strength has waxed and waned, in "normal" times committees are strong and the parties weak and divided. This is true in part because localism produces heterogeneous preferences, which limits leaders' ability to enact policy shifts (Rhode and Shepsle, 1985). The policy choices emanating from this system have normally been incremental in nature.[6]

This section has emphasized the confluence of forces and interactions that have led the House from its projected role as a populistic body to one that has developed deliberate, incremental processes. It should be mentioned there are many historical periods when inertia or incrementalism accords with the wishes of the majority of both the public and the House. When this is the case, the congressional system is in harmony with the people's desires. However, as Walter Dean Burnham has argued, political systems must over time adjust to majority pressures for change (1970, chap. 1). It is from this perspective that we examine how the U.S. House has, at times, overcome the psychological, geopolitical, constitutional, and institutional forces that foster incrementalism to produce significant policy changes.

Nonincremental Change in the House of Representatives: The Role of Critical Elections

It is obvious that elections do not generate changes in federalism, separation of powers, checks and balances, and single-member-district plurality elections. These have survived many elections and continue to reinforce incrementalist tendencies. It is equally clear, however, that certain critical elections reflecting partisan realignments have introduced radical, though temporary, changes in the policy-making process. To understand how these realigning elections affect major public policy changes, we must emphasize again that House elections normally are determined by local factors (local interests, organizations, and issues), thereby assuring the dominance of localism in House politics. In partisan realignments, however, elections are dominated by national issues. Prior to realignments, crosscutting issues arise that do not fit within the framework of the existing two-party system. Ultimately, the parties take positions on the issues that offer clear-cut alternatives to voters. When a realigning election occurs, a new congressional majority party is elected on national, not local, issues. Moreover, historically, the new majority party has maintained uninterrupted control of the presidency and both branches of Congress for over a decade (Clubb, Flanigan, and Zingale, 1980).

The most important effect of realigning elections on the House policy-making process is that they enhance the integrative capacity of political parties. During realignments, representatives are elected on the basis of party positions on national issues, and the majority party is united on the issues that led to the realignment. Local factors do not constrain policy choices, and a unified majority party can initiate major policy changes. Realignments also strengthen the congressional party vis-à-vis committees. The influx of new members reduces committee stability, and new leaders support the party position for major policy innovations. The result is increased party voting, especially on the issues that precipitated the realignment.

If this notion of realignment is correct, it should be possible to show that during partisan realignment the following occur: (1) the dominant parties take polar positions on the crosscutting issues; (2) the critical election is characterized by national voting; (3) there is an influx of new members; (4) the new majority party controls the presidency and the Congress for at least a decade; (5) committee turnover is high; (6) party voting increases; (7) party structures voting on the realignment issues; and (8) significant policy changes occur. We turn now to an empirical examination of these points using data from three major realignments: the Civil War realignment, 1854–60; the 1890s realignment, 1894–96; and the New Deal realignment, 1932–36.

Party Positions in the Three Realignments

In the case of these realignments, a principal crosscutting issue dominated the election. The second U.S. party system was broken up by the rise of slavery and, ultimately, the secession issue. The two dominant parties of the 1832–56 period were the Whigs and the Democrats. Each party had northern and southern wings that ultimately could not accommodate the slavery issue. The Missouri Compromise and the Compromise of 1850 were valiant efforts to patch over differences of opinion, but the introduction of the Kansas-Nebraska Act led to the demise of the Whigs. The Republican party replaced the Whigs as the second major party in the 1856 elections, and by 1860 the Democrats were the proslavery party, while the Republicans were the antislavery party. The electorate was thus offered a clear-cut choice between parties and policies.

The crosscutting issue of the 1890s realignment was the issue of "what future for America—industrial or agricultural?" The rise of industrialization in the aftermath of the Civil War generated the displacement of farmers and a change from a society of local, self-sufficient communities to a highly interrelated industrial society. The result was the displacement of agricultural interests and the end of a way of life. The overriding issues involved gold, silver, the protective tariff, and U.S. expansionism. Agricultural interests favored the inflationary coinage of silver (since they were debtors), free tariffs, and antiexpansionism. Industrial interests favored exactly the opposite. The rise of the profarmer Populist party is testimony to

Table 1. Partisan Platform Differences on Major Issues
in Three Realignment Eras

Era	Slavery	Capitalism	Depression
Civil War			
1848	.00		
1852	.10		
1856	.24		
1860	.71		
1890s			
1884		.08	
1888		.04	
1892		.44	
1896		.55	
New Deal			
1920			.02
1924			.30
1928			.19
1932			.26

Source: Adopted from Ginsberg (1972:612).

the existence of crosscutting issues in the 1896 realignment. The Democrats, under William Jennings Bryan, adopted the Populist position, while the Republicans adopted positions favoring gold, protective tariffs, and expansionism.

The New Deal realignment was precipitated by a single event—the Great Depression. The question was, Would the government adopt policies to combat the effects of the depression? The Republican incumbent, Herbert Hoover, would not adopt policies to aid farmers, workers, cities, and the unemployed. The Democratic party had, by 1932, answered by proposing relief funds and programs to aid those most affected by the depression. Once again, voters were offered clear-cut choices between candidates and parties.

To demonstrate this point, Table 1 shows the party differences on these issues in each of the realignment periods, as presented in Benjamin Ginsberg's (1972) analysis of party platforms; the higher the value, the greater the disagreement. Table 1 clearly shows that the Civil War and the 1890s realignments were characterized by deepening party differences in regard to the crosscutting issues leading up to the critical elections. For the New Deal realignment, the pattern is somewhat different. The parties differed in 1924, but it was not until 1932 that the Democrats could convince the electorate to send a new majority party to Congress. In addition, the magnitude of these figures suggests that the parties were less polarized in the positions they took during the New Deal than they were during the Civil War and 1890s realignments (Brady and Stewart, 1982). Still, in each of the realignment eras, the major political parties took opposing positions on the issues of major concern; when voters went to the polls in the elections of 1860, 1896, and 1932, they were offered "a choice, not an echo."

Nationalization of Voting

If realigning elections are precipitated by crosscutting national issues, the congressional election results should reveal the reduced effects of local forces. The standard technique used to determine the effect of national factors is to calculate the variance across House election results over the relevant time period. The argument is that when variance around the mean is low, national factors are at work; conversely, when variance is high, local factors are predominant (Butler and Stokes, 1969). The point of the Butler and Stokes analysis is that variance around the mean swing in pairs of elections measures the uniformity of change, that is, the extent to which national forces are at work. Their analysis, however, compared elections in the United States and Great Britain; analyses within a single country testing for change over time must be interpreted more carefully because realignments can be either compensating or across the board (Flanigan and Zingale, 1974).[7]

The strategy for analyzing electoral change here is first to examine the mean swing in the vote and the coefficient of variation[8] for the following time periods: 1846–76, 1884–1900, and 1924–46. We want to take into account both the mean swing for or against a party and the variance around that mean. The argument is that as the standard deviation increases relative to the mean, local variation is greater than the national trend, whereas as the mean swing increases relative to the standard deviation, national trends eclipse local factors. In short, the lower the value of the coefficient of variation, the greater the likelihood of an election's reflecting national rather than local factors. The data in Table 2 show the average swing in the vote and the average of the variation coefficient for the prerealignment, realignment, and postrealignment periods. The

Table 2. Aggregate Vote Swings and *V*
Coefficients during the Civil War, 1890s, and New Deal Realignments

	Pre-realignment	Realignment	Post-realignment	Controlling Elections
CIVIL WAR REALIGNMENT	1846–1852	1854–1860	1862–1876	1860
Mean change in				
% Democrats	3.26	−5.31	2.87	−6.07
Coefficient of variation	8.09	−4.34	8.15	—
1890S REALIGNMENT	1884–1892	1894–1896	1898–1900	1896
Mean change in				
% Democrats	−1.79	−5.45	−3.13	3.30
Coefficient of variation	−15.41	−3.05	6.27	—
Mean change in				
% Republicans	−2.62	4.39	−2.13	3.67
Coefficient of variation	−8.21	3.20	5.46	—
NEW DEAL REALIGNMENT	1924–1930	1932–1936	1938–1946	1932
Mean change in				
% Democrats	1.40	9.12	−3.79	7.20
Coefficient of variation	8.32	3.04	−9.64	—
Mean change in				
% Republicans	−1.56	−9.60	4.01	−8.00
Coefficient of variation	−16.60	−4.15	13.47	—

table also shows the mean swing and *V* coefficient for the single election that gave the new majority party control of the presidency, the House, and Senate—1860, 1896, 1932, the controlling elections.

Certain structural problems in the years before the Civil War limit us to an analysis of Democratic vote patterns only for that realignment era.[9] Examining that data for the prerealignment period, we can see that the average swing was 3.26 and the average *V* coefficient was 8.09, which indicates a relatively low swing and considerable variation in voting patterns. In contrast, the realignment period (1854–60) has a mean swing of −5.31 away from the Democrats and an average V coefficient of -4.34, indicating national electoral factors at work. The postrealignment period (1862–76) has a mean swing of only 2.87 and a mean V coefficient of 8.15. These data support the hypothesis of increased nationalization of electoral results during the Civil War realignment. The figures for the 1860 election are even more dramatic, with a swing vote of -6.07 away from the Democrats and a low V of -2.81.[10]

The late 1890s realignment also shows national trends at work. In the 1894 and 1896 elections, the Democrats lost 5.45 percent while the Republicans gained 4.39 percent, and the corresponding Vs were at or below 3.20 in each case. This contrasts sharply with the prerealignment period (1884–92), where the Democrats lost 1.79 percent swing and the Republicans lost 2.62 percent swing, with Vs of -15.41 and -8.21, respectively. The postrealignment period is characterized by smaller swing votes and Vs approximately twice as high as during the realignment. The election that shows the most dramatic effect was the 1894 election. This election gave the Republicans a large majority in the House as voters swung away from the Democrats (-7.60 percent) and to the Republicans (5.50 percent). The election of 1896, normally considered the realigning election, was an increase for the Democrats as well as the Republicans (3.30 and 3.67 percent swing, respectively) at the congressional level. The fact that both major parties gained in the Fifty-fifth House elections (1896) over their totals for the Fifty-fourth House is clearly the result of the Democratic merger with the Populist party; the loss for both parties in the Fifty-third House reflected Populist party gains in the 1892 election. Thus, the election pair that most clearly meets the criterion for a shift toward national electoral factors over local factors is the change between 1892 and 1894.

The results for the New Deal realignment (1932–36) provide the clearest example of the nationalization of electoral factors. The coefficient of variation is 3.04 for the Democrats and -4.15 for the Republicans. The Democrats gained 9.12 percent over their prerealignment vote totals, while the Republicans lost 9.60 percent from their respective prerealignment totals. The largest portion of the Democratic gain came in the shift from 1930 to 1932 (7.20 percent) and the concomitant Republican loss of 8.00 percent. The mean swings and the V coefficients in the prerealignment and postrealignment periods support the nationalization hypothesis. Before the prerealignment period, both parties' mean swing was less than 2.00 percent and the Vs were at least twice as high as during the realignment. In the postrealignment period, the mean swings for both parties were around 4.00 percent and the *V*s were between three and four times higher than during the realignment period.

The results for the New Deal realignment are so much clearer than those for the other eras because it was an across-the-board realignment. The realignments of the Civil War and the 1890s era were compensating realignments that involved substantial regional shifts in partisan affiliations, a matter that has been examined elsewhere (Brady, 1985). This does not mean, however, that the Civil War and 1890s realignments did not result in significant shifts in the makeup of the House, which is our prime concern here. Indeed, each of the three realignments resulted in the undisputed control of the House of Representatives, the Senate, and the presidency for at least fourteen years. To understand how the less dramatic electoral shifts in the Civil War era and the 1890s achieved such dramatic results, we must turn to an analysis of the seats-to-votes ratio and its impact on the distribution of seats and policy outcomes.

House Composition, the Seats-to-Votes Ratio, and Policy Outcomes

In the U.S. electoral system, representatives are elected in single-member districts, where a plurality determines the winner. This first-past-the-post rule often distorts the translation of popular votes in legislative seats. For example, a party could win 50 percent of the votes and 70 percent of the seats, a 20 percent distortion. The argument in this section is that during the major electoral realignments in the United States, there was a high seats-vote distortion. We use the percentage difference between seats won and votes won as a measure of this disparity. The seats-votes difference should be greater during realignments than it was during other periods because relatively small swings in vote distributions affected the outcome of marginal districts. This distortion should be particularly evident in the Civil War and 1890s realignments because, as we have seen, there was not a major national shift of votes to Republicans during either of these realignments. In those realignments, about 5 percent of the voters in the northern states shifted to the Republicans.

The results for the Civil War and 1890s realignments corroborate this argument. In the elections to the Thirty-fourth Congress, the Republicans, who became the majority party in the House, enjoyed a differential of plus 20 percent in seats to votes. The 1855–56 elections were fairly even in terms of seats to votes, while in the 1857–

Table 3. Turnover and Unified Party Government: Three Realignments

Era	Turnover in House (percent)	Years of Undivided Party Control	Turnover on Ways and Means (percent)
Pre–Civil War	49.6	2 years since 1840	38.5
Realignment	56.4	14 years (1860–74)	67.9
Pre-1890s	38.7	2 years since 1876	26.5
Realignment	43.4	14 years (1896–1910)	76.5
Pre–New Deal	19.5	10 years since 1912	15.0
Realignment	27.8	14 years (1932–46)	80.0

58 elections, the Republicans again benefited by over 20 percent. The major distortion in the series occurs in the presidential election of 1859–60—over 25 percent. The Republican victory in 1860 grossly increased the seats-votes difference in favor of the new majority party. In the elections that followed, the Republicans retained their advantage but by far narrower margins. In the 1894 elections in northern states, the seats-votes difference was very high, about a 30 percent advantage to the Republicans. The election of 1896 in the northern states also heavily favored the Republicans, creating a 20 percent difference. Thus, in the two critical elections of 1894 and 1896, the Republican victories in the House can be attributed to the seats-votes advantage enjoyed in the northern states. The results for the New Deal realignment show only a slight seats-votes advantage for the Democratic party. In the New Deal realignment, the vote shift in the North to the Democrats resulted in a significant seat-vote distortion in that region, but the distortion was masked by the solidly Democrat South.

Regardless of how the House majority was created, by major vote switches or a seats-to-votes distortion, the result of each realignment was a substantial change in the makeup of the House, as suggested earlier. This can be seen in Table 3, column 1. This change in composition is also expected to result in unified control of the government for an extended period of time and substantial changes in committee membership. Table 3 also presents data on these points, using membership on the Ways and Means Committee as an example of the broader pattern of committee turnover. These data suggest that realignment provides the new majority party with unified

Table 4. Percentage of Party Votes in Prerealignment
and Realignment Eras

	50 Percent Majorities		90 Percent Majorities	
Era	Prerealignment	Realignment	Prerealignment	Realignment
Civil War	66.4	74.7	8.9	20.9
1890s	53.8	76.4	21.1	50.1
New Deal	48.7	69.4	7.9	16.4

control for fourteen years and results in higher turnover in House membership and on committees.

We also expect realignments to increase partisan voting, especially with respect to alignment issues. Party voting in the House should increase because members are not cross-pressured by local interests differing from national party positions. Table 4 shows the average percentage of party votes in the five Houses preceding the realignment and the percentage of party votes in the realignment Houses. Party votes are defined in two ways. First, the percentage of votes that pitted a majority of one party against a majority of the other party (50 percent majorities) is presented. Second, a more stringent criterion is used, defining party votes as those where 90 percent of one party opposed 90 percent of the other (90 percent majorities). The results clearly indicate a rise in partisan voting during each of the realignments.

Although these results help to corroborate our argument, it would be better if we could show that party voting increases dramatically on the crosscutting issues associated with the realignments. We thus created a set of scales for each of the following realignments and issues: Civil War—slavery, secession, and civil rights; 1890s—monetary policy; and New Deal—social welfare (for a fuller discussion, see Brady and Stewart, 1982). We expect party to be highly correlated with voting on each of these issues sets. We measured the extent of the relationship by correlating representatives' party identification with their voting score. The higher correlation ($+1.0$ is the highest), the stronger the relationship and the greater the party structuring of the vote. Table 5 presents the results, which support the hypothesis. In each of the realignments, the correlation between party and support for or opposition to the dominant issue increased during the realignment. During the Civil War and the 1890s realign-

Table 5. Correlation (*r*) between Party Voting and the Crosscutting
Issue in Three Realignment Eras

	Civil War Issue: Slavery, Secession, and Civil Rights					
Year	1853	1855	1857	1859	1861	
Congress	33rd	34th	35th	36th	37th	
r	.551	.41	.89	.87	.88	

	1890s Issue: Monetary Policy					
Year	1891	1893	1895	1897	1899	
Congress	52nd	53rd	54th	55th	56th	
r	.02	.42	.71	.96	.96	

	New Deal Issue: Social Welfare					
Year	1925	1927	1929	1931	1933	1935
Congress	69th	70th	71st	72nd	73rd	74th
r	0	0	0	.72	.89	.94

ments, the Republicans became more antislavery and more in favor of gold, respectively. In the 1930s realignment, the Democrats became more in favor of social welfare. In short, during each realignment, the party structured voting in the House, especially on the realignment issues.

Our last point is that clusters of major policy changes occurred during each of these realignments. In one sense, this is obvious. The Civil War realignment ultimately resulted in the end of slavery, the passage of the Thirteenth, Fourteenth, and Fifteenth amendments, and an increased governmental role in modernizing the economy. The 1890s realignment resulted in noninflationary money, protective tariffs, the annexation of Hawaii, and the Spanish-American War. In short, the 1896 realignment ensured America's industrial future. The New Deal introduced the welfare state to America. Social security, unemployment assistance, prolabor legislation, agricultural assistance, and government management of the economy are but a few of the legacies of the New Deal. Benjamin Ginsberg's

(1976) analysis of policy changes shows this same pattern in a more sophisticated fashion. In sum, it is the case that in each of these realignments, election results were transformed into major changes in public policy. Periods of realignment did transform the House of Representatives into the populistic body the founders thought they had created.

Conclusion

It is evident that the founders' efforts to institutionalize a populistic branch of government that would serve as a barometer of the political climate soon became entangled in a thicket of constitutional, institutional, and political thorns. The House had to operate in a constitutional framework that reflected the framers' desires to thwart the tyranny of the majority and manifested the geopolitical realities of the times. Although political parties emerged to facilitate the operation of the cumbersome constitutional design, they too succumbed to the forces of localism embedded in the constitutional design that enveloped and structured the House. Sectional diversity compounded the electoral factors that reinforced localistic concerns of election-conscious representatives; these concerns also manifested themselves in the committee structure as it emerged during the course of the nineteenth century.

These factors inhibited the ability of political parties to perform the integrative functions that would have allowed the House to act as a populistic body. Instead, they fostered deliberative, incremental forays through the thicket. But it is equally evident that the pace of these forays was quickened during crucial times in the nation's history. Realignment eras introduced new blood into the House and enabled parties to coordinate the cumbersome constitutional system and implement nonincremental change efficiently. We might hail the realignment mechanism as an effective political adaptation to systemic deficiencies, as evidence that the system does work when it must work and that incrementalism prevails in normal times because it is consistent with the desires of the people. Historically, this characterization might be defensible. To assert that realignments will continue to act as political lubricants for the constitutional gristmill, however, ignores some ominous changes in the structure of congressional elections. These changes have reduced the likelihood of future critical elections that will affect the House's role in the policy-making process.

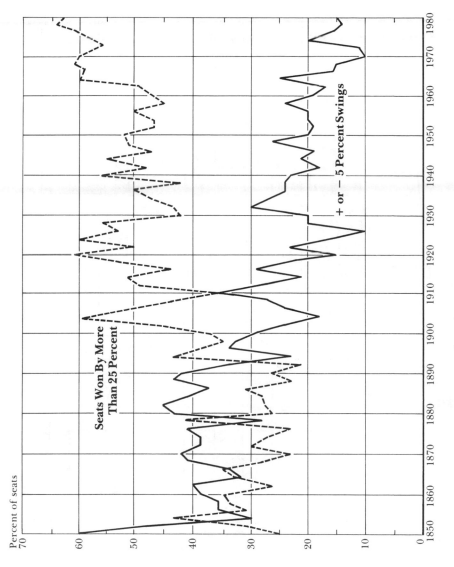

Figure 1. Safe and Competitive Seats, 1850–1980

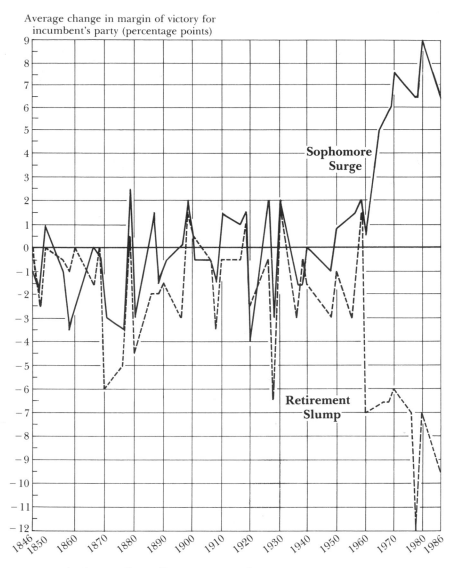

Note: The figure reflects all House races with major party competition. Retirement slump is the difference in a party's share of the vote from one election to the next when the incumbent retires and leaves the seat open. The difference between the two votes is viewed as the amount of the vote that was the incumbent's personal share. Sophomore surge is the increase in the newly elected representatives' vote from their first election to their second.

Figure 2. Sophomore Surge and Retirement Slump, 1846–1986

In the post-1946 era, the number of safe congressional seats has risen dramatically, thereby reducing the number of marginal seats that might be affected by realignments, such as those that occurred around the Civil War and during the 1890s. Figure 1 shows the decline of competitive seats and the rise of safe seats from 1850 to 1980. Moreover, the security of House seats has become increasingly personalized in the post–World War II period. That is, a good share of incumbent representatives' vote totals is based on personal, not party, characteristics. Figure 2 shows the rise of the personal affect in House elections, as measured by retirement slump and sophomore surge.[11] The trend lines reflect the enhanced ability of newly elected members to use the advantages of incumbency to create their own personal vote. The data clearly show that the personal vote factor increases dramatically in the mid-1960s and continues to the present.

The point here is not to elaborate on this well-known theme. Rather, it is to suggest that the decline in marginal districts and the increase of votes on the basis of incumbents' personal characteristics will reduce the president's coattails. House members will owe little to either the president or their party. This will reduce the likelihood that partisan realignments will continue to act as effective brokers of political change in our constitutional quagmire.

NOTES

1. The standard works on this era are Rossiter (1966, 1953), Brandt (1961), Madison (1893), and Wood (1969).

2. For an excellent general statement of the point, see Cooper (1977). For specific studies, see Oppenheimer (1978, 1980), Oleszek (1978), Peabody (1977), and Rudder (1977).

3. This phenomenon is deeply rooted in the American federal system. The Republican party was divided over the gold-silver question prior to 1896 and was divided over the question of welfare and government management of the economy during the post–Franklin D. Roosevelt period. The Democrats were divided on questions of civil rights through a large part of the twentieth century.

4. In the following section, I rely on the work of Cooper (1975, 1977).

5. For a review of committee selection, see Eulau (1985).

6. The formation of the Democratic Study Group (DSG) was a response to this fact. The group was founded to press liberal policy alternatives in a House dominated by cross-party conservative interests (Stevens, Miller, and Mann, 1974). The founders of the DSG found the policy process in the

House cumbersome to operate and weighted toward interests (minority or otherwise) that sought to block legislation, thus preserving the status quo (Burnham, 1970).

7. In a compensating realignment, both parties gain some votes while losing others. Of course, one party gains more than it loses. In an across-the-board realignment, one party gains votes while the other party loses votes. In both cases, as one moves to the realigning election or elections, the variance around the mean is affected because vote totals in districts are shifting, and measures of variance are squared differences; thus, the direction of change is irrelevant. Determining whether a realignment is compensating or across the board is particularly important in the U.S. case because of the regional and cultural variation across the states (Elazar, 1966).

8. The coefficient of variation is

$$V = \frac{S}{X}$$

where S is the standard deviation and X is the mean.

9. Testing for national effects during the Civil War realignment constitutes a problem because the demise of the Whigs, the rise of the Republicans, the secession, and the later readmission of eleven southern states complicate analysis of electoral results. A time series testing for national effects should be run on both major parties for all points in the set (Clubb, Flanigan, and Zingale, 1980), but this is not possible for the 1846–76 period. The analysis for the Civil War period thus focuses on the Democrats' percentage of the vote in each national election. The Democrats contested elections throughout the era, including the period of secession. During the Civil War itself, the Democrats almost won control of the House in the 1861–62 election, and they only narrowly lost the presidency in 1864. Testing for national versus local factors is possible because the Democrats were both stable and competitive over the entire time period. The analysis of electoral changes for the other two realignments is straightforward, given that the Democrats and Republicans are stable in both eras.

10. Unlike either of the two other realignments, the Civil War era had major structural changes that affected the electoral results: the replacement of the Whig party by the Republicans, the secession of the southern states, and their readmission. The elections of 1853–54 and 1855–56 were the two decisive elections that replaced the Whigs as a major party. The analysis of these elections shows a dramatic increase in the mean swing relative to the variance—scores of -2.80 and 2.90, respectively. The Republicans actually won a plurality of House seats in the Thirty-fourth House.

The election of 1859–60, which brought the Republican party full control of the government—president, Senate, and House—also had a coefficient of variance of less than 3.00. In this election, the Democrats lost 6.07 percent of the vote, while the standard deviation was 17.60. The only other election pair with a coefficient of variation under 3.00 was the Fortieth–Forty-first (1866–68) pair. Here, the Democrats gained 3.80 percent, while the variance was only 8.40 percent. The Democratic gain was, in part, a repudiation of radical Republicanism, plus the strong Democratic returns from border states. In sum, elections with low variation coefficients correspond to the structural changes mentioned above.

REFERENCES

Anderson, James. 1979. *Public Policy Making*. New York: Holt, Rinehart and Winston.

Benedict, Michael. 1974. *A Compromise of Principle: Congressional Republicans and Reconstruction, 1863–1869*. New York: W. W. Norton.

Bensel, Richard. 1984. *Sectionalism and American Political Development, 1880–1980*. Madison: University of Wisconsin Press.

Brady, David. 1985. "A Reevaluation of Realignments in American Politics: Evidence from the House of Representatives." *American Political Science Review* 77:331–33.

Brady, David, and Charles Bullock. 1985. "Party and Factions within Legislatures." In *Handbook of Legislative Research*, edited by Gerhard Loewenberg, Samuel Patterson, and Malcolm Jewell. Cambridge, Mass.: Harvard University Press.

Brady, David, Joseph Cooper, and Patricia Hurley. 1979. "The Decline of Party in the U.S. House of Representatives, 1877–1968." *Legislative Studies Quarterly* 4:381–407.

Brady, David, and Joseph Stewart. 1982. "Congressional Party Realignment and Transformation of Public Policy in Three Realignment Eras." *American Journal of Political Science* 26:333–60.

Brandt, Irving. 1961. *James Madison*. Indianapolis: Bobbs-Merrill.

Bullock, Charles. 1972. "Freshmen Committee Assignments and Reelection in the U.S. House of Representatives." *American Political Science Review* 66:996–1007.

Burnham, Walter Dean. 1970. *Critical Elections and the Mainsprings of American Politics*. New York: W. W. Norton.

Burns, James M. 1963. *The Deadlock of Democracy*. Englewood Cliffs, N.J.: Prentice-Hall.

Butler, David, and Donald Stokes. 1969. *Political Change in Britain: Forces Shaping Electoral Choice*. New York: St. Martin's.

Clausen, Aage. 1973. *How Congressmen Decide: A Policy Focus*. New York: St. Martin's.

Clubb, Jerome M., William H. Flanigan, and Nancy H. Zingale. 1980. *Partisan Realignment: Voters, Parties, and Government in American History*. Beverly Hills, Calif.: Sage Publications.

Cooper, Joseph. 1970. *The Origins of the Standing Committees and the Development of the Modern House*. Houston: Rice University Studies.

———. 1975. "Strengthening the Congress: An Organizational Analysis." *Harvard Journal on Legislation* 12:307–68.

———. 1977. "Congress in Organizational Perspective." In *Congress Reconsidered*, edited by Larry Dodd and Bruce Oppenheimer. New York: Praeger.

Cooper, Joseph, and David Brady. 1981. "Institutional Context and Leadership Style: The House from Cannon to Rayburn." *American Political Science Review* 75:412–25.

Dahl, Robert. 1965. *A Preface to Democratic Theory.* Chicago: University of Chicago Press.

Davidson, Roger. 1981. "Subcommittee Government: New Channels for Policy Making." In *The New Congress*, edited by Thomas Mann and Norman Ornstein. Washington, D.C.: American Enterprise Institute.

Elazar, Daniel. 1966. *American Federalism: A View from the States.* New York: Thomas Y. Crowell.

Epstein, Leon. 1980. "What Happened to the British Party Model?" *American Political Science Review* 74:9–22.

Eulau, Heinz. 1985. "Committee Selection." In *Handbook of Legislative Research*, edited by G. Loewenberg, S. Patterson, and M. Jewell. Cambridge, Mass.: Harvard University Press.

Fenno, Richard. 1973. *Congressmen in Committees.* Boston: Little, Brown.

Ferejohn, John. 1974. *Pork Barrel Politics: Rivers and Harbors Legislation, 1947–1968.* Stanford: Stanford University Press.

Flanigan, William, and Nancy Zingale. 1974. "The Management of Electoral Change." *Political Methodology* 1:49–82.

Ginsberg, Benjamin. 1972. "Critical Elections and the Substance of Party Conflict: 1844–1968." *Midwest Journal of Political Science* 16:603–25.

———. 1976. "Elections and Public Policy." *American Political Science Review* 70:41–49.

Goodwin, George. 1970. *The Little Legislatures: Committees in Congress.* Amherst: University of Massachusetts.

Holcombe, Arthur. 1950. *Our More Perfect Union: From Eighteenth Century Principles to Twentieth Century Practice.* Cambridge, Mass.: Harvard University Press.

Huitt, Ralph. 1954. "The Congressional Committee: A Case Study." *American Political Science Review* 48:340–65.

———. 1957. "The Morse Committee Assignment Controversy: A Case Study." *American Political Science Review* 51:313–29.

———. 1961. "The Outsider in the Senate: An Alternative Role." *American Political Science Review* 55:566–75.

Huntington, Samuel. 1965. "Political Development and Political Delay." *World Politics* 17:386–430.

Key, V. O., Jr. 1966. *Politics, Parties and Pressure Groups.* New York: Thomas Y. Crowell.

Lowell, Lawrence A. 1909. "The Influence of Party upon Legislation in England and America." In *American Historical Association, Annual Re-*

port for the Year 1901, vol. 1. Washington, D.C.: American Historical Association.

Lowi, Theodore. 1979. The End of Liberalism. New York: W. W. Norton.

McConnell, Grant. 1966. Private Power and American Democracy. New York: Alfred A. Knopf.

Madison, James. 1893. Journal of the Federal Connection. New York: G. P. Putnam's Sons.

Mann, Thomas. 1978. Unsafe at Any Margin. Washington, D.C.: American Enterprise Institute.

Mayhew, David. 1974. Congress: The Electoral Convention. New Haven, Conn.: Yale University Press.

Miller, John. 1969. Alexander Hamilton. New York: Harper and Brothers.

Neustadt, Richard. 1976. Presidential Power. New York: John Wiley and Sons.

Oleszek, Walter. 1978. Congressional Procedures and the Policy Process. Washington, D.C.: Congressional Quarterly Press.

Oppenheimer, Bruce. 1978. "Policy Implications of Rule Committee Reforms." In Legislative Reform: The Policy Impact, edited by Leroy Rieselbach. Lexington, Mass.: D. C. Heath.

———. 1980. "Policy Effects of U.S. House Reform: Decentralization and the Capacity to Resolve Energy Issues." Legislative Studies Quarterly 5:5–30.

Peabody, Robert. 1977. "The Enlarged Rules Committee." In New Perspectives on the House of Representatives, edited by Robert Peabody and Nelson Polsby. Chicago: Rand McNally College Publishing.

Polsby, Nelson. 1964. Congress and the Presidency. Englewood Cliffs, N.J.: Prentice-Hall.

———. 1968. "The Institutionalization of the United State House of Representatives." American Political Science Review 62:144–68.

Redford, Emmett. 1966. American Government and the Economy. New York: Macmillan.

Reed, John. 1983. Southerners: The Social Psychology of Sectionalism. Chapel Hill: University of North Carolina Press.

Rhode, David, and Kenneth Shepsle. 1985. "The Ambiguous Role of Leadership in Woodrow Wilson's Congress." Paper presented at the annual meeting of the American Political Science Association.

Riker, William. 1982. Liberalism against Populism. San Francisco: W. H. Freeman.

Rossiter, Clinton. 1953. Seedtime of the Republic. New York: Harcourt, Brace.

———. 1966. 1787: The Grand Convention. New York: Harcourt, Brace.

Rudder, Katherine. 1977. "Committee Reform and the Revenue Process." In Congress Reconsidered, edited by Lawrence Dodd and Bruce Oppenheimer. New York: Praeger.

Shepsle, Kenneth. 1978. The Giant Jigsaw Puzzle. Chicago: University of Chicago Press.

Sinclair, Barbara. 1977. "Party Realignment and the Transformation of the Political Agenda: The House of Representatives, 1925–1938." *American Political Science Review* 71:940–53.

———. 1982. *Congressional Realignment, 1925–1978*. Austin: University of Texas Press.

Stevens, Arthur, Arthur Miller, and Thomas Mann. 1974. "Mobilization of Liberal Strength in the House, 1950–1970: The Democratic Study Group." *American Political Science Review* 68:667–81.

Turner, Frederick. 1910. *Essay in American History.* New York: Henry Holt.

———. 1932. *The Significance of the Frontier in American History.* New York: Henry Holt.

Wilson, Woodrow. 1885. *Congressional Government.* Boston: Houghton, Mifflin.

Wood, Gordon. 1969. *The Creation of the American Republic.* Chapel Hill: University of North Carolina Press.

★ 3 ★

Responsiveness in the Upper Chamber: The Constitution and the Institutional Development of the Senate

CHARLES STEWART III

The constitutional convention of 1787 created two distinct chambers in the U.S. national legislature. It is well known that the Senate and House of Representatives differ with respect to both their official duties and their constituencies. The duties and constituency of the House define it as the branch of both federalism and shared executive power.

What is most remarkable about this legislative division of labor is how resilient the Senate has been as an institution over the past two hundred years. The Senate was designed to be far removed from citizens and especially resistant to popular clamorings for change. Given developments in the rest of the world, it might not have surprised us if the Senate had gone the way of the other upper chambers of Western parliaments. Yet the Senate is going strong, while the English lords are but a vermiform appendix in the British body politic and such chambers as the Canadian Senate infrequently make a political mark.

Marveling at the political vitality of the U.S. Senate for most of its history, one is compelled to ask why. Clearly, the chamber that was to be the "saucer that cooled the tea" of national controversy has been anything but a conciliatory legislative arena. There are many ways to approach this question of senatorial vitality; the lens through which this essay approaches it is the Constitution.

The Constitution is a relevant starting point for addressing the question of the institutional development of the Senate for three reasons. First, the framers had several ideas in mind when they endowed the Senate with institutional characteristics fundamentally different from the House's. Even though this vision was occasionally murky at the Philadelphia convention, a clear enough notion of the Senate emerged during the writing of *The Federalist Papers* that we can plausibly claim that the framers had expectations about how the Senate would operate and that they expected it to be different from the House. We can therefore meaningfully compare those expectations with actual historical developments.

Second, even if the Senate did not develop as the framers anticipated, it may still be the case that elements of constitutional design had an unintended influence on how the Senate collectively and senators individually have behaved over the years.

Finally, the issue of the relationship between the Constitution and the evolving behavior of senators and the collective structure of the Senate is appropriate, given political scientists' reinvigorated interest in the question of institutional design, best exemplified by public choice theories of legislatures. Scholars in this tradition have reawakened our awareness to the fact that rules and institutions constrain the behavior of legislators in systematic ways and that policy outcomes are ultimately a patterned product of the institutions through which policy is chosen. The Constitution of 1787 was the quintessential moment of institutional design in the American case; if public choice has any relevance, it should be able to address such real-world questions as the development of the Senate in the light of the Constitution.

In this essay, I first summarize the highlights of public choice theories of legislatures and briefly discuss why the theory suggests that the interaction of preferences with institutions is the focus for understanding patterns of legislative outcomes. To the degree that any constitution can manipulate legislative results, it will do so by circumscribing the preferences of its members and its rules of procedure. Because the U.S. Constitution directly addresses the question of the preferences of senators, the second section examines constitutional provisions relating to senatorial elections, first asking whether the membership of the Senate evolved as anticipated and then discussing why the framers got more than they bargained for. The Senate is far from being a conservative body, judging by its responsiveness to changes in popular sentiment. In fact, the electoral connection between the Senate and its constituents looks a lot like the electoral nexus between citizens and the House. Since the Constitution indirectly addresses the rules of procedure in the Senate, the third section briefly examines how the lack of constitutional constraints on procedures, along with initial expectations about the

Senate's role in the federalist system, guaranteed that the Senate would be an institutionally conservative body.

Legislatures and Public Choice

Research into legislative behavior has undergone a major theoretical reorientation over the past decade. During this time, a theory of legislative behavior rooted in microeconomics has emerged, variously labeled social choice, public choice, political economy, and the new institutionalism. Regardless of the appellation given this approach, there are a few basic premises that distinguish it from past research. In the new institutionalism, legislators are posited as utility maximizers, and legislative institutions emerge as a consequence of the individual utility calculus of each member of the legislature. This approach differs markedly from the sociological approach, which provided the theoretical research categories for the previous generation of legislative scholars.

The sociological and economic approaches to studying Congress differ primarily in terms of the relative weights placed on collective and individual behavior. To the sociologically oriented, legislative behavior is constrained by the operation of norms perpetuated through such processes as socialization and the imperatives of group maintenance. Scholars in the public choice tradition turn this relationship around and see institutional practices, such as formal rules and informal norms, as instruments for the achievement of the individual goals of legislators. Where traditional scholars took formal and informal legislative rules for granted, new institutionalists view these practices in a more instrumental light, assuming they are a product of deliberate choice and subject to change at any time.

There is not one public choice theory of legislative behavior; instead there are several theories, all sharing a core of theoretical presuppositions. While the theoretical and methodological tools of this approach are diverse, the general findings themselves have been replicated and extended, using a number of different research languages. Before proceeding with our empirical examination of the relationship between Senate behavior and the Constitution, we should review some of the findings of this theoretical genre in a general sense, relying more on intuition than on the mathematical formalization that usually characterizes this mode of research.

The earliest theoretical work in public choice analyzed simple generic settings where a group of people had to make a collective choice, such as approving a budget or electing a candidate for office. Through a variety of avenues, a consensus of opinion emerged about the operation of pure majority rule institutions.[1] In a result associated with Kenneth Arrow's (1951) "general impossibility theorem," it has been shown that even if individuals have transitive preferences across feasible policies, there is no guarantee that there is a transitive preference ordering for the entire society.[2] As others confirmed in a spatial voting setting, where legislators prefer proposals to be "close" to their own policy ideals, a diversity of preferences among legislators is usually sufficient to make it impossible to locate a policy outcome that would remain unambiguously the social choice of the entire group (Enelow and Hinich, 1984). Worse, it has been shown that there is rarely one outcome that beats all others in a pure majority rule setting if preferences are spatial; if legislators are free to make motions and continue voting until they hit upon a policy that beats all other possible motions, they will be voting forever. Worst of all, it has been proven that given this "chaos result" in majority rule voting, if anybody is given the right to control the order in which proposals are voted on, then she can manipulate the process so that, in the end, the legislature would choose her position regardless of how bad off this made the rest of the members of the legislature.

These findings are very unsettling. Normatively, they suggest it is vacuous to talk about *a* majority rule or *a* democratic outcome (Riker, 1983). Indeed, the quintessential method of democratic rule, majority voting, seems ill suited to yield final outcomes that are judged "fair" by most standards. Empirically, the "anything can happen" result hardly seems to describe any real-world legislatures, where substantive outcomes typically seem quite stable. Theoretically, these findings are disturbing because it is unclear why rational legislators would endure such a procedure as pure majority rule, which is so unstable and prone to manipulation and perverse policy outcomes.

The theoretical answer to these objections was found in exploring the implications of the following empirical observation: no legislatures we would be interested in studying in fact operate by pure majority rule. Legislatures in real life have numerous rules that limit the operation of majority rule and, in the process, induce outcome stability, reduce problems of agenda manipulation, and allow legislative majorities to ensure against being made worse off by voting on a series of legislative proposals. Reasonable outcomes apparently emerge because legislative institutions limit the ability of legislators to make all possible policy trade-offs and consider all alternatives.

For instance, such institutional practices as establishing standing committee jurisdictions, perfecting bills seriatim, and making germaneness requirements can produce final outcomes that are near the "center" of all legislative preferences. The practice of (implicitly) pairing an amended bill against the status quo as the last vote in legislative consideration ensures that the majority can guarantee it will not be made worse off by passing a bill, although it cannot guarantee the majority will be made better off.

One of the major theoretical points of three decades of work in public choice theory is that so long as legislators are rational and "sophisticated,"[3] and so long as they get to select the rules under which they operate, their legislative rules are likely to guarantee final outcomes somewhere close to the "center" of policy preferences in the legislature. This is not the same as saying rules will guarantee that the "best" or "most preferred" policy will be chosen. It is to say debate will be carried out around the center of legislative opinion, with "fringe" solutions unlikely to be the final outcome. As a corollary, changes in the location of the center of legislative opinion—due to membership turnover, for instance—are likely to alter the set of feasible outcomes.

A second major theoretical conclusion of public choice is that debates over rules of procedure are likely to inherit characteristics of debates over substance. If structure limits what will finally be chosen from the feasible set, then legislative antagonists will fight to ensure that, at the very least, their ideal solutions can be reached through the legislative process. Stated more strongly, they will push to give their own solutions some privileged position within the feasible set.

To conclude with an eye toward the particular case of the Senate, theory tells us that policy outcomes are reached legislatively through an interaction between legislative preferences and legislative rules. There is therefore no guarantee that a shift in legislative preferences will translate into a shift in policy; policy is contingent upon the rules. Although naive theories of democracy may state that shifting policy majorities in the Senate through elections is a necessary and sufficient condition for changing policy outcomes, it is in fact neither. Preferences may delineate the set of all feasible legislative outcomes when structure is endogenously chosen, but rules of procedure are likely to have more influence in determining precisely which outcome is chosen in the feasible set.

Ironically, social choice theory thus emphasizes procedures as much as, if not more than, preferences in predicting which policy will finally emerge in the collective choice in any legislature. Yet the Constitution was written with an eye toward manipulating preferences rather than institutional procedures in Congress. The framers created the Senate and gave it an electoral system designed to insulate it against hasty shifts in opinion, yet, at the same time, they gave the Senate majority a free hand in setting its procedures. If one's focus is on policy outcomes, the framers provided a very blunt instrument—elections—through which to manipulate policy choices. Yet if one's focus is on why the Senate has remained a vital legislative arena over the past two hundred years, the answer lies in the operation of that blunt instrument.

The Senate and the Electoral Connection

Article I of the U.S. Constitution clearly sets out a different set of electoral relations between the Senate and the House, on the one hand, and their respective constituencies. First, it defines altogether different constituencies for the two chambers. As originally designed, members of the House of Representatives were accountable to the voting citizens in the various states—which, in the days preceding universal manhood suffrage, varied markedly cross-sectionally—while senators were accountable to the majorities in the state legislatures.

This bifurcation of constituencies was cemented as a key element of the Great Compromise as a way, in part, to minimize the loss in voting power that small-population states had to endure because of the demise of the Confederation Congress. State legislators presumably had a set of pressing concerns and reasons for being directly represented in the national government that differed from those of ordinary voting citizens. To assuage state legislatures for their loss of a de facto veto over the implementation of national legislation in their states, the compromise enabled state legislators to retain a direct say in making national legislation.

Electing senators through state legislatures was the first of several mechanisms that were supposed to buffer the Senate against the fickle swings of popular mood and maintain "a defense to the people against their own temporary errors and delusions" (*Fed-*

eralist No. 63). Although the state legislatures themselves were ultimately subject to the vagaries of public opinion, they did not respond in lockstep to major changes in public opinion; legislators in the various states had different terms of office, different electoral calendars, and the like. Thus, even if the arena of election had been the only difference between the Senate and the House, we would have expected the Senate to have been a less sensitive indicator of popular sentiment, because it was elected through a series of political middlemen who themselves were responsive to varying electoral systems.

Of course, this was not the only electoral difference between the Senate and the House. The second key electoral difference between the two chambers concerned the term of office and the related division of the Senate into three electoral classes. By requiring only one-third of the Senate to seek reelection every two years, the framers hoped that short-term fluctuations in public opinion would be leveled out in the Senate, allowing only enduring shifts in sentiment to take hold. In addition, because each individual senator had the luxury of six years between elections, while members of the House had to face reelection almost immediately upon taking office, the framers expected individual senators to take the long view in addressing national problems.

Finally, the framers anticipated that the Senate and the House would simply attract different types of individuals, in part because of the different types of electoral incentives offered by the Constitution. They thought the Senate would attract individuals who were more comfortable with insider politics, while the House, with the potential to "go public" guaranteed from the start, would attract those who reveled in the rough-and-tumble of electoral politics.

Early in the nation's history, however, things began to diverge markedly from the expectations of the framers, especially on the Senate side. The greatest divergence from the framers' expectations was the degree to which the Senate became a "popular" institution, as the overtly federal character of Senate membership began to be undermined early in the nineteenth century (Riker, 1955; Haynes, 1906, 1938).

As the nineteenth century progressed, state legislatures had an increasingly difficult time controlling their senators in Washington. Instructions to a senator might or might not be heeded. Lacking the right to recall senators who ignored the wishes of their legislatures, a right that had existed under the Articles of Confederation, the state legislatures had few sanctions with which to induce compliance with their wishes. A few senators resigned when they could not comply with the instructions of their state legislatures, but these acts were few and far between and occurred only as a result of the individual's sense of honor. Counting on their own abilities to explain away their behavior come reelection or hoping the legislative majority would change in their favor before their seats came up again, senators mostly ignored the instructions of their state legislatures when they differed over desired national policy.

The most potent factor weighing against the maintenance of the Senate as a consciously federal institution, as well as dashing hopes that senators would be buffered from the vicissitudes of electoral politics, was the de facto popularization of senatorial elections starting in the early nineteenth century. Prior to the 1830s a candidate for the Senate would typically wait until the state legislature had been elected before campaigning for office among the elected legislators (Riker, 1955). In the 1830s the practice of public canvasing emerged as an electoral device for Senate candidates. The canvas in this case was not of legislators but of voters. Making it clear which state legislative candidates favored and opposed their election to the Senate, candidates for the Senate would effectively run for the Senate among the voting population. Many candidates for the Senate transformed the mechanism of senatorial election much the same way that Andrew Jackson and his successors transformed the electoral college during this period.

In so doing, senators began to reverse the power relationship between state legislators and themselves, so that it eventually favored the senators. In many states senators became the power behind the throne in state legislative races and, ultimately, in state politics. It is therefore not surprising that this system reached its peak by the 1890s, when the Gilded Age Senate became in part a college of state party bosses.

The reform era changed this relationship even further, but only in form, not direction. Popular primaries to pick party nominees for the Senate began in the 1880s and spread quickly throughout the South, Northwest, and Midwest. "By 1910, 44 of the 46 states had primary election laws and 28 of these provided in one way or another for the nomination of party candidates for the Senate at the party primary" (Riker, 1955:466).

The "Oregon system" further whittled away the federalist orientation of the Senate and its popular insulation. In the early 1900s, Oregon went beyond popular party nomination for the Senate to provide for a plebiscite in the November election to choose among the candidates who had been nominated in the party primaries. Oregon's state legislators were pledged to elect to the Senate the winner of the plebiscite at the next meeting of the legislature.

Troubles with the Oregon system, along with popular reform momentum, carried the formal transformation of the senatorial election system to its logical conclusion in 1911, when the Senate sent to the states what became the Seventeenth Amendment, providing for the direct, popular election of senators.[4] In a handful of states, the passage of the Seventeenth Amendment occasioned a radical departure from the past manner of choosing senators. For most states, however, the Seventeenth Amendment merely ratified a clear trend toward centralization of government authority and popularization of elected offices. Instead of *causing* such a realignment, the amendment *was caused* by the changing relationship between citizens, states, and the federal government.

Still, we should not lightly dismiss the Seventeenth Amendment as a mere epiphenomenal expression of popular will and part of inevitable historical progress. Once the amendment passed, there was no going back to a system of elite-dominated politics to the degree that existed in prior generations. For all the power that senators managed to exercise over their state legislators in the late nineteenth century, the state legislatures still had some residual, independent authority over senators that was permanently destroyed by the Seventeenth Amendment. It is therefore important to examine whether the Seventeenth Amendment did indeed have any effect on the nature of senatorial membership or, at the very least, whether changing patterns of Senate membership coincided with the popularization of the Senate that gathered steam at the beginning of the twentieth century.

The Effects of Electoral Popularization Reconsidered

We can never be entirely certain how the informal and formal inauguration of popular elections of senators changed the U.S. Senate. Given the development of popular elections, it is unlikely that the Seventeenth Amendment effected a radical departure from the immediate past, since most senators were already being elected through quasi-direct procedures. Even in the few states that had resisted the advances of popularization, state legislatures were popularly elected; state legislators would not have survived very long politically if they had made a practice of sending individuals to the Senate who were perversely unrepresentative of state preferences.

Circumstantial evidence of this conjecture is provided by the fate of three cohorts of senators: those who sought reelection between 1908 and 1912 (immediately before the Seventeenth Amendment took effect), between 1914 and 1918 (the first cohort to fall under the Seventeenth Amendment), and between 1920 and 1924. For the 1908–12 cohort, the best data available indicate that 73 senators sought reelection to the Senate. Of these, 45 (62 percent) won reelection, 9 (12 percent) were defeated in a primary, and 15 (21 percent) lost in the legislature.[5] Of the 1914–18 cohort, 78 sought reelection. Of these, 58 (74 percent) were ultimately successful, 5 (6 percent) lost in a primary, and 15 (19 percent) were defeated in the general election. Finally, the electoral fate of the 1920–24 cohort was similar: 89 sought reelection, of whom 58 (65 percent) were reelected, 8 (9 percent) lost in a primary, and 23 (26 percent) were defeated in the general election. Thus, although more senators might have sought to remain in office after 1914, reelection rates did not change significantly during this transition period to the formal direct election of senators.

Although the last Senate cohort elected by state legislators stood the test of formal direct election very well, that does not mean the electoral dynamics—and thus the patterns of membership change— had begun to mimic perfectly those of the House. Nor does it necessarily mean that the Senate has become as popular an institution as the House is. For evidence on this score, we need to turn to a series of explicit comparisons of Senate and House elections over the past two centuries.

It is nearly impossible to test directly whether the framers succeeded in creating, through the electoral system, a Senate that was more contemplative, more reasoned, and less parochial than the House. It is equally difficult to tell how the Seventeenth Amendment changed all that. It is easier to examine whether other characteristics—principally stability—were instilled in the collective membership of the Senate by the constitutional design and implementation of the electoral process, and whether that stability became unsettled at the beginning of the twentieth century. Specifically, we can hypothesize that (1) because senators serve longer terms of office, the average senator should serve more years in the Senate than the average representative serves in the House; (2) because senators are divided into classes for election, the Senate should be less susceptible to wild swings in its membership than the House is; and (3) because senators' terms are longer and staggered, shifts in policy majorities in the Senate and House should rarely coincide. If the Seventeenth Amendment had any influence on the electoral differences between the two chambers, electoral swings in the Senate should more closely mirror those in the House after 1914, although the remaining constitutional differences should keep the Senate and House from converging entirely.

For the remainder of this section, I examine the evidence for different electoral patterns between the two chambers. Because so little research has been done on the electorally induced differences between the Senate and House—especially historical research—some of these findings must remain preliminary. Yet, by examining the membership differences between the two chambers that are a product of the Constitution of 1787, popularization, and the Seventeenth Amendment, we will be on the way to a greater understanding of issues of constitutional design.

Average Chamber Service. The first empirical question to be addressed is whether senators, on average, have served in their chamber longer than members of the House over time. The simplest way to answer this question is to examine the average prior service of senators and representatives at the beginning of each Congress (see Figure 1). Between approximately 1820 and 1900, the Senate clearly

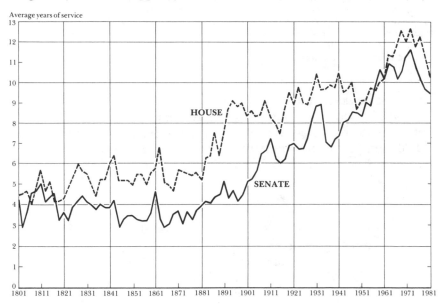

Figure 1. Average Years of Service for Senators and Members of the House, 1801–1981.

Table 1. Rookies Serving in the Senate and House, 1901–21

		Senate			House		
Congress	Year	Percent rookies	6-election moving avg.	Diff.	Percent rookies	6-election moving avg.	Diff.
57	1901	0.213	0.217	−0.004	0.282	0.418	−0.136
58	1903	0.172	0.207	−0.035	0.355	0.396	−0.041
59	1905	0.204	0.208	−0.004	0.248	0.362	−0.114
60	1907	0.216	0.211	0.005	0.274	0.322	−0.048
61	1909	0.243	0.210	0.033	0.229	0.288	−0.059
62	1911	0.327	0.229	0.098	0.350	0.290	0.060
63	1913	0.248	0.235	0.013	0.383	0.307	0.077
64	1915	0.130	0.228	−0.098	0.327	0.302	0.025
65	1917	0.279	0.241	0.039	0.232	0.299	−0.067
66	1919	0.178	0.234	−0.056	0.279	0.300	−0.021
67	1921	0.234	0.233	0.001	0.307	0.313	−0.006

Note: *Percent rookies* is the percentage of members in the House or Senate who were serving their first term during that Congress. The column of figures labeled *6-election moving average* reports the average percentages of rookies in the House and Senate over the previous six elections. The columns reporting the differences between these two figures indicates whether the number of first-term legislators in a chamber during a particular Congress was higher or lower than recent history. The figures reported in the difference columns do not always equal percent rookies minus the 6-election moving average because of rounding.

had a more stable membership, with its members serving on average one to two years longer than representatives. Increased longevity and careerism also arrived earlier in the Senate, beginning in the 1880s compared with the 1890s in the House. The peak difference in longevity occurred at the beginning of the Fifty-fifth Congress (1897), when senators served an average of 8.8 years, while representatives served an average of 4.2 years.

This difference changed abruptly at the turn of the century. Senate elections between 1906 and 1912 produced higher-than-average turnovers in the chamber, while the House experienced high turnover levels in the elections between 1910 and 1914 (see Table 1). Because representatives already served fewer years in Washington than senators did, average service fell more precipitously in the Senate. In subsequent years, senators have on average served slightly longer tenures than representatives have, but the difference has been small.

Table 2. Average Percentage of Senators and Representatives
Returning upon Expiration of Their Terms, 1789–1981

Congresses	Years	Senate	House
1–10	1789–1809	42.7	59.0
11–20	1809–1829	43.3	51.8
21–30	1829–1849	40.2	45.6
31–40	1849–1869	36.4	43.7
41–50	1869–1889	39.4	52.3
51–60	1889–1909	52.0	64.7
61–70	1909–1929	53.6	73.3
71–80	1929–1949	54.4	73.0
81–90	1949–1969	69.0	82.9
91–97	1969–1981	59.7	81.6

The principal reason behind the continuing longer service for senators (albeit fewer years difference) is their longer terms of office, because they are less likely to be reelected when their terms expire than are members of the House (see Table 2). Yet the rapid convergence of the average length of service in the Senate and House that occurred at the beginning of the twentieth century (see Figure 1) suggests that popularization and the Seventeenth Amendment must also be involved.

We have to credit both informal forces and the Seventeenth Amendment at this point. Extraconstitutional forces must be credited because the major convergence in years of service occurred before the Seventeenth Amendment took effect. In fact, it is likely that the rapid turnover in Senate membership before 1911 was actually a cause of the Seventeenth Amendment, since the senators who entered in the elections immediately prior to 1911 were much more likely to vote in favor of the amendment (see Table 3).

Once average length of service in the Senate and House had become nearly equal, the Seventeenth Amendment might have helped perpetuate the House-Senate convergence.[6] Popular election enabled the Senate to be more directly affected by the same swings in popular sentiment that buffeted the House. It also gave a larger number of ambitious state politicians a reasonable shot at running for the Senate, resulting in more frequent and serious challenges to incumbent senators seeking reelection.

In summary, from around 1810, when the Senate emerged as an institution whose members valued Senate service enough to serve

Table 3. Senate Votes on Seventeenth Amendment
by Length of Service, June 12, 1911

		First Year in Senate	
		1907 or Earlier	After 1907
Vote	Yes	20	44
	No	12	12

full terms, senators served longer than did members of the House. For formal and informal reasons this pattern of longer tenure has diminished in the twentieth century, at times disappearing altogether.

Partisan Swings. The second empirical question to be addressed is whether the Senate has been less susceptible than the House to wide swings in its policy majorities. The answer to this question was anticipated in the process of answering the first, since a legislative body that has a longer average tenure is also likely to have less turbulent policy majorities. But there is no guarantee that this will be the case, so we need to add substance to this answer by analyzing the partisan character of membership fluctuations in each chamber. The simplest way to examine whether the Senate's policy majorities have been more enduring than the House's is to ask (1) whether the Senate has typically exhibited less partisan imbalance than the House, and (2) whether swings in partisanship from one Congress to another have been smaller in the Senate.

Although it would seem that the Senate is guarded against having extreme partisan compositions, it is the case that the partisan composition of the Senate has been no more "moderate" on average than that of the House. Before 1914, the average plurality of the majority party in the Senate was 64 percent, while the average plurality in the House was 63 percent. Subsequent to 1914, the average plurality has been 59 percent in the Senate and 60 percent in the House.[7]

Although the size of partisan majorities in the two chambers has been about equal throughout history, the Senate has exhibited more muted partisan swings from one Congress to the next. Before 1914, the partisan composition in the Senate would change on average 6.4 percent after each election, compared with the average change in the House of 9.6 percent.[8] After 1914, these figures become 5.5 percent for the Senate and 7.0 percent for the House. Thus, throughout history the Senate has been less likely than the House to experience a dramatic change in partisanship between Congresses. Since both chambers have had less volatile changes in partisanship since 1914, it is unlikely that the Seventeenth Amendment had much affect on the partisan variability of the Senate in the twentieth century.

Simultaneity of Partisan Swings. The third and final question about differences in electoral patterns between the Senate and House concerns the degree to which shifts in policy majorities have occurred simultaneously in the two chambers and whether the Seventeenth Amendment influenced that pattern.

Throughout U.S. history it has been common for a congressional election to alter the partisan control of at least one of the chambers of Congress. Counting the number of times since 1787 that the various branches of the federal government have changed partisan hands, and the number of times we have had a divided government, is complicated by the fluidity of U.S. political parties in the eighteenth and nineteenth centuries. If we make some simplifying assumptions, for instance treating the Jeffersonian, Democratic- Republican, and Democratic parties as being the same, then the House has changed partisan hands 23 times since 1789, the Senate 17 times, and the presidency 18 times (U.S. Bureau of the Census, 1976: tables Y204-10). This means the House changed partisan control following about one-fourth of all biennial elections, the Senate after one-sixth of all biennial elections, and the presidency after one-third of all quadrennial elections.

In keeping with the expectations of the framers, the Senate has been less likely to change partisan hands over the years—17 versus 23 times. Yet this difference disappears, and even changes direction, when we divide our analysis before and after 1914. Before 1914, there were 62 biennial elections, during which the Senate changed partisan hands 9 times (15 percent), while the House changed hands 17 times (27 percent). Since the institution of popular elections for senators, the House has changed hands 6 times in 38 biennial elections (16 percent) and the Senate 8 (21 percent).[9] Thus, in any given election, the Senate is now slightly more likely to change partisan control than the House is.

We are left with some inconclusive results about the relative partisan volatility in the two chambers. The average party majority in each chamber has been about 60 percent throughout U.S. history, and partisan swings are likely to be smaller in the Senate than in the House. On the other hand, where it really counts—in determining which party has a majority—the Senate has moved from being significantly less volatile than the House to being slightly more mercurial since the onset of popular Senate elections.

There is no easy way to resolve this puzzle, other than to note that partisan pluralities and swings operate at such close tolerances that such a paradox is possible. One thing is clear, however: whatever greater partisan stability the Senate might once have had is now gone. By two measures—average annual partisan swing and probability of party control changing hands—the Senate and House are nearly identical.

By probing deeper into electoral dynamics, we see how the six-year, staggered term for senators helps insulate it from even greater partisan swings than it currently exhibits. For this analysis, I divided the Senate into three electoral classes and examined the degree of partisan variability from election to election within electoral classes.[10] Since 1914, the average partisan swing in each class of senators has averaged 16 percent—over twice the average partisan swing in the House. Among the individual classes, Class 3 is the most volatile, with an average 20 percent swing; classes 1 and 2 both exhibit average 14 percent swings.

There is one final way in which we can observe the substantive effects of the different electoral calendars facing senators and representatives: by examining the swing ratios of the two chambers.[11] Since the passage of the Seventeenth Amendment, the Senate has exhibited an overall swing ratio of 1.33, meaning that a 1 percent shift in the electorate toward the Democratic party would add another 1.33 percent Democrats to the Senate.[12] This is almost identical to the swing ratio of the House of 1.35 during the same period. The Senate and the House thus have had nearly equal swing ratios since the formal institution of direct senatorial elections. This is quite surprising, considering that in any given election two-thirds of the Senate cannot change partisan hands.

We can disaggregate the Senate figures a bit more to demonstrate greater sensitivity of individual Senate classes to shifts in national partisan sentiments. When we use as a base of comparison only those Senate seats up for election in any given year, the swing ratio of the Senate more than doubles, from 1.33 to 2.69. Further dividing into individual classes reveals even greater variability: Class 1 has a swing ratio of 3.03, Class 2 of 2.06, and Class 3 of 3.58. Classes 1 and 3 have swing ratios that are statistically indistinguishable from each other; Class 2's swing ratio is statistically smaller than the other two. The reason for this is unclear, although Class 2 appears to contain more one-party Democratic states than do the other two classes.

Summary. Let me conclude this section by returning to the framers' expectations and the conventional views about the Senate that pertain to the electoral system. Has the Senate had a more stable membership than the House? Has the Senate provided a check against hasty shifts in public sentiment?

On the issue of stability, the evidence points in divergent directions. On net, however, we must conclude that the greater stability that characterized the Senate through the nineteenth century has all but disappeared in the twentieth; senators and representatives now serve about the same amount of time in Congress.

On the issue of providing a check against the turbulence of public sentiment, the evidence is clearer that the framers achieved what they wished. First, recall that the Senate simply changed partisan hands less frequently prior to 1914. In addition, because the electoral settings of the chambers do not coincide, the Senate and the House have rarely changed partisan control at the same time. To return to the data, the Senate and the House have switched party control simultaneously only 9 times in American history, although the House and Senate, considered alone, have changed hands 23 and 17 times, respectively.

Interestingly, partisan change in the two chambers has become more synchronized since the onset of popular senatorial elections. Before 1914, partisan shifts in the two chambers coincided only 4 times, or 24 percent of the House shifts and 44 percent of the Senate's. Since 1914, partisan shifts have coincided 5 times, consisting of 83 percent of the shifts in the House and 63 percent of the shifts in the Senate. It is impossible to know for sure, but it is likely that this greater coincidence in partisan shifting since 1914 is a consequence of both senators' and representatives' responding to the same constituents—the public.

The electoral system envisioned by the framers no longer exists in fact, although fragments of it might have existed at one point. The one electoral provision of the 1787 Constitution that continues to meet the framers' expectations is the division of the Senate into electoral classes. That provision alone appears to keep the Senate from actually having a more volatile membership than the House.

It is quite ironic that in the late twentieth century the Senate has in many ways become at least as "democratic" as the House, when electoral effects are examined. Counterbalancing the staggering of-Senate terms is a number of factors—both constitutional and extra-constitutional—that have resulted in the Senate's increasing susceptibility to swings in public sentiment. Among these are:

1. *The Seventeenth Amendment.* As discussed earlier in this section, by the 1910s the Senate was already becoming a popular electoral institution through a series of ad hoc mechanisms, although at an uneven pace across the states. The Seventeenth Amendment ratified what was becoming a common understanding about the relationship between citizens and the federal government and extended that understanding evenly throughout the nation. The Seventeenth Amendment also ended any pretense the Senate had of being a uniquely federalist institution that formally united the state and federal governments. From 1914 to the present, senators have had to express allegiance to the voters and not even a hortatory allegiance to the state governments as such.

2. *Six-year terms.* After the Senate became fully and formally a popular electoral institution, the six-year term of senators actually might have helped popularize the institution, ironically, by removing senators from the electoral arena long enough to allow potential opponents to hone their skills for a future challenge (Fenno, 1982). During the same period in which senators are spending six years attending to legislation, members of the House are attending to legislation and running for reelection twice; governors may also run for reelection once or twice during the term of a single senator. Thus, once a senator returns to the campaign trail in earnest, she may be facing an opponent who has had opportunities to run other races in the state more recently than the incumbent senator, and she thus may not be an entirely advantaged candidate for reelection. Although the six-year term may improve the quality of Senate legislation, it probably works to the detriment of senators-as-candidates.

3. *State-level constituencies.* Having an entire state as one's constituency is certainly part of what adds to the prestige of being in the Senate, but it also adds to the factors increasing senatorial vulnerability under a regime of popular election. In part because senators cannot dominate statewide media markets as easily as members of the House can dominate local media markets, much of what voters know about senators is beyond the control of senators. In contrast, voters know less about their representatives in the House and what they do know is more likely to be controlled by House members themselves (Jacobson, 1987).

In addition to having to deal with more unwieldy media markets, senators must face an electoral landscape littered with more potential challengers than members of the House confront. Research has revealed that senators, like members of the House, are more likely to lose reelection when they face "high-quality" challengers (Abramowitz, 1988; Stewart, 1989). The key difference here, however, is that Senate challengers are of significantly higher quality than are challengers running against incumbent members of the House. The final consequence of this is that senators are more likely to fail in their reelection attempts, producing on aggregate a chamber that is more volatile from Congress to Congress and therefore more responsive to changing national policy sentiments.

For these and other reasons, the Senate has not lived up to the hopes of the framers, who anticipated that the Senate, compared with the House, would be characterized by an added "permanency to provide for such objects as require a continued attention and a train of measures" (Federalist No. 63). This is not to say that the constitutionally defined electoral system causes senators to be like members of the House. The longer term of office may very well make individual senators more likely to take the long view about policy; having a state for a constituency rather than a subdivision of a state may make individual senators less parochial than their House counterparts. Yet, because of electoral dynamics, the contemporary Senate as an institution is no more conservative than the House, and it has not been for a long time. If recent developments are any predictor of the future, the Senate may be in the process of becoming an even more turbulent, partisan arena.

The electoral dynamics of the Senate are a big part of what has helped maintain its viability in an epoch when parliamentary upper chambers have generally declined. In much the same way that presidential candidates began to cultivate mass followings in the second quarter of the nineteenth century, senators took advantage of the constitutionally mandated electoral regime, wresting control of the process from state legislatures beginning in the 1830s. Senators thus began to appeal directly to voters. Because their indirect constituencies were so large, senators were allowed to engage in debates about the major issues of the day. Senators, such as Daniel Webster, Henry Clay, and John Calhoun, became very popular national politicians as a result of addressing the great questions of their day from the venue of the Senate (Peterson, 1987).

The degree to which senators and the Senate could address voters directly and circumvent state legislatures all but formally was demonstrated in the Lincoln-Douglas debates of 1858. It is often forgotten that these debates were part of a popular canvas for the Senate, and the fact that the debates took place in numerous public gatherings, rather than in the closed confines of Springfield, indicates the level of public attention paid to senatorial attitudes and the audience to which senators addressed themselves at this time.

When the Senate became the "Millionaires' Club" during the Gilded Age, reformers could legitimately complain that the Senate was moving away from historic practice, if not constitutional design. By then it was expected that senators would serve the people and that the Senate would not be an isolated bastion of conservatism. Progressive reformers thus continued what the senators themselves had begun, opening up the Senate to all voters, once and for all, through the Seventeenth Amendment.

The actual practice of senatorial elections helped open up the Senate, make it a popular body, and save it from the scrap heap of history. Citizens, aroused by issues as far-flung in time as slavery and the nomination of Robert Bork to the Supreme Court, have felt it their legitimate right to pressure their senators into action, and the Senate has maintained its legitimacy by responding as a popular electoral institution. Yet elections are only half of what makes the Senate what it is. The other part of the equation involves the procedural rules of the Senate, the topic to which we now turn.

Rules of Procedure

Article I, Section 5, of the Constitution gives both the Senate and House the right to "determine the rules of its proceedings." Beyond this clause, the document gives Congress very little guidance as to how to structure itself.

Potentially significant restrictions are found elsewhere in Article I: Section 7 gives the House gatekeeping authority over tax legislation, which presumably prohibits the Senate from changing tax laws without previous House action; Section 8 delineates the expressed powers of Congress, therefore limiting the range of policies open for motion and consideration; and Section 9, the so-called little bill of rights, prohibits Congress from enacting, and implicitly from considering, certain types of legislation, such as bills of attainder and ex post facto laws.

Over time, however, these restrictions have proven very yielding. Section 7 has been frequently violated, if not in letter, certainly in spirit. For instance, in 1911 the Senate substituted a corporate tax in a House-passed inheritance tax bill, and the Supreme Court rejected a challenge to this action. More recently, the 1982 tax bill that increased revenues by $98 billion over three years was first considered by the Senate Finance Committee. The committee tacked the package onto H.R. 4961, a miscellaneous tax bill that had already passed the House. Before doing so, the committee removed all the House-passed provisions from the bill, leaving only the Senate language. After passing the Senate, H.R. 4961 went immediately to conference, where a final version was hammered out. Thus, when the House finally approved the conference report on H.R. 4961, it was voting for the first time for the tax increase (Fessler, 1982).

Section 8 has been liberally interpreted through expansive readings of both its commerce and "necessary and proper" clauses. The enforcement of Section 9 has been a mixed bag as well. Congress and the courts have acquiesced to blatant violations of the section, as Lincoln's suspension of habeas corpus during the Civil War illustrates. The restriction that "no money shall be drawn from the Treasury, but in consequence of appropriations made by law; and a regular statement and account of the receipts and expenditures of all public money shall be published from time to time" is certainly violated by the provision for "black" (i.e., secret) line items in the federal budget hidden from public scrutiny due to claims of national security.

The degree to which congressional practice has deviated from the letter of the Constitution is one indication of how hard it is to design *ex post* institutional self-restraint *ex ante*. Relying on James Madison's device of "ambition counteracting ambition" to ensure that its strictures were followed (*Federalist No. 51*), the Constitution was silent on enforcing its prescriptions about congressional behavior. Yet even if the political ambitions of the incumbent politicians in the different branches are usually at loggerheads, they are not always so, which allows constitutional practice to begin a slow drift away from its letter and to set new precedents guiding future behavior. The Supreme Court, which has emerged as the most enduring third-party enforcer of the constitutional contract, has rarely waded into institutional issues, leaving them to be resolved as "political questions."

The issue of constitutional interpretation as it relates to congressional behavior, and especially as it informs relations between Congress and the presidency, is a wide-ranging topic, the intricacies of which are beyond the scope of this essay.[13] Suffice it to say that even where the Constitution explicitly delineates congressional power and limits institutional practice, there is no guarantee that its limits will be respected. In an era such as the present, in which constitutional issues are seen as being in the purview of the courts, members of Congress have spent less time worrying aloud about the constitutionality of their actions. Rather, they are willing to rely on the Supreme Court to rule, knowing that the Court may dismiss a suit about congressional action on the grounds that it is a political question—in which case the legislative majority has achieved its desires—or the court might overturn congressional action—in which case the congressional majority can use the Court as a convenient scapegoat.

Where there is no question about congressional discretion is in setting the rules of procedure of the two chambers: they have full rein, subject only to minimal judicial oversight.[14] Yet this discretion means that the Constitution actually has very little effect on the internal structure of the Senate. This is not to say that the Constitution has no effect. Although the direct effect has been weak, there are indirect influences that are quite significant.

The most important indirect constitutional effects on senatorial procedures grew out of the Senate's initial role as a federal chamber, its small size relative to the House, and the provision for a weak presiding officer in the Senate. Its size and its function helped maintain procedural egalitarianism once the House became more hierarchical. When the Senate did become large and more senators became interested in expanding the federal government's role in society, it was nearly impossible to control senatorial proceedings to the degree that the House had been controlled. Two institutional practices that emerged as a consequence and continue to set the Senate apart from the House—complex unanimous consent agreements and the filibuster—ultimately served to increase the Senate's conservatism, materially affecting the development of policy.

The Constitution also established the vice-president as the presiding officer of the Senate. This occurred almost as an afterthought in the Philadelphia convention. Originally, the Committee on Detail made provisions for the Senate to elect its own president; this arrangement was adopted without opposition and remained unquestioned for a month. Eventually, however, concerns were expressed about presidential succession and the lack of a "casting" vote in the Senate. These two issues came together to produce the vice-president's role as president of the Senate.

Although the installation of the vice-president as the Senate's presiding officer allowed a few vice-presidents to have greater political leverage, such as John Adams, Thomas Jefferson, and Lyndon Johnson, vice-presidents have generally been extraordinarily weak senatorial leaders. The reason for this weakness is found in Article I, Section 5; if the Senate can write its own rules, it does not have to give its presiding officer any independent power. Even if the presiding officer had independent power, the Senate can challenge any ruling of the chair, a check on the power of the presiding officer that has been exercised more frequently in the Senate than in the House.

Because the Senate's presiding officer comes from outside the Senate, and thus rarely shares senators' political concerns in a visceral sense, there is little reason to expect that a majority of senators would give great discretion to the vice-president. Lacking discretion and independent authority, the vice-president has never had a toehold to acquire any greater power in the Senate. In the House, toeholds were provided that permitted some Speakers, like Henry Clay and Thomas B. Reed, to gain even greater power and expand the political role of the House's presiding officer.[15] Lacking strong procedures (as I will discuss below in more detail), the Senate also has lacked strong leaders with unilateral authority, and it probably never will have them as long as its presiding officer is imposed on it from the outside.

The formal and informal differences in Senate and House operations are well known. The Senate is the more collegial of the two bodies, and has less formal structure, including looser rules of debate and fewer amendment restrictions on the floor. One consequence of this relative lack of hierarchy and control is that it is easier for the Senate to get tied in procedural knots. The restrictions in the House serve to move legislation along by limiting the number of individuals who directly affect the content of legislation, the number and scope of amendments, and the amount of time that legislation is considered on the floor.

Whence come these differences? Most of the general explanations for the genesis of these differences have focused on the relative size of the two chambers. Indeed, when the House was a relatively small institution in the late eighteenth century, it, too, operated with few rules and little hierarchy.[16] There were few limits on debate and few standing committees. Legislation was initially considered and debated on the House floor through a motion by one of its members.

After the House debated the issue and arrived at a sense of its members, a special committee was appointed to draft specific legislation for final passage (Young, 1966). As the House grew in size, however, it became harder to reach initial agreement on the floor, since more members meant more people wanting to speak and a larger country meant more problems to be addressed.

The rapid growth of the House in its early years thus led to the imposition of a number of limits to legislative egalitarianism. The motion for the "previous question," which was originally created for other purposes in 1789, was extended in the House to cut off debate in 1811. In addition, as the size of the House grew, the legislative practice of first debating an issue on the House floor and then having a committee draft a bill was reversed. Throughout the early nineteenth century, the right of committees to act on their own initiative was expanded, as was the roster of standing committees (Sklandony, 1985; Cooper, 1970).

The Senate grew much more slowly than the House and thus encountered institutional strains more gradually. It took the Senate forty-eight years to double its size from its original twenty-six members, when Michigan was admitted to the Union in 1837; the House, on the other hand, took only fourteen years to double its original size, after the reapportionment of 1800 took effect. On the eve of the Civil War, the Senate was just reaching the same size as the 1789 House (see Table 4).

On top of these size differences—which affected transaction costs of legislating—early common expectations led the House to become the more active legislative body. Indeed, senators in the early years often remarked about their lack of work, and Senate sessions frequently adjourned early in the afternoon so that senators could watch the more active, raucous, and interesting House at work.

In the early years, the combination of size, activity, and role led senators to have little desire to follow the House's lead in structuring and circumscribing the activity of its members. Debate was free and unfettered. Scheduling legislation and coming to a final agreement were facilitated in the cozy confines of the small Senate club.

These early beginnings would limit the ability of policy majorities to guide the Senate's action easily, once legislating and partisan conflict became more pointed in the late nineteenth century. At the same time that Speakers were acquiring greater power to control debate on the House floor, senators were honing the filibuster to a fine art. While the House was empowering the Rules Committee as an instrument of partisan agenda control, the Senate was having to

Table 4. Size of the Senate and House Following Decennial Censuses

Year	Senate		House	
	Size	Percent Change	Size	Percent Change
1789	26	—	65	—
1793	30	15.4	105	64.1
1803	34	13.3	141	34.3
1813	36	5.9	181	28.4
1823	48	33.3	213	17.7
1833	48	0.0	240	12.7
1843	54	12.5	221	−7.9
1853	62	14.8	223	0.9
1863	50	−19.4	241	8.1
1873	74	48.0	292	21.2
1883	76	2.7	326	11.6
1893	88	15.8	356	9.2
1903	90	2.3	386	8.4
1913	96	6.7	435	12.7
1923	96	0.0	435	0.0
1933	96	0.0	435	0.0
1943	96	0.0	435	0.0
1953	96	0.0	435	0.0
1963	100	4.2	435	0.0
1973	100	0.0	435	0.0
1983	100	0.0	435	0.0

Note: The size of the House in each year reflects the size of the House set following the previous apportionment; the size of the Senate reflects the number of states in the Union at the commencement of the Congress in which the House reapportionment took effect.

schedule and structure debate on the floor, often through complex unanimous consent agreements.

The filibuster is the best known of the delaying tactics available to senators, playing a role in guiding policy outcomes in most important issues of the twentieth century, from the debate over the League of Nations to civil rights, from energy regulation to abortion. As important as the filibuster has been in guiding policy outcomes in the Senate, it is important to remember that even without the filibuster the Senate has always had few mechanisms to expedite action and many with which to impede it.

I should reiterate that nothing in the Constitution mandated the Senate to maintain a set of rules that effectively prohibited legislative action. The Constitution's effect on Senate obstructionism has been indirect, through setting the initial conditions and assumptions about the Senate's governing role. In an institution with numerous vehicles for a small minority to obstruct majority action, it was likely some minority would obstruct attempts to change the rules that made obstruction possible in the first place—witness the battle over cloture from the 1950s through the 1970s (Sundquist, 1968; Oleszek, 1988).

In a more practical vein, the filibuster threat, the lack of a strong agenda committee, and a weak presiding officer increase the number of people who must agree to a policy change in order for legislation to pass in the Senate. Before the passage of Rule 22 (cloture) in 1917, the most important legislation had to please everybody—or, more likely, it could not be so onerous that any nontrivial minority would be willing to pay the cost of talking endlessly so legislation would die on the floor.

Since the advent of cloture, the size of the aggrieved minority sufficient to block legislation has grown, but it is still true that on very important issues, at least 60 percent of the Senate—the current number necessary to invoke cloture—must approve the legislation.[17] The threat of the filibuster gives strength to all other blocking mechanisms and guarantees that almost every bill of consequence must please a supermajority (i.e., a majority greater than 50 percent).

What are the consequences of this? Not surprisingly, it makes changing policy more difficult in the Senate than in the House, other things being equal. From a theoretical standpoint, as one increases the number of individuals necessary to agree to change policy, the set of feasible alternatives gets smaller. There is less room for bargaining, and there is less chance that radical departures from the past will be chosen.

Finally, it is interesting to note that the Senate betrays surprising similarities with the pure majority rule institution of spatial voting models. Debate is difficult to cut off, amendments are difficult to limit, and, with no germaneness rule in the Senate, even the dimensionality of legislation is difficult to confine. It is thus more likely that "anything can happen" in the Senate, including the inability to reach an equilibrium policy solution. It is this inability to guarantee cloture—of both the technical and more general kind—that frequently keeps the Senate from acting and makes it inherently, over the long term, a more conservative institution than the House.

Conclusion

The Senate as an institution manifests many of the characteristics anticipated by the writers of the Constitution, even as it has evolved into a very different entity. In general, it is an institution that is slow to change and slow to act. Yet, over time, the Senate has become a more popular institution, even rivaling the House in the degree to which it is a legislative body responsive to voters. Indeed, in the twentieth century, Senate membership has been more volatile than the House membership, presumably meaning that turnover in policy preferences has at times accelerated in the Senate while languishing in the other body.

At this point, it is natural to wonder what the consequences of the dual senatorial character in this half of the twentieth century—greater responsiveness to electoral shifts in its membership, yet greater conservatism in its institutional practices—are for senatorial policy-making. For the 1950s and 1960s, the answer to that question would be relatively straightforward. This was a period when presidents were leading the way as the federal government actively expanded its role in society. Analyses of domestic policy-making during this period (e.g., Sundquist, 1968) convey the sense that it was a story of House activism and Senate recalcitrance. Because there is little evidence that the median senator and representative were radically different in their policy preferences during this era, much of the explanation for senatorial recalcitrance must lie with its institutional forms that encourage obstructionism.[18]

Civil rights legislation is an interesting case in point. While it is true that the passage of legislation through the House and Senate was influenced by institutional factors in each chamber, the Senate was much more likely to be handcuffed from action than was the House.

For instance, the House passed a four-part civil rights bill in 1956, providing for a civil rights commission, institutional elevation of the civil rights division in the Justice Department, authority for the attorney general to intervene on behalf of those whose civil rights were being violated, and voting rights' guarantees. Following House passage, the bill languished in the Senate Judiciary Committee for the rest of the session; proponents were unable to get the bill to the floor both because the Senate Judiciary Committee was chaired by John Eastland of Mississippi, who kept the bill bottled up, and because efforts to have the bill considered on the floor through shrewd parliamentary maneuvers failed with the threat of a filibuster. Once the bill passed the House again in 1957 on a 286-126 vote, the Senate was hampered from acting on a strengthened measure. In fact, instead of addressing the bill directly, civil rights supporters unsuccessfully tried first to amend Rule 22. The bill was finally considered on the floor only after a rare parliamentary maneuver that intercepted the bill before it could be referred to the Judiciary Committee. In this instance, the filibuster still played an important role, since the threat of staging a talkathon prompted supporters to accede to gutting the bill of its most potent provision, which would have allowed the attorney general to intervene on behalf of any individual whose civil rights were violated (the famous Part 3 of the bill).

Most telling in the journey of civil rights legislation through Congress was 1959, following a landslide that swept liberal Democrats into the Senate, almost all of whom favored a dramatic extension of civil rights laws. Even though Senate Democrats were much more liberal on civil rights measures than they had ever been (Carmines and Stimson, 1986) and were more liberal than House Democrats, Rule 22 was still left unchanged, and the Civil Rights Bill of 1960 that finally passed both chambers was significantly weaker than a majority of each chamber would undoubtedly have approved. It is not implausible to suspect, although impossible to prove, that a high threshold for cloture delayed the passage of tough, effective civil rights legislation for a decade, while discrimination continued and the nation's racial climate turned ugly.

Imagining the consequences of greater institutional conservatism since the mid-1960s becomes a murkier issue. The major difficulty in assessing the final consequences is that so much of this period has been characterized by deeply divided government, both between and within the branches. During much of the Nixon and Reagan administrations, Democratic majorities in Congress found themselves skirmishing with Republican presidencies to such a degree that any institutional conservatism endemic to senatorial action was overwhelmed by the inherent conservatism induced by partisan division of power between the branches. Absent a clear, coherent national agenda in both branches of the federal government, it is difficult to draw any conclusions about the role of the Senate's institutional conservatism in policy-making in recent years.

This past decade brought the most telling piece of evidence concerning senatorial conservatism: the tremendous turnover in Senate membership that accompanied Ronald Reagan's election in 1980. Interestingly, this radical departure from past membership was met with a radical departure in policy. The new conservative Senate quite easily moved to endorse the broad outlines of Ronald Reagan's economic and fiscal program—certainly more easily than did the House. Moreover, the Senate did so without the threat of the filibuster hanging over its head. It must be said that by 1980 the threshold for cloture had been lowered, so it was less of a threat, given the size of the Republican majority. In an ironic twist, it was the Senate, not the House, that reinforced the conservative electoral shift of 1980, giving Ronald Reagan the partisan beachhead he needed to effect a fiscal and domestic policy revolution in Washington.

To conclude, I want to return to the question that began this essay: how has the Senate retained its vitality in a world of declining upper parliamentary chambers? The primary answer here is electoral. Had the Senate remained the chamber of federalism, elected to promote the interests of the state governments rather than of the state electorates directly, it, too, probably would have faded from political relevance. The vitality of the Senate, therefore, rests with the actions of entrepreneurial senators who, in the middle part of the nineteenth century, began going over the heads of state legislators, seized the initiative in the electoral arena, and transformed the Senate as an institution in the eyes of the public. It is this popularization of the Senate that has allowed it to survive, even though other similar chambers have faded and even though it occasionally failed to act in important policy areas.

NOTES

1. In a pure majority rule institution, a member of the institution makes a motion to replace the status quo (the current policy or the policy that exists absent any positive legislative action) with something else. The members all vote. If the motion carries, it becomes the new status quo and another motion is permissible. If the motion fails, there is no change in the status quo, but another motion is still permissible. Motions continue to be made until the legislature reaches a point where (1) nobody wants to make a motion to replace the current status quo, (2) no possible motion could upset the status quo, or (3) the legislature votes, by majority rule, to cease the process and accept the last motion that passed as the final outcome. Classic examinations of pure majority rule can be found in Black (1958), Arrow (1951), and Riker (1962).

2. Transitivity can be understood as follows. Imagine that A, B, and C are feasible policy outcomes. An individual is said to have transitive preferences across A, B, and C if she prefers A to B, B to C, and therefore A to C.

We write this relationship as $A > B > C$. Her preferences would be intransitive if she preferred A to B, B to C, but C to A.

Transitivity for groups is defined similarly. If the group unambiguously prefers A to B, B to C, and A to C, then the social preference ordering is said to be transitive.

The possibility of *social intransitivity* arising from *individual transitivity* can be seen in the following simple example. Imagine three individuals, X, Y, and Z, who order outcomes A, B, and C as follows:

	Individual		
	X	Y	Z
First preference	A	C	B
Second Preference	B	A	C
Third Preference	C	B	A

Each individual has a transitive preference ordering over the three alternatives. Now, allow the three to vote for the three alternatives, pairing two against each other in a series. If A is paired against B, A gets 2 votes (because X and Y prefer A to B) and wins. Now, pair the winner, A, against C. Here C wins, because Y and Z both prefer C to A. If the social choice ordering were transitive, then C would beat B in a pairing because we have already established that $C > A > B$. Yet in this case, X and Z both prefer B to C and therefore (socially) $B > C > A > B$.

A common mistake made in interpreting the Arrow impossibility theorem is to assume that social intransitivity is a *necessary* consequence of social choice settings. All Arrow shows is that social transitivity is not guaranteed and that intransitivity is therefore *possible* when all individuals have transitive preferences. Monte Carlo simulations, in which fictional legislators are endowed with random preferences, show that the probability of social intransitivity emerging from individual transitivity rises either as the number of individuals increases or as the number of dimensions on which proposals can be evaluated grows larger (Ordeshook, 1986:58).

3. *Sophisticated voting* is a technical term in game theory, but its definition is easy to understand intuitively. It is contrasted with *sincere voting*, in which legislators never misstate their preferences when called upon to vote between two proposals. Sophisticated voting requires legislators to weigh all ballots and issues to be considered later when casting a vote. Thus, sophisticated legislators might vote against a proposal they prefer at one step in a sequence of votes if it would prevent an even worse proposal from ultimately passing. The classic treatment of sophisticated voting is found in Farquharson (1969). See also Denzau, Riker, and Shepsle (1985).

4. The Senate had been the sticking point for several decades in getting this amendment out of Congress and to the states. The House had resolved to submit such an amendment to the states as early as 1894, but the Senate demurred for the next seventeen years. The Senate was finally spurred into action by the membership turnover produced by the 1910 election and by

the large number of states that had memorialized Congress for a constitutional convention to consider this and other amendments.

5. We are, at this point, unable to differentiate between senators who simply lost in the state legislative election and those who lost in a plebiscite that was ratified by the state legislature.

The data used here and in the rest of this chapter to examine Senate membership patterns were taken from the Interuniversity Consortium for Political and Social Research (ICPSR) data set, "Roster of United States Congressional Officeholders and Biographical Characteristics of Members of the United States Congress, 1789–1985: Merged Data." The original investigators and the ICPSR bear no responsibility for the analysis that follows.

6. Average career length in the Senate and House became more alike in the twentieth century because of changes in career patterns in both chambers. The literatures of political science and history have explored changes in House careers in some detail. Increasing stability of House membership between 1890 and 1910 has been attributed to the polarization of partisan sentiments in congressional districts, along with an increase in the value of House service due to the institutionalization of seniority (Cooper and Brady, 1981; Price, 1971, 1975, 1977; Polsby, 1968; Polsby, Gallaher, and Rundquist, 1969).

7. Neither do the other summary moments about the mean—variance, skewness, or kurtosis—reveal that the two "partisan plurality distributions" are different.

8. These percentages are based on the entire membership of the chamber. For instance, a gain in Republicans in a 100-member Senate from 55 to 61 would be a 6 percent partisan swing.

9. The presidency has exhibited similar volatility since then as well. Starting with the 1916 election, there have been 19 elections, 7 (37 percent) of which have resulted in a change in partisan control of the presidency. Between 1792 (Washington's second election) and 1912, there were 31 elections, 11 (35 percent) of which resulted in changing the party of the president.

10. Class 1 faced election in 1916, 1922, 1928, 1934, 1940, 1946, 1952, 1958, 1964, 1970, 1976, 1982, and 1988; Class 2 in 1918, 1924, 1930, 1936, 1942, 1948, 1954, 1960, 1966, 1972, 1978, and 1984; and Class 3 in 1914, 1920, 1926, 1932, 1938, 1944, 1950, 1956, 1962, 1968, 1974, 1980, and 1986.

11. The swing ratio is a much-used measure in political science that indicates the relationship between the change in the vote received by a party over two elections and the change in the seats held by that party. In a purely proportional electoral setting, the swing ratio would be exactly 1, indicating that a 1 percent change in votes received by a party between two elections would yield a 1 percent change in the number of legislative seats held by that party. Because the United States is not a proportional system, but instead elects its legislators in districts using the plurality rule (in most cases), the swing ratio is unlikely to be 1. Seen another way, the swing ratio

is a measure of the responsiveness or sensitivity of the electoral system. As the swing ratio gets larger, shifts in partisan sentiment have a greater impact on sentiments in the legislature. As the swing ratio gets closer to zero, shifts in partisan sentiment within the electorate are less likely to translate into partisan swings within the legislature. The swing ratio in the House has frequently been examined, but the Senate has rarely been studied using this measure.

12. Another way of thinking about this result is that for each 3 percent change in partisan sentiment in the electorate from election to election, 4 Senate seats change from one party to the other on net (because $3 \times 1.33 = 3.99$).

The calculation of the swing ratio here is made by regressing seats on votes since 1914. Stephen Ansolabehere, David Brady, and Morris Fiorina (n.d.) define the measures of votes used as the average plurality the Democratic party received in each state for a particular election year. Traditionally, one would simply use the percentage of aggregate votes received by the Democrats nationally. As Ansolabehere, Brady, and Fiorina show, however, the traditional measure is a biased estimate of two-party vote share and yields a biased estimate of the swing ratio if turnout is correlated with partisanship, as is true in the United States.

13. The best politically sensitive exploration of these issues can be found in Fisher (1978, 1988).

14. The classic example of judicial intrusion into congressional prerogatives defined by Article I, Section 5, is *Powell v. McCormack* (1969). For a general discussion of court rulings on the application of Article I, Section 5, see Corwin (1978) and Congressional Reference Service (1987:120–22).

15. For Clay, this toehold was the appointment of representatives to committees. For Reed, this was the power to recognize members during floor debate.

16. The apportionment of the House provided by the Constitution allowed for sixty-five representatives.

17. An interesting recent development in the use of the filibuster as an obstructionist tactic has been the willingness of senators to stall in order to block legislation for a more local concern. Historically, the filibuster had been reserved for broad national, or at least regional, issues such as civil rights. This extension represents two developments: first, learning on the part of senators; second, the fact that once the federal government began providing more domestic programs to citizens there were simply more programs of local economic import for senators to try to protect (Calmes, 1987).

A development mitigating the effectiveness of the filibuster as a delaying tactic is the practice of putting legislation on parallel "tracks," which effectively allows the Senate to consider legislation while other bills are being filibustered.

18. A good analysis of senatorial and House preferences during this time in the area of civil rights is found in Carmines and Stimson (1986).

REFERENCES

Abramowitz, Alan. 1988. "Explaining Senate Election Outcomes." *American Political Science Review* 82: 385–404.

Ansolabehere, Stephen, David Brady, and Morris Fiorina. N.d. "Turnout and the Calculation of Swing Ratios." Stanford University Graduate School of Business, Research Paper Series, no. 990.

Arrow, Kenneth J. 1951. *Social Choice and Individual Values.* New Haven, Conn.: Yale University Press.

Black, Duncan, 1958. *Theory of Committees and Elections.* New York: Cambridge University Press.

Calmes, Jacqueline. 1987. " 'Trivialized' Filibuster Is Still a Potent Tool." *Congressional Quarterly Weekly Report* 45:2115–20.

Carmines, Edward G., and James A. Stimson. 1986. "The Politics and Policy of Race in Congress." In *Congress and Policy Changes,* edited by Gerald C. Wright, Leroy N. Rieselbach, and Lawrence D. Dodd. New York: Agathon.

Congressional Reference Service. 1987. *The Constitution of the United States of America: Analysis and Interpretation.* Washington, D.C.: Government Printing Office.

Cooper, Joseph. 1970. *The Origins of the Standing Committees and the Development of the Modern House.* Houston: Rice University Studies.

Cooper, Joseph, and David Brady. 1981. "Institutional Context and Leadership Style: The House from Cannon to Rayburn." *American Political Science Review* 75:411–26.

Corwin, Edward S. 1978. *The Constitution and What It Means Today.* 14th ed. Princeton, N.J.: Princeton University Press.

Denzau, Arthus, William Riker, and Kenneth Shepsle. 1985. "Farquharson and Fenno: Sophisticated Voting and Home Style." *American Political Science Review* 79:1117–34.

Enelow, James, and Melvin Hinich. 1984. *The Spatial Theory of Voting.* New York: Cambridge University Press.

Farquharson, Robin. 1969. *Theory of Voting.* New Haven, Conn.: Yale University Press.

Fenno, Richard F. 1982. *The United States Senate: A Bicameral Perspective.* Washington, D.C.: American Enterprise Institute.

Fessler, Pamela. 1982. "House Members' Suit Disputes Constitutionality of '82 Tax Bill." *Congressional Quarterly Weekly Report* 40:2761–62.

Fisher, Louis. 1978. *The Constitution between Friends.* New York: St. Martin's.

———. 1988. *Constitutional Dialogues.* Princeton, N.J.: Princeton University Press.

Haynes, George H. 1906. *The Election of Senators.* New York: Henry Holt.

———. 1938. *The Senate of the United States.* 2 vols. Cambridge, Mass.: Riverside.

Jacobson, Gary. 1987. *The Politics of Congressional Elections.* 2d. ed. Boston: Little, Brown.

Oleszek, Walter. 1988. *Congressional Procedures and the Policy Process.* 3d. ed. Washington, D.C.: Congressional Quarterly Press.

Ordeshook, Peter. 1986. *Game Theory and Political Theory.* New York: Cambridge University Press.

Peterson, Merrill D. 1987. *The Great Triumvirate.* New York: Oxford University Press.

Polsby, Nelson. 1968. "The Institutionalization of the United States House of Representatives." *American Political Science Review* 62:144–68.

Polsby, Nelson, Miriam Gallaher, and Barry S. Rundquist. 1969. "The Growth of the Seniority System in the U.S. House of Representatives. *American Political Science Review* 63:787–807.

Powell v. McCormack. 1969. 395 U.S. 486.

Price, H. Douglas. 1971. "The Congressional Career—Then and Now." In *Congressional Behavior,* edited by Nelson Polsby. New York: Random House.

———. 1975. "Congress and the Evolution of Legislative Professionalism." In *Congress in Change,* edited by Norman Ornstein. New York: Praeger.

———. 1977. "Careers and Committees in the American Congress: The Problem of Structural Change." In *Parliamentary History,* edited by William Aydelotte. Princeton, N.J.: Princeton University Press.

Riker, William. 1955. "The Senate and American Federalism." *American Political Science Review* 49:452–69.

———. 1962. *Theory of Political Coalitions.* New Haven, Conn.: Yale University Press.

———. 1983. *Liberalism against Populism.* San Francisco: W. H. Freeman.

Sklandony, Thomas. 1985. "The House Goes to Work: Select and Standing Committees in the United States House of Representatives." *Congress and the Presidency* 12:165–87.

Stewart, Charles. 1989. "A Simultaneous Determination Model of Senate Elections." *Legislative Studies Quarterly* 14:567–601.

Sundquist, James. 1968. *Politics and Policy.* Washington, D.C.: Brookings Institution.

U.S. Bureau of the Census. 1976. *Historical Statistics of the United States.* Washington, D.C.: Government Printing Office.

Young, James Sterling. 1966. *The Washington Community, 1800–1828.* New York: Columbia University Press.

⋆ 4 ⋆

Entrepreneur in the Constitutional Marketplace: The Development of the Presidency

BERT A. ROCKMAN

The principal question posed in this essay is, How has the Constitution influenced the development of the presidency as an institution? From one standpoint, the answer seems painfully clear, especially to every incumbent president. The occupant of the presidency is often stymied and frustrated by countervailing political forces. Constitutional doctrines of the delegation and separation of powers—the package of checks and balances—lead presidents of the modern era to think the deck is stacked against them. From their perspective, the theory of checks and balances becomes checkmate in practice. The constitutional doctrines, of course, reflect the framers' rejection of a centralized, hierarchical, command mode of government. They ensure that presidents are usually in competition with other agents and institutions of government.

Ironically, though, the most important long-term trend in American government is the enhancement of the central government and, consequently, the ascendancy of the presidency. Paradoxically, this long-term trend means that modern presidents are expected to make policy, yet lack the exclusive ability to choose the policy course. The forces structured by the Constitution impinge on presidential power, but they do so amidst long-term trends that seem to have increased the presidential role. The fragile institutional balance established as a result is thus linked both to the Constitution and to the historical trends that have focused more political attention on Washington and the presidency. The Constitution provides for the emergence of a political marketplace. As a result of the long-term trends, presidents strive to become monopolists in this marketplace, but they are constitutionally deterred from fulfilling that aspiration.

The Constitutional System as Marketplace

The thesis of this essay is that the American political system is analogous to an economic marketplace in which suppliers of public goods (political authorities) compete. The system is designed to create many suppliers through federalism and the separation of powers. The market shares held by each supplier, however, are only partially demarcated by the Constitution itself. Actual practice, stemming from the evolution of norms and legal interpretations, tends to define these shares more clearly but often only temporarily. That is why Richard Neustadt's (1980) characterization of the American political system as a system of separate institutions sharing powers is correct.

In this conceptualization of the system, collusion occurs as well as competition. Even in economics, collusion is not always bad. Shared risk and joint capital ventures for large-scale undertakings can be desirable. In politics, collusion also may be good when similar risks—decisions to make large commitments, for instance—must be undertaken. Decisions to go to war, to raise taxes, to cut expenditures, or to restructure allocations may involve sufficiently large risks that collusive behavior among suppliers leads to an efficient outcome. More frequently, though, such collusive behavior occurs when policy goods rather than their costs are to be distributed (i.e., when the incentives for logrolling dominate those for syndicating risk).

How shall we think of collusive and competitive behavior? What are the goods and bads each of these behaviors produces? A lot depends on our prior assumptions about human behavior—on our views about the role of stability and conflict processes. Competition brings excitement, conflict, and instability, and also promotes entrepreneurship. Collusion brings stability and peace but also the potential for a static equilibrium and a willingness to allow the supply of public goods to be determined by the convenience and comfort of the prevailing players, not by demands made in the political marketplace. Unfortunately, we lack a clear theory of how each form of behavior contributes to, or subtracts from, the public welfare.

The framers, in the end, rejected a system of hierarchy and command but not necessarily one of collusion. Indeed, in a system of competitive suppliers, equilibrium is likely to be induced only through collusion (cooperation) rather than through hierarchy. By scorning the construction of a hierarchical framework, the framers created a unique system that could oscillate between competition and collusion but would be remarkably resilient in its capacity to resist command. In any competitive market, of course, one or more of the suppliers may seek to establish dominance. Throughout U.S. constitutional history, two sets of suppliers have become increasingly ascendant. The first of these is the federal government itself vis-à-vis the states and local governments; the second is the president. This must be kept in perspective, however, because all suppliers of public goods have become more active. By any measure, government, even in these times of contracting pressures, is more active than it was, say, a century ago. That means the states and local governments, as well as the federal government, supply more public goods. Yet it is the federal government whose presence, even as it operationally flows through other levels of government, has grown most sharply. This is so even while public policy in the U.S system is still strongly characterized by state and local influences.

As the influence of the federal government itself has been extended, so too the role of the president within the political system has grown. The presidency has grown more powerfully in expectation and public visibility than in the legal or political means for performance, but that, in turn, gives rise to the legitimacy of presidential entrepreneurship in the system (Lowi, 1985). This evolution means that presidents often are frustrated, because despite the development of the entrepreneurship norm, presidents typically cannot dominate the system in the sense of generating a monopolistic position. Nonetheless, they will have strong incentives to seek to do precisely that (Moe, 1985).

By modern standards, the U.S. system of government still remains splendidly diffuse (or disastrously so, depending on one's outlook) in its design of authority and its actual operations. Most certainly, it is a government in competition with itself. The growth of public policy, a consequence of modernity, is itself a stimulant to further competitiveness on the part of all suppliers.

When all the suppliers are actively competing to determine public policy, the result is often a competitive disequilibrium in which no supplier clearly predominates, though each typically is striving to do so. Such is the normal condition of American politics, which is fundamentally derived from the Madisonian principles of setting ambition against ambition, articulated in *Federalist No. 51*.

I focus here on one aspect of this competition: the division of authority within the federal government itself, more specifically, between the two actively competitive agencies—the presidency and Congress. In this competitive market, no institutional actor is better positioned than the president to gain an upper hand. Centrality, visibility, and initiation are the powers that inhere in the office. Constitutionally, the branches of government are reputed to have been born equal, but the realities of modern political and social life have steadily eroded that presumption. The presidency holds a disproportionate market share in modern public life but, to the regret of most modern presidents, not a monopoly. Presidents often try to turn the system of shared powers into a system of presidential monopolization. This tendency has been at the heart of contemporary controversies regarding accountability and, particularly, the operational powers of Congress. Whatever the powers endowed to presidents, many in recent times have deemed them insufficient in relation to the ones they believe are needed.

The reasons for this development are complex. Certainly sheer growth in the supply of public goods has elevated expectations about the minimum standards for government performance (Rose, 1976a). The visibility and centrality that enable presidents to be policy entrepreneurs also serve to increase their risks. Whereas members of Congress are able to blame institutional shortcomings while promoting themselves personally (Fenno, 1978), no president can afford a similar luxury. The incumbent is the institution.

In recent times, the role of the United States as an imperial power also has exacerbated conflict between branches, because no domain of behavior is as ambiguously demarcated as that which has become ubiquitously characterized as national security policy. In national security decision making, presidents have especially powerful advantages in the political marketplace. Decisiveness, initiation, and the fusion of policy (government) and symbolic (head of state) roles give presidents a powerful, yet not monopolistic, share of the policy market. The norm of presidential preeminence here exists in the minds of presidents and scholars alike. As one of the latter recently has lamented, "The design of the Framers was such that the functioning of institutions depends on small balances, and the balances underlying the presidency have shifted. The result is that the president has not been able to carry the public very far in foreign policy" (Horowitz, 1987:26). Here, however, the problem is not so much public fickleness about minimal standards for government performance (dictating, for example, the management of short-run macroeconomic forces) as it is the application of maximum expectations held by presidents themselves as crisis managers (and agitators).

Metaphors can be powerful but also fragile. They easily become more entertaining than exacting. Their power is to evoke persuasive images and analogues that bring about compelling insights. Their frailty is that they are always in danger of being pushed too far and of forcing more straightforward explanations and descriptions into a confining mold.

The institutional features of the American system, however, lend themselves to metaphors derived from economics. This is largely because the fundamental principles of the Madisonian logic are analogous to those of market economics. In this regard, Adam Smith's economics and moral philosophy may be a more central analogue than Newtonian physics. Competition is an all-important value, deterring the accretion of power (monopoly share) by any single authority (supplier). Yet, as we know, a situation that is often highly satisfactory to the consumer is, for exactly that reason, often unsatisfactory to the supplier. Presidents thus understandably try to increase their market share, lessen the chaotic struggle for policy control, and expand their resources to meet public expectations and presidential goals.

There are times, of course, when policy supply is rejected in favor of shirking behavior, a condition that arises precisely because of the existence of an alternative supplier. When the costs of supply are high and collusive behavior becomes impossible, Congress and the president can blame one another for failing to supply policy. Consider, for example, the federal budget situation during the Reagan administration. Neither institution was willing to supply policy except, of course, one that would not be accepted by the other branch. Each branch, recognizing the structure of this market, had an incentive to be a shirker. Government thus operated through continuing resolution, a mark of its continuing irresolution. But in such seeming irresolution, a fragile equilibrium was established. The status quo looked better to each institutional actor than the preferences of the other.

The central constitutional question posed by these conditions is whether such outcomes or deadlocks are an inevitable consequence of the design of American institutions. The short answer is no, as I have argued at greater length elsewhere (Rockman, 1990). Deadlock and shirking are the products even of governments in which power legally is fused. Nonetheless, the American system contains powerful incentives toward institutional collision in the absence of a mutual interest in collusion.

It is certainly the case that the U.S. Constitution is overwhelmingly biased against simple majoritarianism. The institutional design is fully a part of the same fabric that emphasizes the use of concurrent majorities and outsized coalitions. If a competitive disequilibrium is normal, there are two potential evolutionary paths toward resolving the problem of authority in the American system. The first points to the establishment of a normative and legal hierarchy. This undoubtedly would favor presidents, since presidents, by virtue of their role, are best positioned to become the hierarch. To a certain extent, this already seems to have occurred in the minds of some presidents, but hierarchical notions hardly have gone unchallenged. The other potential path points to collusion, particularly over issues in which it is in the interest of the authorities to share political risks, as in the case of the 1990 budget agreement. To say the least, there are numerous obstacles to such tendencies, but that, of course, is the constitutional logic—to prevent the monopoly of power.

Alternatively, there is the path of least resistance, which is to deny that there is a problem of authority or that the prevailing competitive disequilibrium is a wholly acceptable outcome. This outlook suggests that the status quo should prevail, except under exceedingly rare circumstances. The power of decision inherently is the power to alter the status quo. If decision is made difficult, the status quo is advantaged. From this standpoint, competition among suppliers brings an acceptable equilibrium among policy consumers when they have little desire to diverge from the status quo. Based on the public's propensity for split-ticket voting, there is reason to think this is a fair assumption.

One line of argument about the U.S. Constitution and its bias against concentrations of power has been precisely this: on matters of critical importance, the status quo should be advantaged in the absence of a far-reaching consensus, or, to put it in the language of our metaphor, the status quo should be altered only when demand for a new policy product is both deep and extensive. Whether or not this is regarded as acceptable no doubt depends on one's view of the status quo. Nonetheless, even if acceptable to the consumers of public policy, the status quo is almost always unsatisfactory to the suppliers who struggle for competitive advantage.

The struggle was constitutionally preordained, though the balance of forces has had long- and short-term shifts. Much also has turned on particular leaders, especially presidents, and their ambitions. Over time and by virtue of modern media, the president has come to accrue certain advantages in the competition, but the advantages remain far short of the market share over public policy that presidents have come to desire. Much of American political history, however, occurred in an era of limited media, of policy dominance by the states, of selected rather than elected senators, and of centralized congressional leadership. Under these conditions, the balance of competitive advantage belonged to Congress.

For the most part, changes in the balance of competitive advantage between the president and the Congress fit reasonably well into three broad epochs of American political history. The first covers approximately the first full century of U.S. politics. The second coincides with the period of the premodern presidency and the decline of congressional leadership. The final period coincides with the development of the modern presidency. Never absent at any time in our history, the norm of presidential entrepreneurship nevertheless has been a growing one, and the assumption that what presidents want they should try to take, equally, has been on the rise.

In sum, viewing the constitutional system as a marketplace leads to thinking about the forms of relationships that can exist among the institutional providers of public policy. Such forms can be of a cooperative, competitive, or command nature. In all but rare instances, the constitutional system obviates the command relationship. It does not, however, specifically determine whether institutional relationships will be predominantly competitive or cooperative. A system of multiple suppliers of policy, though, is likely to breed competition unless otherwise manipulated.

Competing providers holding market shares in a constitutionally structured marketplace inhibit the emergence of monopolistic supply. The actual nature of the market shares held by institutional providers and the nature of the relationships that emerge between providers, however, are determined by the character and magnitude of policy demands, the arenas to which policy demands are directed, and the way in which the demand structure meshes with the institutional characteristics of a particular policy provider. These conditions, in turn, are shaped by historical developments. The interaction between such developments and the constitutional system are at the core of this essay.

The First Century

I am about to characterize long stretches of time in exceedingly generalized and simplified terms. While this is perilous, for my purposes, the question is whether the broad tendencies are essentially correct, even when we know they are not always correct.

A broad sweep across the first century (and somewhat more) of American history suggests the following characteristics of American government in this period: (1) its basic functions are those of state maintenance, followed by an emphasis on developmental activities (many of which are privatized or dependent on private capital) and, toward the end of the period, increased emphasis on regulatory behavior; (2) the major governmental players in supplying public goods are the states and local communities (which is still the case in many respects, despite the growth of federal involvement); and (3) within the federal government, Congress and the political parties are the major players, although the parties, especially during the later stages of this period, are essentially the products of regional, state, and local politics rather than national politics.

In regard to its functions, Richard Rose's (1976b) analysis of the development of cabinet functions across governments since 1848 shows a clear and steady progression by which government moves from being a small business with a clear product line (collective goods) to a conglomerate performing a wide variety of functions consistent with the existing welfare state. Over time, governments clearly have been producing more public goods as their activities and constituencies have expanded and as the rights associated with citizenship have enlarged. Taken to its extreme, then, big government becomes bloated government. It is large but pockmarked with interests. It can, in other words, be simultaneously large and leaderless. Large government—and America's on most standardized dimensions is relatively small for countries of its class—does not inherently increase the market share of public goods controlled by its central leadership.

Although there is evidence that the expansion of the welfare state and regulatory functions also have expanded bureaucratic operations and the apparatus of government, most of this activity, once legislated, moves outside the orbit of presidential concern and into the realm of delegation. Studies of cabinet interaction in both the United States and Britain, for example, emphasize, beyond pro forma settings, the notion of an inner cabinet with privileged access to the president or the prime minister (Cronin, 1980:253–96; Rose, 1980:1–49). The inner cabinet leans heavily on the side of the core state maintenance functions—foreign affairs, defense, finance, and justice, especially the first three. Ironically, the expansion of public goods supplied by government affects mainly the realm presidents are held responsible for rather than the realm they wish to be responsible for. Their real involvement is with the nonroutine, hence their involvement with the inner cabinet.

While presidents did have problems with even the small bureaucracy of the early period (Crenson, 1975; Skowronek, 1982; Nelson, 1982), early government was austere and performed mainly the essential functions of the state. Even as the developmental activities of government grew in the United States, they often resulted in privatization rather than the extension of the public realm. The Homestead Act, granting public lands for private settlement, exemplified the frequent use of private means to forge goals of national development. Often, too, state instruments were the favored means for federal policy. The Morrill Act, which created the nation's land grant colleges as agencies of the states, exemplified the process of devolving national goals to state instrumentalities. In a federal system, of course, central governments do control fewer resources than in unitary states, and the primary responsibility for delivering most public goods and services rests with states and local governments. The key issue here, of course, is more law than money—namely, what instruments are possessed at the federal level of government to control the behavior of officials delivering public goods at other levels. That is a matter that presidents ultimately would take an interest in, but one that would not become relevant until the emergence of a more active government.

Insofar as the players are concerned, developments requiring large sums of capital investment typically were financed and initiated by the states through private means. The creation of the Erie Canal, for instance, was mainly a creation of the capital market rather than a direct government subsidy (Goodrich, 1960:chap. 3). Indeed, one of the unique aspects of the U.S. government is its dependence on fundamentally autonomous financial markets for the provision of public investment capital.

On what would prove to be the most fundamental issue of the first half of the nineteenth century, the slavery issue, the federal government ultimately could not supply policy at all; it could only arbitrate and mediate the balance between states that supplied their own policies on whether to permit or forbid slavery in their territory. Only the logic of continuous development through territorial expansion would place the prior balance of proslavery and antislavery states in a politically precarious position. The system ironically would be torn between the survival of its unity as a nation-state and its needs and opportunities for territorial expansion. Lincoln's proclamation to abolish slavery, occurring under wartime conditions, could hardly have been countenanced under any other circumstances. Except during the Civil War, the American system was one in which state sovereignty was a powerful norm and through which institutions of representation in Congress were organized to reinforce this norm. With only modest amendment, this sentence also can be put in the present tense.

In regard to the players within the federal government, the balance of power was not favorable to the presidency, particularly compared with the contemporary situation. Today, it is usually assumed that a sitting president controls the party apparatus, if not always the hearts of its partisans or the support of congressional party members. The parties of yesteryear, however, were too sturdily constructed from the bottom up to be taken over by momentarily incumbent presidents. If a president had a party, the party also had him. Whereas, as James Ceaser (1978) observes, contemporary renditions of party government emphasize presidential direction over party, earlier conceptions emphasized the peer quality of party governance. Parties, in short, did organize politics more completely, but they, in turn, were much less capable of being organizationally penetrated by presidents.

Inside the national legislature, party began to define political division as early as the Second Congress (Hoadley, 1980). Counter-tendencies, however, were prevalent in the formative years of the Republic as well. The development of congressional committees and their influence over the president's cabinet and the departments produced primitive subgovernments of the day, moving influence toward Congress and away from the presidency (Young, 1966). The basic point here is that in spite of both nationalizing and regionalizing tendencies, in spite of both party-centeredness and fragmenting structures, the presidency lacked its present role and visibility as the putative principal policy entrepreneur.

Within broad expanses of history, there are, of course, powerful cycles of long- and short-term leadership influences (Rockman, 1984; Hargrove and Nelson, 1984; and Skowronek, 1990). Some of these depended on crystallizing broader political change, and some were certainly induced by presidential temperament. Thus, while Thomas Jefferson's presidency represented a more direcional style of party government, James Madison's was ensnarled by the convoluted system of his construction. Andrew Jackson and Martin Van Buren not only were politicians of considerable temperamental difference but also operated under substantially different short-run conditions. In the intense crisis of the Civil War and with the disappearance of the southern Democratic opposition that had joined the Confederacy, Abraham Lincoln also was able to make dramatic moves that would not have been likely otherwise.

For the most part, however, the wherewithal for presidential entrepreneurship was limited. This was so partly because the power of the states vis-à-vis the federal government was greater then. At that time, the Senate more deeply reflected the power of state leadership, which was greatly reduced after the introduction of direct election. The organization of the military also was far more dependent on the state militias than it now is. Both party organization and congressional leadership were also more powerful than the president, particularly the congressional leadership during the later part of that era. This last point is particularly ironic because contemporary reformers pushing for presidential monopolization of policy supply usually embrace vital party organization and more powerful congressional leadership as instruments for enhancing presidential leverage over the system. Until the revenue-raising capabilities of the federal government were enhanced by the income tax amendment, the ability of the federal government to generate policy supply also was more limited. For many reasons, including U.S. dependency on international capital, the ability to act forcefully from the center was at best sporadic and usually crisis-driven. In many respects, the American state was still in process of being patched together, especially after having been undone by the Civil War. American society in the postbellum era was in process of becoming industrially modern, even while the American state was decentralized and administratively weak.

In brief, the central state was a limited supplier of public goods, and the institutional competitors to presidents were relatively stronger, in part because their power bases largely derived from the states. Above all, an expectation of centrally driven initiative (i.e., presidential government) was not yet fully developed.

Modernizing Impulses in the Premodern Presidency

At the onset of the second century of U.S. government, the organizational problems of the American state became increasingly obvious in the face of burgeoning industrialization, a continent-wide nation, and a growing profile in the world. While the faces of reform were many, one consistent emphasis was to create the fabric of a modern state, one that would be less vulnerable to "vested" interest, more immune to the small-minded urges of politics and politicians, and better able to define a norm of professional service to the state above and beyond the realm of party politics and political particularism. There were sharp conflicts over the goals of reform, but most agreed that one of the main purposes was to break through the web of organizational incompetence saddling the development of the American state and to create an efficient and effective source of public authority, with a professional support structure operating on its behalf. In other words, among the most strongly felt needs were to strengthen leadership around a core set of national values and to empower that leadership with a professionally competent and incorruptible civil service.

The "new nationalism" articulated many of these values clearly. As a proponent of the new nationalism, Teddy Roosevelt proclaimed the presidency a "bully pulpit," thus clearly signalling it as the driving force of leadership in a system with need of a center. Although Woodrow Wilson was not, as such, a "new nationalist," he too thought constitutional evolution had produced a leaderless state (Tulis, 1990). Within the presidency, however, lay the potential for the activation of powerful national purposes; indeed, only the presidency could generate a truly national leadership that expressed both public will and public interest. This new interpretation of presidential legitimation is at the heart of what Jeffrey Tulis (1990) refers to as the second Constitution.

As Wilson made clear in *Congressional Government* (1885), the system had drifted into a set of legislative satrapies, better able to impede than to mobilize effective support for national purposes. Politics itself fell increasingly under the domination of local bosses and their fiefdoms. In Tulis's very interesting argument, Wilson's conception of the Constitution was not that it inevitably failed (because there were occasions when excellence in leadership was produced through it), but that it must be evolutionary. A key element in this evolution was the emergence of the presidency as the preeminently popular political institution for purposes of defining national goals and generating support on their behalf.

This evolution did not occur in isolation. Many ideas came together in this era, during which the nation moved from debtor to creditor, from industrializing to industrial, and from hemispheric influence to imperial pretension. The twin drives of nationalism as the embodiment of high purpose and of managerial competence to fulfill such purpose were at their peak. Nonetheless, politics remained rife with spoils, corruption, particularism, and localism. The creation of a state able to cope with and direct change in an increasingly complex and urbanizing society was viewed by reformers as a necessity. During this era, not only had practical changes occurred in the Constitution that reduced the grip of the states and state party leaders on the Senate (the Seventeenth Amendment) and increased the coffers of the federal government (the Sixteenth Amendment), but numerous other changes in the governmental sphere were taking place through less dramatic means. The federal government's role in regulating facets of the society and economy, from food and drugs to the banking system, had surged.

The policy supply of the federal government was clearly growing. Policy supply was increasing in the states as well (e.g., the regulation of professions and of professional standards). In short, government was being called upon to cope with complexity and the externalities induced by industrialization and rapid economic and social change. Rationalizing the state for these purposes was the major focus of reform. This followed naturally from changes taking place in the general sphere of ideas and industrial management (e.g., the influence of Frederick Winslow Taylor and the theory of scientific management). Even the newly created field of political science sought to bring ideas to public application. Scholars such as Frank Goodnow, Lawrence Lowell, and Woodrow Wilson brought their ideas to the world of public affairs. No doubt, the high tide in the influence of political science on government came in the profession's earliest years.

Also on the rise was democratization, a condition that mostly strengthens the legitimacy of popular mandates—and no one could more clearly articulate being the recipient of one of these than a freshly elected president. The Progressive movement certainly was wide-ranging and frequently reflected contradictory tendencies, but one of its tendencies was to enhance the role of direct democracy through referenda, recalls, initiatives, and so forth, albeit at the level of the states and local municipalities. In the meantime, of course, the Progressives pushed strongly for executive leadership and competence that would be above partisan interests, notably the city-manager system of local government. The implications for the presidency were obvious.

In the House of Representatives, rebellion against authoritarian leadership came to full boil in the revolt against Speaker Joseph Cannon, although it did not spring from the same sources as the ones just discussed. Certainly, we now know that the effects of strengthening the hand of committee chairs against the central leadership were to contribute further to producing the kind of fragmentation and narrowly focused outcomes that Wilson had railed against. Indeed, in one sense, the very nature of this outcome, and the kind of legislature it fostered, later delegitimized (without deeply diminishing) congressional power relative to executive power. The expectation that only the president could supply policy in the national interest fit the evolutionary course of the two institutions—or at least how they would be perceived. One was seemingly national in concern and decisive; the other seemingly parochial, intensely local, and hopelessly inefficient.

The new nationalism also produced a new internationalism in the United States. A regional power was rapidly becoming an international power. The implication was that presidents were becoming more important because of the implicit standing the Constitution seemingly confers in the domain of foreign affairs. Presidents earlier took controversial initiatives—James K. Polk on behalf of Texas and against Mexico, for example, and a great many others. But the pressures for policy supply in foreign affairs clearly were growing, perhaps reflected most immediately by the initiation of the war against Spain in William McKinley's presidency and the subsequent invasion of the Philippines and the struggle against indigenous guerrilla forces there. The role of American diplomacy was on the rise and so was the deployment of the armed forces, as imperial ambition waxed under Theodore Roosevelt and was righteously translated into a moral force under Woodrow Wilson. Seemingly, these new energies peaked after World War I. Wilson's campaign on behalf of U.S. involvement in the new League of Nations was the last gasp of this now exhausted movement toward presidential domination of the policy market. Immediately succeeding presidencies drew back from activism and certainly from high-flown moral objectives. New nationalism dissipated and new internationalism became the old isolationism. In the midst of the Great Depression, President Herbert Hoover attempted to restore some presidential policy resources.

These met with little success, however, in large part because Hoover himself was a premodern president with little capacity to elicit feeling or to stir enthusiasm.

Modernity and the Expanded Policy Market

The defining characteristic of the modern presidency is the assumption that presidents are at the center of the political system; that if they fail, the system fails. New technologies of communication would strengthen this perspective for better and for worse. As a distinctive part of their strategy of influence, presidents would be compelled to "go public" (Kernell, 1986). Executive leadership was to become the expected norm. Congress was thought to be better equipped to deal with problems of representation and review rather than ones of national policy-making (Huntington, 1965). This was particularly true as the long-term results of the revolt against Speaker Cannon in the House and the dissipation of strong central leadership in the Senate became evident. Committee chairs became ever more powerful, and the ability to stifle legislation grew. Reformers at the height of the committee chairs' power in the 1950s and early 1960s decried congressional paralysis and the lack of legislative vitality. The demand for public policy seemed to be growing, but Congress in particular appeared to be unable to supply it.

The nationalization of policy that developed with the New Deal, along with major demographic, technological, and social changes, eroded the local organizational base of the political parties, robbing them of a relatively immobile set of dependent constituencies. Over time, then, the dependencies of presidents (and presidential candidates) on local party organizations and their leaders would fade. Presidents would rely mostly on their own personal political organization to do the job, because they could trust only organizations committed to them. The brokerage functions of local party leaders became increasingly less relevant because local party leaders presided over increasingly hollow organizations. Moreover, even when local party organizations were vital, local needs always took priority. Brokerage was not absent, of course. It just had become more national and mediated through party constituencies that were outside of local party organizations.

The movement of the federal government toward a welfare/warfare state in the 1930s and 1940s increased not only its scope but also its professionalism. The growth of the welfare state, followed by the growth of a wartime state, vastly increased the numbers and professional qualities of those in the service of the government. The great development of the administrative state coincided with the New Deal and World War II. Policy supply clearly was on the upsurge, and the entrepreneurial force was believed to reside in the combination of executive leadership and the competence of career public servants. In those heady times, the executive was deemed to be a unity—presidential aspirations and the enthusiasm of career officials were regarded as coincident.

The postwar period brought a flurry of additional government instrumentalities and laws to mandate desirable outcomes, such as found in the Full Employment Act. It became increasingly clear that even though the New Deal had receded, the New Deal romance with the presidency had not. No doubt this was reinforced by the Republican Eightieth Congress and, ironically, also by the quiescent interlude of Dwight Eisenhower's presidency, whose absence of activist fervor stirred the intellectuals' desire for "The New Frontier." What Thomas Cronin (1980) later referred to as "the textbook presidency" was in full bloom. The presidency was regarded as the engine of government, especially by those whose imagery of presidential leadership was forged experientially by Franklin Roosevelt.

Clearly, one result of this imagery, particularly given the rapid development of the electronic media, was that presidents were now expected to be agenda-setters, movers and shakers, and necessarily adept at mastering symbols. Although John Kennedy's appeal to elect him "to get the country moving again" was a substanceless slogan, it generated an expectation that Kennedy would act and that from his actions public good would follow. Presidents whose acts included requests for legislative enactments, however, were bound to be frustrated. It wasn't until Jimmy Carter that presidential enthusiasts replaced their sympathy toward a president's plight with derision of his abilities. For brief periods, Lyndon Johnson in 1964–65 and Ronald Reagan in 1981, presidents dictated the supply of policy. Otherwise, they wrestled with Congress (and other sources of policy influence) and rarely met with consistent or overwhelming success. The rare episodes of extensive policy change may not be any rarer in modern times than in the past, but the expectation that presidents need to succeed in full lest they be thought to fail is of more recent vintage, and it corresponds to the rise of what Theodore Lowi (1985) has called "the personal presidency."

In contemporary times, presidents have strong symbolic political needs. They need to appear to be doing well. That is the essence of the personal presidency, to use Lowi's term, or the plebiscitary presidency, as I have elsewhere called it (Rockman, 1986). Approval is presidential currency for getting things done, but getting things done (or seeming to) often is necessary for approval. Despite these political needs, presidents also can have strong policy desires. One of the most persistent of these desires lies in foreign policy, which presidents think of as being, principally, their realm. Here, they alone want to supply policy, if at all possible.

Since the U.S. entry into World War II and its continuous interventionist role following the onset of the Cold War, presidents have been at center stage as crisis managers and fomenters. National security has been a shield used to cover a great many presidential decisions and executive actions. In theory, foreign policy is designed to produce a collective good, namely, the security and well-being of the United States and its citizens. The collective goods function is one that tends to be associated with the presidential role. However, the means to these desirable ends, to say the least, have been and remain much in dispute (Rockman, 1987). Because the national security state has become so pervasive and disagreements about the proper direction and instrumentation of U.S. policy in the world so strong, there has been a tendency for presidents to try to manage policy exclusively through the executive branch or, even more restrictively, through the White House alone. The key variable contributing to the growth in presidential policy supply has been the prominence of the national security state. That the U.S. role in world affairs has been contentious rather than consensual also has led presidents to seek as great a monopoly over foreign policy as possible. Evidence strongly suggests, for example, that the so-called bipartisan consensus on foreign policy was mostly a phenomenon of the Eisenhower presidency and reflected the fact that congressional Democrats liked Ike (in foreign policy at least) better than many members of the president's own party did.

In many important aspects, the Kennedy presidency appears to be a turning point in the extent to which foreign policy–making was deinstitutionalized and monopolized by the president. Kennedy's activation of his commander-in-chief role during the Berlin crisis of 1961 and the Cuban missile crisis of 1962 was given ex post facto support in light of the prevailing outlooks of the day, but significant actors outside the United States, such as General Charles de Gaulle, were not so easily consoled. Even if members of Congress did not then so clearly recognize (or care about) the distinction between advice and consent, de Gaulle did. That recognition clearly lent impetus to the eventual French decision to disengage militarily from NATO.

Vietnam changed congressional acquiescence to crisis activity because it also revealed essential cleavages over U.S. foreign policy. The protracted involvement in Vietnam painfully revealed divisions in perceptions about the nature of the world and the U.S. role in it (Holsti and Rosenau, 1984). In addition, the last stages of the Vietnam involvement coincided with Richard Nixon's demise over Watergate, which also overlapped with increasing congressional involvement in the policy entrepreneur role (Walker, 1977; Salisbury and Shepsle, 1981). This transformation was the result of internal congressional change, personnel turnover, and executive challenge.

It is clear that especially since the Nixon years, the competition between the president and Congress has become fierce. One reason is that, with the exception of the Gerald Ford years when Congress was the primary policy entrepreneur, distrust between the branches has been strong. This has been fed to a significant degree by the party differences between one or more chambers and the White House. The party split across branches should not be discounted, because it is clear that in the past two decades partisan differences have been rising (Miller and Jennings, 1986; Aberbach and Rockman, 1990). Not only is there sharper party polarization but a lot of that polarization occurs over foreign policy issues.

Beyond the party differences, though undoubtedly buoyed by them, Congress, like the executive, also has become more professional. Staffs abound in Congress, and so too do information and knowledge. The capabilities for congressional policy-making have never been higher, and the incentives to engage in it are strong. All of the factors making for strong competition between the president and Congress are therefore in place, and the incentives for collusion are accordingly weak.

A Heightened Competition

Strong institutional competition endured even during the first six Reagan years of a Republican Senate (or at least from 1981 to 1986). This strongly competitive condition has led some recent presidents to exert through executive authority what otherwise may be denied them through legislative opposition. The proposition that the nature of the system forces presidents to do this—to politicize the bureaucracy, for example—has been articulated with both stunning clarity and analytic power by Richard Nathan (1986) and especially Terry Moe (1985). Their argument is that presidents simply have no choice if they are to have a chance at being successful. Surrounded by competitors, who it is assumed wish them no good, presidents must gain control over whatever they can—and the bureaucracy is fair game as a policy and political resource in the competition. In short, a president has to do what a president has to do.

The effort to govern by executive authority alone means straight-away an attempt to monopolize policy supply. This monopolistic presumption denies the prospect of collusion and, by implication, political bargaining. It assumes, instead, the necessity for domina-tion which, in turn, is derivable from the political support presi-dents often seek to claim as the only nationally elected official in the country. From their perspective only they carry a mandate. Thus, the normal frustrations that presidents historically have had with Congress in getting the system to tick to their beat are en-larged because each actor is seeking a larger policy share and is dis-trustful of the other's motives.

The outcomes typically remain uncertain, with no conclusive winner. That does not mean an equilibrium is reached; rather, it means a competitive disequilibrium exists, with each actor seeking to alter the existing state of affairs within an uncertain market for policy demand. The framers themselves might have been more di-rectly influenced by Newton than by Adam Smith, but their solu-tion to the problem of competitive policy supply either had to be the equivalent of Smith's invisible hand (the nature of demand will de-termine the principal supplier) or assumed a talent for collusion (po-litical bargaining).

In the meantime, presidents have not been bashful about assert-ing their prerogatives, and Congress has not been timid about seek-ing to constrict these. Uncertainty reigns because we are in exactly the situation James Madison foresaw—a clash of ambitions with no definite resolution. That situation is what Alexander Hamilton sought to prevent, seeing in this otherwise unresolved competition the hopeless paralysis of authority and leadership. Although the competition may be stiff, presidents have on their side the power of initiation, which in some matters is also the power of accomplish-ment. Where authority to act is implied, presidents also have that on their side. In many respects, their constitutional authority de-rives less from the specificity of what they are empowered to do than from the roles conferred on them that imply what they must do. That, so to speak, is the hole in the donut. In the case of the U.S.

Constitution, it is oftentimes advantageous for an actor to have the powers of office implied rather than specified.

The Hole in the Constitutional Donut

Article I of the Constitution stipulates, at relatively great length, the powers and responsibilities of Congress. Articles II and III, setting forth the execution and judicial functions, are shorter. The doctrine of judicial review that seems to be implied by Article III, Section 2, is nowhere explicitly stated in the discussion of judicial functions. Yet the role given to the Supreme Court almost inevitably conferred on it the right of judicial review. A similarly expansive interpretation of presidential prerogatives inheres in the constitutional logic. The powers of the office tend to be ones conferred implicitly by role rather than by exact stipulation.

There is good reason to think that the power to act decisively is inherent in the president's role. The power to act, as Alexander Hamilton put it in *Federalist No. 70*, is to act with dispatch and secrecy. The "take care" clause of Article II, Section 3, confers powerful authority on the president and, by norm, so too does the commander-in-chief role. There is no doubt that presidents attempt to stretch their ability to act in unrestricted fashion, but we know they are not always successful.

As I have argued elsewhere, there is little that can be done to prevent presidents from acting in *a priori* fashion, but that does not mean *a posteriori* sanctions cannot be applied (Rockman, 1986). How much force such sanctions have, however, frequently depends on the third branch—the judiciary, which, in the *Immigration and Naturalization Service v. Chadha* decision (1983), removed an important monitoring function that Congress had.

The power to initiate can be a power of awesome proportions. Increasingly, presidents have become infatuated with that power. Reinterpreting congressional intent often has been accomplished through administrative means (Aberbach and Rockman, 1988). Especially in matters of foreign affairs, the power to initiate is a prodigious power. Even so, what presidents can get away with (or try to get away with) is determined by their standing with the public.[1] How Congress reacts is affected by the extent of presidential political vulnerability. Politicians calculate the demand for policy supply and translate that into market shares the various political actors can supply. For example, pressure for constraint on the president's ability to commit forces rose formidably as Richard Nixon's stock declined dramatically. Because of Ronald Reagan's popularity, Congress interpreted the War Powers Act very timidly and expressed little opposition to Reagan's decision to commit U.S. "peacekeeping" forces in Lebanon. Once there was public criticism of Reagan over the 1983 bombing of the marine barracks there, however, congressional opposition strengthened to the point that Reagan concluded he could become as vulnerable as the marines unless he cut his (more tragically, their) losses. In short, if modern conditions give presidents an edge in what they can get away with, they also increase the risks that presidents must absorb.

By inducing competition among the agents of government, the U.S. system escalates ambition, risk, and the potential for deadlock. This deadlock takes the form of a competitive disequilibrium. The policy suppliers are always dissatisfied with the status quo, though each can do relatively little about altering it. If incentives for collusion are strong, however, moderation can be induced. Notwithstanding President George Bush's early overtures to Congress, these incentives generally seem to have grown weaker or at least less attractive to the political actors. Until the incentives in the political environment change, ambition will continue to clash as the actors seek enhanced market shares. Eventually, consistent market signals come about, and these are perceived as changes in the nature of policy demand. Clear and unequivocal signals for policy demand come rarely, though. Ronald Reagan benefited from this rare occurrence in 1981, until more normal (and ambiguous) conditions returned.

The Constitution unavoidably shapes our politics. Yet political signals also determine definitions of constitutional prerogative and restriction—who can get away with doing what. Those signals sometimes can be powerful and consistent; at least they are so perceived by the policy suppliers. Mostly, however, the signals are mixed and ambiguous. This is the normal state of affairs, and under such conditions our system weighs heavily on behalf of the status quo. Efforts toward change are to be expected, but success is another matter. When the suppliers want to provide different policy products yet cannot read the market for them, there is no clear means for them to resolve their dispute except by seeking to dominate the other until the market sends clearer signals or by colluding.

Given the contemporary definitions of the presidential role—that of entrepreneur for the system—this situation is necessarily frustrating to presidents, since the presidency continues to be the central source of political and policy energy in the government. Having evolved in this manner, our system effectively gives presidents more power than powers, and it usually gives presidents the largest say without granting them the final word. The evolution of the system is remarkably faithful to the Madisonian framework. That framework compels collision and invites collusion. There is no doubt, however, as to which of these alternatives has been the more powerful in our present era.

NOTE

1. Note the following conclusion by Simon and Ostrom (1988:754): public support will influence the relative balance of authority between the executive and legislative branches. At high levels of support, the president is likely to be the dominant partner in the relationship. Congress will be inclined to grant broad delegations of authority (e.g., the Gulf of Tonkin Resolution) and not challenge presidential actions that impinge on its prerogatives (e.g., Eisenhower's dispatch of troops to Lebanon).

REFERENCES

Aberbach, Joel D., and Bert A. Rockman. 1988. "Mandates or Mandarins? Control and Discretion in the Modern Administrative State." *Public Administration Review* 48:606–12.

———. 1990. "From Nixon's Problem to Reagan's Achievement—The Federal Executive Reexamined." In *Looking Back on the Reagan Presidency*, edited by Larry Berman. Baltimore: Johns Hopkins University Press.

Ceaser, James W. 1978. "Political Parties and Presidential Ambition." *Journal of Politics* 40:708–41.

Crenson, Matthew. 1975. *The Federal Machine: Beginnings of Bureaucracy in Jacksonian American*. Baltimore: Johns Hopkins University Press.

Cronin, Thomas E. 1980. *The State of the Presidency*. 2d ed. Boston: Little, Brown.

Fenno, Richard. 1978. *Home Style: House Members in Their Districts*. Boston: Little, Brown.

Goodrich, Carter. 1960. *Government Promotion of American Canals and Railroads, 1800–1890*. New York: Columbia University Press.

Hargrove, Erwin C., and Michael Nelson. 1984. *Presidents, Politics, and Policy*. New York: Alfred A. Knopf.

Hoadley, John F. 1980. "The Emergence of Political Parties in Congress, 1789–1803." *American Political Science Review* 74:757–79.

Holsti, Ole R., and James N. Rosenau. 1984. *American Leadership in World Affairs: Vietnam and the Breakdown of Consensus.* Boston: Allen and Unwin.

Horowitz, Donald L. 1987. "Is the Presidency Failing?" *Public Interest* 88:3–27.

Huntington, Samuel P. 1965. "Congressional Responses to the Twentieth Century." In *The Congress and America's Future,* edited by David B. Truman. Englewood Cliffs, N.J.: Prentice-Hall.

Immigration and Naturalization Service v. Chadha. 1983. 462 U.S. 919.

Kernell, Samuel. 1986. *Going Public: New Strategies of Presidential Leadership.* Washington, D.C.: Congressional Quarterly Press.

Lowi, Theodore J. 1985. *The Personal Presidency.* Ithaca, N.Y.: Cornell University Press.

Miller, Warren E., and M. Kent Jennings. 1986. *Parties in Transition: A Longitudinal Study of Party Elites and Party Supporters.* New York: Russell Sage Foundation.

Moe, Terry M. 1985. "The Politicized Presidency." In *The New Direction in American Politics,* edited by John E. Chubb and Paul E. Peterson. Washington, D.C.: Brookings Institution.

Nathan, Richard P. 1986. "Institutional Change under Reagan." In *Perspectives on the Reagan Years,* edited by John L. Palmer. Washington, D.C.: Urban Institute.

Nelson, Michael. 1982. "A Short, Ironic History of American National Bureaucracy." *Journal of Politics* 44:747–78.

Neustadt, Richard E. 1980. *Presidential Power: The Politics of Leadership from FDR to Carter.* New York: John Wiley and Sons.

Rockman, Bert A. 1984. *The Leadership Question: The Presidency in the American System.* New York: Praeger.

———. 1986. "The Modern Presidency and Theories of Accountability: Old Wine and Old Bottles." *Congress and the Presidency* 13:135–56.

———. 1987. "Mobilizing Support for National Security Policy." *Armed Forces and Society* 14:17–41.

———. 1990. "The American Presidency in Comparative Perspective: Systems, Situations, and Leaders." In *The Presidency and the Political System,* edited by Michael Nelson. 3d ed. Washington, D.C.: Congressional Quarterly Press.

Rose, Richard. 1976a. *Managing Presidential Objectives.* New York: Free Press.

———. 1976b. "On the Priorities of Government: A Developmental Analysis of Public Policies." *European Journal of Political Research* 4:247–89.

———. 1980. "British Government: The Job at the Top." In *Presidents and Prime Ministers,* edited by Richard Rose and Ezra N. Suleiman. Washington, D.C.: American Enterprise Institute.

Salisbury, Robert H., and Kenneth A. Shepsle. 1981. "U.S. Congressman as Enterprise." *Legislative Studies Quarterly* 6:559–76.

Simon, Dennis M., and Charles W. Ostrom, Jr. 1988. "The Politics of Prestige: Popular Support and the Modern Presidency." *Presidential Studies Quarterly* 18:741–59.

Skowronek, Stephen. 1982. *Building a New Nation-State: The Expansion of National Administrative Capacities, 1877–1920.* Cambridge: Cambridge University Press.

———. 1990. "Presidential Leadership in Political Time." In *The Presidency and the Political System,* edited by Michael Nelson. 3d ed. Washington, D.C.: Congressional Quarterly Press.

Tulis, Jeffrey. 1990. "The Two Constitutional Presidencies." In *The Presidency and the Political System,* edited by Michael Nelson. 3d ed. Washington, D.C.: Congressional Quarterly Press.

Walker, Jack L. 1977. "Setting the Agenda in the U.S. Senate: A Theory of Problem Selection." *British Journal of Political Science* 7:423–45.

Wilson, Woodrow. 1885. *Congressional Government.* Boston: Houghton, Mifflin.

Young, James Sterling. 1966. *The Washington Community, 1800–1828.* New York: Columbia University Press.

★ 5 ★

Democratic Constitutionalism and the Evolution of Bureaucratic Government: Freedom and Accountability in the Administrative State

DAVID H. ROSENBLOOM

During the past century, the relationship between the Constitution and large-scale public administration became central to politics and government in the United States. Neither the framers of the Constitution nor the founders of modern American public administration in the 1880s provided comprehensive blueprints for combining our twentieth-century administrative state with our eighteenth-century governmental framework (Rohr, 1986). Public administration is necessary to fulfill the constitutional purposes set forth in the Preamble, and the Constitution has strongly conditioned public administrative development and practice. Yet there has been a long-standing tension between the norms, values, and structural features of the constitutional and administrative states. Moreover, presidential, congressional, and judicial efforts to gain better control over public administration, though not wholly inefficacious, have led to serious political dysfunctions and distortions of constitutional integrity. These tensions, and attempts to deal with them, are the subject of this essay.

Specifically, this essay considers the broad strains that public administration and the Constitution place on one another and how each of the constitutional branches has responded to the rise of bureaucratic power. The essay argues that today a new administrative culture is emerging. In the past, public administration was viewed primarily as an extension of elite dominance, an adjunct of political parties, or as a businesslike, managerial, or professional enterprise (Mosher, 1968). The new administrative culture considers public administration to be "governance." It consequently emphasizes the relevance and legitimacy of introducing constitutional norms, values, and processes into public administration. It promises to develop a public administration that can effectively incorporate strong protections of individual rights, representativeness, participation, and structural checks and balances. It also stresses the desirability of holding public administrators personally responsible to constitutional values in their official performance. Various aspects of the emerging administrative culture stem from different concerns, but together they form a coherent basis for making public administration and the Constitution more compatible.

Public Administration versus Democratic Constitutionalism

The rise of the administrative state in the United States transformed the character of the regime. To be sure, the framers were experienced with administration and considered it a central facet of government. In *Federalist No. 68*, Alexander Hamilton even proclaimed that "we may safely pronounce that the true test of a good government is its aptitude and tendency to produce a good administration" (Rossiter, 1961:414). Their provisions in the Constitution for public administration were rudimentary, however. Subsequent generations consequently have faced the task of "retrofitting" the administrative state into the constitutional order. In the process, the Constitution has shaped administrative development, and large-scale public administration has altered the government's traditional structure and processes, as well as the nation's politics.

The development of large and powerful administrative components is virtually a worldwide phenomenon. Bureaucratization is a common response to the social and economic complexity and mutual interdependence brought about by industrialization and urbanization. Governmental agencies are established to aid in the coordination of the division of labor, to regulate conflicts and other relations among competing units and antagonistic sectors of the economy, to protect the public's health and the nation's future productive capacity, to provide public goods (including defense), to subsidize and direct technological development, and to control harmful externalities (Krislov and Rosenbloom, 1981:4–7; Jacoby, 1973).

In the United States, public administration has also been relied on to bridge the separation of powers, to simplify governmental processes, and to coordinate federalism. Public administration enables executive, legislative, and judicial functions to be combined in single governmental units. Kenneth Davis notes, "The volume of the legislative output of federal agencies far exceeds the volume of legislative output of Congress" (1975:8), while Peter Woll writes, "In terms of the day-to-day activities of the citizenry administrative adjudication is probably more ubiquitous than that carried out by the courts of law, with the exception of criminal actions" (1963:10). Combining these functions in administrative agencies enhances the government's ability to coordinate its exercise of power in specific areas of public policy. Moreover, because administrative procedures for rule making and adjudication are generally more flexible than the legislative and judicial processes provided for directly under the Constitution, reliance on administration allows the government to deal more effectively with the huge demands it now confronts.

Public administration has also been a vehicle for coordinating federalism. Samuel Beer presents a lucid analysis, noting that "dual federalism" or "the mutually exclusive allocation of powers between the general and the state governments" has a base in the original constitutional design; however, "given the realities of our times, [dual federalism] could not be made to apply, to that system today" ([1978] 1986:82). Rather, "vertical bureaucratic hierarchies cutting across different levels of government have become a main feature of the present phase of American federalism" and one that "has facilitated cooperation" (93).

From the perspective of bridging the separation of powers and coordinating federalism, public administration, like political parties, can be seen as essential to effective constitutional government. But there are also serious tensions between the contemporary administrative state and traditional democratic constitutionalism in the United States (Nachmias and Rosenbloom, 1980; Waldo, 1980; Redford, 1969). First, there is the structural tension. Constitutional government based on a threefold separation of powers has not easily accommodated the rise of large-scale public administration. As Justice Robert Jackson noted in 1952, administrative bodies have become "a veritable fourth branch" of government that has "deranged" our thinking about a three-branch separation of powers (*Federal Trade Commission v. Ruberoid Co.*, 1952:470). Just as "there is no doubt that the development of the administrative agency in response to modern legislative and administrative need has placed severe strain on the separation-of-powers principle in its pristine formulation" (*Buckley v. Valeo*, 1976:280–81), there is no doubt that classical American public administrative theory was continually confounded by the division of constitutional authority among three branches of government. Woodrow Wilson ([1887] 1941), Frank Goodnow (1900), Luther Gulick ([1937] 1978), and others claimed that government had two functions, politics and administration, rather than three. As a result, they failed to develop a public administrative theory that could combine legislative and judicial values, such as representation and due process, with managerial values.

Nor could the traditional constitutional view of federalism, as articulated by the Supreme Court, remain intact in the face of contemporary administrative practice. As Justice Sandra Day O'Connor observed, "In 1954, one could still speak of a 'burden of persuasion on those favoring national intervention' in asserting that 'National action has . . . always been regarded as exceptional in our polity, an intrusion to be justified by some necessity, the special rather than the ordinary case.' . . . Today [1985], as federal legislation and coercive grant programs have expanded to embrace innumerable activities that were once viewed as local, the burden of persuasion has surely shifted, and the extraordinary has become ordinary" (*Garcia v. San Antonio Metropolitan Transit Authority*, 1985:587). Effective protection of state interests under the Constitution now lies neither in the limits of the commerce clause nor in the Tenth Amendment but primarily "in the structure of the Federal Government itself" (*Garcia v. San Antonio Metropolitan Transit Authority*, 1985:550–51).

A second historical tension between public administration and constitutional democracy has been procedural. Constitutional processes emphasize election, rotation in office, checks and balances, the promotion of pluralism, citizen participation, open discussion of governmental affairs, and accountability to the electorate. Classical public administrative theory, often matched by behavior, favored selection for governmental service based on expertise, seniority in office, unity of command, the promotion of uniformity (Rosenbloom, 1983; Hummel, 1982), limited involvement by the citizenry in the government's "business," secrecy, and accountability to hierarchical authorities. There has been a large number of instances in which the federal judiciary has been called on to adjudicate the conflicts between administrative and constitutional processes. Justice William O. Douglas's dissent in *United States v.*

Richardson encapsulated the problem well: "The sovereign of this Nation is the people, not the bureaucracy. The statement of accounts of public expenditures goes to the heart of the problem of sovereignty [Article I, Section 9]. If taxpayers may not ask that rudimentary question, their sovereignty becomes an empty symbol and a secret bureaucracy is allowed to run our affairs" (1974:201).

Dissenting in *Garcia v. San Antonio Metropolitan Transit Authority,* Justice Lewis Powell presented a bleak, though accurate, description of how the administrative state has sometimes eroded constitutional democracy at the state and local levels:

> Federal legislation is drafted primarily by the staffs of the congressional committees. In view of the hundreds of bills introduced at each session of Congress and the complexity of many of them, it is virtually impossible for even the most conscientious legislators to be truly familiar with many of the statutes enacted. Federal departments and agencies customarily are authorized to write regulations. Often these are more important than the text of the statutes. As is true of the original legislation, these are drafted largely by staff personnel. The administration and enforcement of federal laws and regulations necessarily are largely in the hands of staff and civil service employees. These employees may have little or no knowledge of the States and localities that will be affected by the statutes and regulations for which they are responsible. In any case, they hardly are as accessible and responsive as those who occupy analogous positions in state and local governments.
>
> ... My point is simply that members of the immense federal bureaucracy are not elected, know less about the services traditionally rendered by States and localities, and are inevitably less responsive to recipients of such services, than are state legislatures, city councils, boards of supervisors, and state and local commissions, boards, and agencies. It is at these state and local levels—not in Washington as the [majority of the] Court so mistakenly thinks—that "democratic self-government" is best exemplified [1985:576–77].

Another tension concerns legitimacy. Since the 1880s, American public administrative thought has sought to legitimize the role of administrative decision makers on the basis of scientific expertise and performance. Constitutional democracy, by contrast, relies on popular consent for legitimacy. Woodrow Wilson noted the implication of this tension in 1887: "We have enthroned public opinion;

and it is forbidden us to hope during its reign for any quick schooling of the sovereign in executive expertness or in the conditions of perfect functional balance in government" ([1887] 1941:491).

Sometimes the efforts of leading administrative theorists to square the authority of unelected experts with democratic consent led to statements that made the fundamental problem all the more visible. For instance, Luther Gulick wrote that "democracy is a way of government in which the common man is the final judge of what is good for him," and "efficiency is one of the things that is good for him because it makes life richer and safer. That efficiency is to be secured more and more through the use of technical specialists" in public administration ([1937] 1978:45). Similarly, in proposing the creation of the modern administrative presidency, the Brownlow Committee could argue for the combination of the two factors necessary for governmental efficiency—"the consent of the governed and good management"—in the president, who "is indeed the one and only national officer representative of the entire Nation" (U.S. President's Committee on Administrative Management, [1937] 1976:111, 113). These approaches obviously fail to deal seriously with the complex and fundamental character of the concepts of consent and representation in our constitutional scheme.

They also are lacking in political realism. As Justice Powell, dissenting in *Branti v. Finkel*, observed, "the implementation of policy often depends upon the cooperation of public employees who do not hold policymaking posts. . . . The growth of the civil service system already has limited the ability of elected politicians to effect political change" (1980:530). Moreover, as Chief Justice Warren Burger noted for the majority in *Immigration and Naturalization Service v. Chadha*, from a constitutional perspective, efficient administrative performance does not legitimize governmental action: "it is crystal clear from the records of the [Constitutional] Convention, contemporaneous writing and debates, that the Framers ranked other values higher than efficiency" (1983:958–59).

The administrative state has also threatened to diminish the scope of individual rights guaranteed by the constitutional state. This threat has been the outgrowth of several factors. The constitutional state is based largely on eighteenth-century liberalism. It assumes that government is to be a limited actor in society and that individuals retain their natural rights as a shield against governmental action. "Negative liberties" ensure that the government will leave the people alone in many spheres of economic, social, and political activity (Berlin, 1969). The Ninth Amendment is a clear expression of the view that the government is restrained by individuals' natural rights: "The enumeration in the Constitution, of certain rights, shall not be construed to deny or disparage others retained by the people." The administrative state, by contrast, is a more positive form of government. It engages in a variety of forms of economic, social, and political regulation. Theorists such as Friedrich Hayek (1944) and Elton Mayo (1933) saw the seeds of a form of totalitarianism in an administrative state that would combine regulation of economy and society under polity.

Others, noting the potential danger of administrative infringement on individual rights and liberties, have urged the adoption of greater constitutional protections against public administration. As Justice Douglas expressed it in *Spady v. Mount Vernon*, "Today's mounting bureaucracy, both at the state and federal levels, promises to be suffocating and repressive unless it is put into the harness of procedural due process" (1974:985). In a more comprehensive analysis, Charles Reich called for the treatment of governmental largess—licenses, welfare benefits, public housing, public employment—as a form of property under constitutional law because "if the individual is to survive in a collective society, he must have protection against its ruthless pressures. There must be sanctuaries or enclaves where no majority can reach. To shelter the solitary human spirit does not merely make possible the fulfillment of individuals; it also gives society the power to change, to grow, and to regenerate, and hence to endure. These were the objects which property sought to achieve, and can no longer achieve [in the modern administrative state]" (1964:787).

The Search for Constitutional Control of the Administrative State

Tensions in the United States between public administration, as it historically developed, and constitutionalism have been fundamental to a great deal of political change and adjustment during the past century. Frederick Mosher put his finger on the basic problem: "The accretion of specialization and of technological and social complexity seems to be an irreversible trend, one that leads to increasing dependence upon the protected, appointive public service, thrice removed from direct democracy. Herein lies [a] central and underlying problem . . . how can a public service so constituted be made to operate in a manner compatible with democracy? How can we be assured that a highly differentiated body of public employees will act in the interests of all the people, will be an instrument of all the people?" (1968:3–4). One approach to making public administration more compatible with constitutional democracy has been for each of the three constitutional branches of government to try to exert more effective control over public agencies. Each branch has responded to the rise of the administrative state; however, even taken together, these responses have not fully or satisfactorily brought public administration into the nation's constitutional framework. Since the responses involved are well known (Nachmias and Rosenbloom, 1980; Rosenbloom, 1983; Dodd and Schott, 1979; Arnold, 1986), it is possible to limit the discussion to a brief review.

The presidential response to the growth of large-scale federal administration continues to be based on the logic developed by the Brownlow Committee in 1937. The president should be "administrator-in-chief." The creation of the Executive Office of the President (EOP) provides the president with the structural wherewithal for becoming so. Delegation of legislative authority, first for reorganization and later for budgetary and other matters, supplies the president with greater power to manage the executive branch (Cronin, 1975). For a variety of reasons, including the essential political nature of the presidency, these changes have not resolved the problem of unchecked administrative action. As Peter Woll and Rochelle Jones note, "The bureaucracy, sometimes with Congress but often by itself, has frequently been able to resist and ignore Presidential commands. . . . bureaucratic frustration of White House policies is a fact of life" (1975:216–17). Recent presidents have been aware of "the inertia or the momentum of the federal bureaucracy," though they may sometimes underestimate it (Barger quoting Jimmy Carter, 1984:166). Top-level political appointees, such as Richard Cheney, chief of White House staff under President Gerald Ford, may find themselves "far more aware of the constraints than . . . of the power. You spend most of your time trying to overcome obstacles getting what the President wants done" (Cheney quoted in Edwards and Wayne, 1985:351).

In the wake of the 1986–87 Iran-Contra affair, it is evident that the reforms of the presidency begun in 1939 in response to the administrative state have become problematic—perhaps even seriously dysfunctional. The increased presidential staff, originally intended to enable the president to manage the bureaucracy more effectively, has been used to evade the traditional constitutional system of checks and balances. Writing in the mid-1970s, Thomas

Cronin warned, "The presidential establishment had become over the years a powerful inner sanctum of government isolated from the traditional checks and balances. Little-known, unelected, and un-ratified aides on occasion negotiate sensitive international commitments by means of executive agreements that are free from congressional oversight. With no semblance of public scrutiny other aides wield fiscal authority over billions of dollars . . . " (1975:138). Moreover, as Stephen Wayne notes and the Iran-Contra record seems to support, the presidency can elude presidential control: "In the process of expansion, the White House aggregated considerable power. By the 1970s, it had clearly become more than the president's personal office" (1978:60). Perhaps Stephen Hess supplies the best epigram here: "With the bureaucratizing of the presidency, it is hardly surprising that the White House fell heir to all the problems of a bureaucracy . . . " (1976:9).

The congressional effort to exercise greater control over federal administration has also involved changes in structure and authority. Beginning with its reorganization in 1946, Congress has sought to promote better oversight of federal administrative agencies by developing further committee and subcommittee specialization, especially the latter. It has also strengthened its own administrative capacity through the enlargement of the General Accounting Office and the creation of such new units as the Congressional Budget Office. The legislature dramatically increased the numbers of its committee and personal staff (Nachmias and Rosenbloom, 1980:105–40). Until it was found unconstitutional in 1983, Congress also placed increasing reliance on the legislative veto as a means of controlling administrative discretion (*Immigration and Naturalization Service v. Chadha*, 1983). These initiatives enhance Congress's capacity to influence the bureaucracy; however, as in the case of the presidency, such changes have led to distortions in institutional roles and dysfunctions. In Leroy Rieselbach's words,

> For all the increased attention Congress has paid to gaining control of a "runaway" bureaucracy, it is not certain that much has been accomplished. More oversight activity—more hearings, more reports required, more legislative-bureaucratic contacts— has not necessarily meant more influence or at least not coordinated management of the executive agencies. This probably suits most members of Congress, who for policy or reelection reasons prefer power over some small segment of the bureaucracy to broader forms of institutional control. It is not that

members lack the capacity to exercise close oversight of the executive branch; rather, they lack incentive to impair the cozy subgovernment relationships with executive agencies and interest groups, relationships that foster their electoral goals [1986:104].

As Morris Fiorina tells us, "the growth of an activist federal government has stimulated a change in the mix of congressional activities. Specifically, a lesser proportion of congressional effort is now going into programmatic activities and a greater proportion into pork-barrel and casework activities" (1977:46).

Congress is now so dependent on its staff that the question "Who's in charge here?" is legitimately raised (Malbin, 1977, 1979). Ironically, according to R. Douglas Arnold, an appropriate answer may sometimes be "the bureaucracy": "bureaucrats appear to allocate benefits strategically in an effort both to maintain and to expand their supporting coalitions. When it furthers their purposes, they broaden their program's geographic scope and increase the number of shares of benefits so that more congressmen can be brought into their supporting coalitions. When necessary, they allocate extra shares of benefits to leaders and to those who are crucial coalition members" (1979:207).

The efforts of judges to exercise greater control over the actions of public agencies and administrators have also amounted to a response to the administrative state, though one which has been less explicit (Rosenbloom, 1983, 1986a). The judiciary's initial reactions to the beginnings of the modern administrative state were hostile. It opposed economic regulation and the delegation of legislative authority to administrative agencies. From the late 1930s until roughly the mid-1950s or early 1960s, the courts tended to acquiesce in the exercise of administrative power (Shapiro, 1968). By the mid-1970s, however, the judiciary had clearly forged a "new partnership" with public administrators (Rosenbloom, 1987). This relationship enabled the courts to play a much greater role in controlling and influencing administrative action and thought. The new partnership has sometimes brought judges not only into a "political thicket" but into an administrative one as well. For instance, in 1981, 48 percent of Boston's budgetary appropriations were "presided over" by federal and state judges (Turner, 1981:12). Among the functions affected were public education, public personnel selection, incarceration, public housing, and care for the mentally retarded. The administrative thicket has often been inhospitable to judges (Horowitz, 1977). However, the new partnership has forced public administrators to change the way they think, evaluate, and act in a manner that is calculated to make public administration not just accountable to democratic constitutionalism but philosophically and practically more compatible with it (Rosenbloom, 1983).

Like the institutional responses of the other two constitutional branches, the judiciary's efforts to influence public administration have carried a price. Their interventions in public administrative institutions and processes have sometimes failed seriously, presumably damaging the courts' legitimacy, and have given rise to charges of "government by judiciary" (Berger, 1977; Boudin, 1932). More fundamental, as Donald Horowitz cautions,

> Retooling the judicial process to cope with the new responsibilities of the courts means enhancing their capacity to function more systematically in terms of general categories that transcend individual cases. Some such innovations are required. And yet, it would seem, there is a limit to the changes of this kind that courts can absorb and still remain courts. Heightened attention to recurrent patterns of behavior risks inattention to individual cases. Over the long run, augmenting judicial capacity may erode the distinctive contribution the courts make to the social order. The danger is that courts, in developing a capacity to improve on the work of other institutions, may become altogether too much like them [1977:298].

In fact, there has already been a perceptible "bureaucratization of the judiciary" (Fiss, 1983).

Taken together, the presidential, legislative, and judicial responses to the administrative state seriously distort the constitutional scheme. The president has become more activist and the legislature more reactive, as epitomized by the now defunct legislative veto. The staffs of both institutions have become central actors in government. Power consequently has devolved from elected officials to appointed ones. The appointive judiciary is also more obviously engaged in policy-making, overseeing public management, and affecting budgetary allocations than it was in the past. To some extent, it has created a "juridical federalism" that makes federal judges the de facto supervisors of state and local public administrators (Rosenbloom, 1986b). These developments do enhance the capacity of the three constitutional branches to control public administration, but they also frustrate popular sovereignty.

Finally, it should be noted that a number of statutory and administrative restraints have also been placed on federal administration in an effort to make it more externally accountable and controllable. In addition to the reorganization power and the legislative veto mentioned above, these controls have included loyalty-security requirements, performance and program-budgeting techniques, government in the sunshine and other informational and notification requirements, such civil service reforms as merit-pay plans and greater political direction of the top levels of the career service, and sunset legislation. In the aggregate, these adjustments and requirements have certainly had an impact on public administration and have made it more compatible with democratic constitutionalism, but they have been insufficient to bring the administrative and constitutional states into full harmony. As Dwight Waldo (1948) argued some four decades ago, the traditional doctrines of public administration, which rely so heavily on unified authority, are themselves problematic from the perspective of democratic constitutionalism. The assumption that public administration does not have to reflect political values because it is a "business" endeavor is a gross oversimplification. It is necessary to place public administration on a fundamentally democratic basis, one that values rights, representation, citizen participation, internal checks and balances, and individualized accountability and responsibility. Today, the United States is in the process of developing an administrative culture that has precisely these elements at its core.

An Emerging Administrative Culture

The concept of administrative culture has been used to encompass the values, cognitive approaches and methods of developing knowledge, and evaluative perspectives that dominate public administration's theoretical and practical orientations in political systems (Nachmias and Rosenbloom, 1978). Administrative cultures vary widely from nation to nation, even though the structural characteristics of administrative organizations may be similar (generally, "bureaucratic"). For instance, some administrative cultures place a high value on formalistic adherence to rules, whereas in others bargaining is a common way of determining outcomes. Similarly, what is deemed appropriate in one culture (e.g., politicization) may be considered corrupt or otherwise undesirable in another (Heady, 1966; Heidenheimer, 1970). Historically, our administrative culture has shifted dramatically on three occasions and is currently undergoing an incremental, but marked, transformation.

The first administrative culture under the constitutional regime is generally referred to as "administration by gentlemen" (Mosher, 1968; White, 1948, 1951). Existing from 1789 to 1828, this culture valued elite social status and general knowledge as determinants of appointment to administrative office. It prized honesty, favored long tenure in office, and tended to treat administrative positions as a form of property. It viewed administrative office as a political resource but did not embrace the politicization of administrative action (Rosenbloom, 1971). The culture was associated with the founding period and was quite consciously promoted by President George Washington on the grounds that it was extremely important to establish the federal service on a sound basis.

The second administrative culture was characterized by a very high degree of politicization and a "spoils system." It was ushered in by President Andrew Jackson in 1829, with a call for extensive administrative reforms aimed at opening administrative officeholding to a much broader segment of the society. The new culture was a central element in the "Jacksonian Revolution" that transformed the governmental and party systems (White, 1954). During this period, which ended in the 1880s, administrative office was viewed as a commodity and tool for partisan use. Several practices that are considered corrupt today were common, including electioneering by public employees, no-show jobs, and political assessments.

The third administrative culture grew out of the civil service reform, Progressive, and scientific management movements during the period from the 1870s to the 1920s (Skowronek, 1982). This culture may appropriately be labeled "reformist." Although it is currently being replaced, it continues to command substantial support. It rests on the politics-administration dichotomy and treats the latter as a field of business that should be informed by science. The major values of the culture were laid out by Woodrow Wilson in 1887: "It is the object of administrative study to discover, first, what government can properly and successfully do, and, secondly, how it can do these proper things with the utmost possible efficiency and the least possible cost either of money or of energy" ([1887] 1941:481). Like the administrative cultures that preceded it, the reformist culture developed as part of a major political change. In fact, to a considerable extent, it was part of the ideology of the Progressive movement. Presidents Theodore Roosevelt and Woodrow Wilson were outstanding proponents of the reformist culture, which became entrenched (indeed, enshrined) in the federal government through a succession of measures, including the extension of the merit system, adoption of political neutrality regulations, development of elaborate position-classification systems, reforms in budgeting, reorganizations, and revisions of managerial doctrines (see Gulick and Urwick, 1937).

By the late 1940s, the shortcomings of the reformist administrative culture were all too evident. Its values were at odds with those of democratic constitutionalism (Waldo, 1948). Its claims to legitimacy based on science were impugned (Simon, 1946; Dahl, 1947). Its insistence that public employees play no role in public policy—making was increasingly viewed as descriptively inaccurate and normatively inappropriate (Appleby, 1949; Long, 1949). The administrative culture emerging today can fully replace the reformist culture. Thus far, however, it has not been accompanied by a coherent political movement. Rather, it has been composed of several diverse elements that have evolved somewhat separately. These elements can be joined together, but it may be up to the public administrative community to make them cohere. Public administration has emerged as such a powerful, central, and professionalized activity in the United States that it may no longer be reasonable to expect changes in its culture to be imposed systematically from outside. The earlier cultures looked at public administration as guardianship by gentlemen, as politics, or as business. The emerging culture views public administration as governance.

Individual Rights

Reflecting the mainstream of the reformist culture, Leonard D. White wrote that "the study of administration should start from the base of management rather than the foundation of law, and is therefore more absorbed in the affairs of the American Management Association than in the decisions of the courts" (1926:vii–viii). In the emerging culture of public administration as governance, the decisions of the courts are of far greater importance. To a considerable extent, contemporary public administration has been constitutionalized through the declaration of new rights for individuals as they come into contact with government agencies and officials (Rosenbloom, 1983). Since the 1960s, clients of administrative agencies, such as welfare recipients, have been afforded far greater substantive, equal protection, and procedural due process rights. Government benefits, once defined as a privilege to which one had no constitutional right, were redefined as a "new property" (Reich, 1964) in which one does have a constitutionally cognizable interest. The constitutional rights of public employees to freedom of speech and association, procedural due process, and equal protection have also been vastly expanded. Individuals involuntarily confined to public mental health facilities have been granted a constitutional right to treatment or training, and some of their ordinary constitutional rights as members of the political community have been granted greater protection. The Eighth Amendment and equal protection rights of prisoners have also been dramatically strengthened through radical departure from earlier legal doctrines. Additionally, some constitutional protections have been developed for individuals engaged in "street-level" encounters with police or other public administrators (see *U.S. v. Brignoni-Ponce*, 1975; *Delaware v. Prouse*, 1979; *Kolender v. Lawson*, 1983). These constitutional developments are a kind of bill of rights for the individual in the administrative state that places new constraints on public administrative activity in several areas of public policy.

The impact of these constitutional changes reaches to the core of the values established by the reformist culture. There has now accumulated a very large body of law in which the actions of public administrators that were squarely within the reformist tradition have been declared unconstitutional violations of individuals' rights to due process, equal protection, and their exercise of substantive liberties. Claims for administrative efficiency, economy, and effectiveness have been rejected in favor of those protecting free exercise of religion, speech, and association; the rights to privacy and travel; the privilege against self-incrimination; the barrier against cruel and unusual punishment; and the requirements of equal protection and procedural due process in a wide variety of settings (Rosenbloom, 1983; *Uniformed Sanitation Men's Association v. Commissioner*, 1968; *Garrity v. New Jersey*, 1967). When coupled with public administrators' legal liability for violating individual rights (discussed below), these changes virtually compel public administrators to think in terms of rights and encourage them to value rights highly.

The reformist culture was perhaps especially challenged by the expansion of the constitutional rights of individual public employees as part of the constitutional changes just described. Historically, the status of public employees was at the center of the development of contemporary constitutional doctrines regarding the distribution of government largess. During the loyalty-security program of the

1940s and 1950s, federal employment became contingent on answers to such questions as "Were you a regular reader of *The New York Times?*" "Do you and your wife regularly attend any organized church services?" "Are your friends and associates intelligent, clever?" and "Have you ever had Negroes in your home?" (Rosenbloom, 1971:160–65). Eventually, these abuses led the courts to reject the view that the receipt of largess (including public employment) was a privilege and that this categorization obviated the assertion of rights pertinent to the conditions under which governmental benefits were received. Today, by contrast, public employment may even be deemed to constitute a "property interest" (*Cleveland Board of Education v. Loudermill,* 1985).

The new protections afforded public employees have enabled them to speak out on political issues and the quality of administrative performance. Organized groups of civil servants publicly opposed the Vietnam War and advocated the elimination of racial and sexual discrimination from the public service (Rosenbloom, 1971:240–43). Individual public employees have spoken out on a wide range of topics, including school bond referenda and racism (Rosenbloom, 1983:99–139; *Leonard v. City of Columbus,* 1983; *Pickering v. Board of Education,* 1968). Others have engaged in whistle-blowing or have publicly exposed improper administration. Unions representing public employees have been critical of public managers and have advocated changes in public policies. These activities have belied the reformist culture's claims that public employees are apolitical, neutral experts engaged in the "science of administration." It is now obvious that public employees have political views upon which they are prepared to act and that their concepts of proper administration vary more widely than a "science" would seem to permit. If neither apoliticality nor scientific expertise can legitimize the governmental role of public administrators, what can? Clearly, if public administration is governance, rather than business or science, the values and processes of democratic constitutionalism become highly appropriate.

Representativeness

In retrospect, the loyalty-security program marked a critical turning point in the nation's reformist administrative culture. By investigating the loyalty of every person in the federal service, not just those in sensitive positions, the program implicitly rejected the politics-administration dichotomy. Technical competence (merit) and moral fitness were now considered inadequate guarantees of proper performance. Political views might prompt public employees to engage in subversive behavior. Inevitably, public administration did contain politicality. If public employees could act on their politically subversive beliefs within the context of their jobs, could they not act on the basis of more conventional political or partisan outlooks (Long, 1949)? Public administration was clearly more than a "field of business"; it was part of government.

Our democratic constitutionalism seeks to legitimize the exercise of political power partly through making public officials representative of the people or some segments of them. The emerging administrative culture seeks to legitimize the governmental role of the public service in much the same way. Concepts of representation and representative bureaucracy vary widely (Krislov and Rosenbloom, 1981). Today, however, public policy in the United States favors the establishment of a direct connection between public administrators and the public as a means of ensuring that the administrative state is responsive to the citizenry. This approach was encompassed in embryonic form in the Administrative Procedure Act of 1946, which requires most federal agencies to publicize information about their organizational structures, procedures, rules, and proposed rules. Informal rule-making procedures require that the public be afforded an opportunity to comment on proposed rules and that the agency involved consider these views prior to propounding its final rules. Formal rule making requires a trial-like procedure in which participants are afforded an opportunity to present their perspectives before a presumptively impartial administrative law judge. Subsequent enactments, including the Freedom of Information Act (1966), Privacy Act (1974), and Government in the Sunshine Act (1976), have developed the Administrative Procedure Act's informational scheme more fully.

The emerging administrative culture's approach to representation now includes far more elaborate elements as well. It embraces the use of advisory committees to provide guidance to administrative agencies. The Federal Advisory Committee Act of 1972 states that advisory bodies "are frequently a useful and beneficial means of furnishing expert advice, ideas, and diverse opinions to the Federal Government['s]" administrative structure (1972:770). It also requires "the membership of the advisory committee[s] to be fairly balanced in terms of the points of view represented and the functions to be performed by the advisory committee" (1972:770). In 1981, there were 853 committees, down about 600 from 1972, with roughly 22,000 members (Steck, 1984:158). More generally, this form of representation is part of the "interest group liberalism" that has become central to the United States political system (Lowi, 1969).

Representation by personnel is another leading element in the contemporary concept of representative bureaucracy (Rosenbloom, 1977). Beginning in the 1970s, public policy makers asserted that there is a connection between an individual's social background and his/her performance in a public administrative position. In 1975, the United States Commission on Civil Rights wrote that had there been no previous discrimination against blacks and other groups in public employment,

> the Nation would have discovered that a civil service, operating in a manner consistent with the equal opportunity guarantees embedded in the Constitution, would more likely have the broad range of experience and skills necessary to address society's problems. Moreover, it would more likely generate support for government programs by all groups in society. Because of the growing tendency of elected representatives to delegate and assign legislative and judicial functions to the Federal bureaucracy, it has become increasingly crucial that the practices which for many years denied equal employment opportunities to citizens because of their race, color, national origin, religion, or sex, and by so doing deprived the Nation of the benefit of their services, be eliminated from public employment procedures [1975:vol. 5:6–7].

The Civil Service Reform Act of 1978 seeks a "Federal work force reflective of the Nation's diversity" that is drawn from "all segments of society." It defines "underrepresentation" as "a situation in which the number of members of a minority group designation . . . within a category of civil service employment constitutes a lower percentage of the total number of employees within the employment category than the percentage that the minority constituted within the labor force of the United States . . . " (1978:secs. 3, 2301, 7151).

More generally, William T. Gormley (1986) writes of the "representation revolution" in state-level regulatory administration. He finds that a number of procedures, such as public hearings, public membership on occupational licensing boards, recourse to ombudsmen, and proxy advocacy in utility regulation, can provide forms of "public representation in state regulation that can promote substantive representation" (190).

These developments indicate that contemporary public administration seeks to promote representation not only to legitimize the governmental roles of public administrators but also to make their substantive policy-making responsive to interested individuals and groups within the general citizenry. An extension of this approach is to allow public participation in public administration.

Participation

The emerging administrative governance culture supports the idea of citizen participation in public administration. It rejects the reformist culture's position that such participation was unnecessary because administration was a field of business and undesirable because it would promote inefficiency. As William Morrow notes, public administration has been caught up in a broader concern with citizen participation: "contemporary politics . . . has been marked by a revolution seeking more direct participation by citizens in policy-making. In contrast to the tendency for institutions to represent organized interests, this resurgence of participatory democracy seeks direct citizen access to decision centers and involvement in decision-making regardless of any connections or affiliations that the participants might have with organized interests. In fact, the participation movement has stressed representation of unorganized publics that have been given only casual concern in policy arenas" (1975:189–90). There are a number of familiar obstacles to participation along these lines. Most notable, perhaps, public participation in politics is frequently limited, as in the case of electoral turnouts. Nevertheless, the emerging administrative culture has been associated with several efforts to induce greater public participation in public administration.

The "war on poverty" under the Economic Opportunity Act of 1964 and the Model Cities Program under the Model Cities Act of 1966 remain the best known of these large-scale federal efforts to include members of the general citizenry in administrative decision making affecting their communities. Both programs were characterized by serious shortcomings, including a lack of sufficient participation and opposition by local governments to community-based access to federal resources (Moynihan, 1970:136–37). Yet Robert Aleshire's evaluation of these programs reflects the emerging administrative culture's perspectives on participation: "The simple conclusion of a comparison of the costs and benefits of participation of the poor in the Community Action and Model Cities Programs is that democracy would not and will not survive without such participation; that a basic reallocation and decentralization of power is required; and that the necessities as well as the benefits outweigh the costs, some of which are produced by the fact that the system itself is not designed to encourage or facilitate participation" (1972:442).

Elaine Sharp (1980) has suggested that the concept of participation can be systematically incorporated into public administration in some areas through "coproduction." She maintains that "the crucial point about the coproduction concept is that it highlights a different understanding of urban service delivery, and of productivity improvement. . . . Here, the assumption is not that government officials perform for citizens, and therefore bear total responsibility for productivity improvements or the lack thereof; rather, the emphasis is upon service delivery as a joint venture, involving both citizens and government agents" (111). Moreover, Charles Levine (1984) argues that coproduction can help rebuild citizenship in the contemporary administrative state.

Some aspects of environmental policy also seek to include public participation in administrative decision making. The National Environmental Policy Act of 1969 requires that impact statements accompany "major Federal actions significantly affecting the quality of the human environment" (1970:852). Such statements can become the basis for broad public discussion of proposed administrative actions and for forums and hearings at which direct public participation can take place. At the state level, environmental agencies may employ specialists in citizen participation, as is the case with New York's Department of Environmental Conservation.

Many aspects of public participation in public administration remain unresolved. The central point, however, is that the emerging administrative culture does not seek to confine the public to the role of "authoritative critic," as Woodrow Wilson ([1887] 1941: 498) and the reformist culture did. Widespread citizen participation is now deemed desirable; only the specific mechanisms remain problematic.

Checks and Balances within Public Administration

The emerging administrative culture also seeks to tame and legitimize the political power of administrative agencies by creating internal checks and balances within public administration. Among the leading developments in this context have been the "judicial-ization" of administrative processes, increased use of inspectors general, and the deliberate incorporation of pluralism into the administrative structure. Judicialization relies on independent administrative functionaries, who operate within the framework of agency hierarchies but are not subject to their authority (Dimock, 1980). By 1980, there were over a thousand administrative law judges (ALJs) in twenty-nine agencies (Heffron, 1983:273). They make decisions concerning the rights, status, and property of private parties that have a direct impact on agencies' rules, budgets, procedures, and authority. By law, ALJs must be independent of the managerial authority of the agencies in which they are employed. Inspectors general, who serve as a check on mismanagement and corruption, have a similar independence. ALJs and inspectors general represent a very pronounced departure from the reformist culture's reliance on "unity of command" (Gulick, [1937] 1978:43) and strict subordination for the sake of coordination. The creation of these positions also denotes a recognition of the desire to augment external checks on administration, such as legislative oversight and judicial review, with internal checks.

The deliberate establishment of administrative pluralism seeks to promote a similar function. There have long been broad overlaps and redundancies among administrative agencies. The reformist administrative culture was strongly opposed to such structural arrangements, viewing them as wasteful, inefficient, and irresponsible. It favored the consolidation of agencies into departments placed tightly under the control of chief executives. By the 1970s, however, it became evident that administrative pluralism could be used to promote checks and balances within administration. The federal civil service reform of 1978 presents an excellent example. Somewhat competing functions, which had previously been housed in a single agency—the Civil Service Commission—were dispersed among three independent agencies: an Office of Personnel Management to perform the major tasks of personnel administration; a Merit Systems Protection Board to protect employees' legal rights and to ensure strict adherence to personnel law; and the preexisting Equal Employment Opportunity Commission to exercise general authority over the government's equal opportunity program. Additionally, the Federal Labor Relations Council, on which the Civil Service Commission had representation, was replaced by a more autonomous Federal Labor Relations Authority. The latter has general responsibility for the operation of collective bargaining in the federal service. These agencies compete with one another and have been involved in a variety of contests over matters of public personnel administration, some of which have been adjudicated in court. The Occupational Safety and Health Act of 1970 presents another example of deliberate administrative pluralism. It established two agencies, the Occupational Safety and Health Administration (OSHA) and the Occupational Safety and Health Review Commission (OSHRC). OSHRC is an independent body to which appeals concerning OSHA decisions can be made.

The idea of agency suing agency, or even competition among agencies, was anathema to the reformist administrative culture. Checks and balances do not promote businesslike administration, but they do make public administration resemble the larger constitutional scheme of governance. The emerging administrative culture recognizes the governmental and political benefits of administrative pluralism, much as the Constitution recognizes the practical utility of bicameralism in promoting deliberation.

Personal Responsibility

The reformist administrative culture placed a strong emphasis on accountability. Its focus, however, was primarily within the framework of an agency's hierarchy. The legal doctrine of respondeat superior lent justification to superordinates' power over subordinates. Clear lines of authority and responsibility within agencies were viewed as a means of guaranteeing substantial accountability. The emerging administrative culture, by contrast, emphasizes the desirability of channels through which public administrators can be held directly and personally accountable to persons or bodies outside the administrative framework. Public administrators' official liability is the clearest example of such personal accountability. The changing view of whistle-blowing is also important in this context.

During the 1970s, the Supreme Court redefined the law of public officials' liability (Rosenbloom, 1983:179–206). It abandoned the presumption that public administrators have an absolute immunity from civil suits seeking damages for their tortious behavior within the scope of their official duties. The new presumption is qualified immunity only. This doctrinal change drastically increased the personal liability of public administrators for violating individuals' constitutional and federally protected statutory rights. Public administrators' liability now generally depends on whether they violate constitutional or other rights of which they are, or reasonably should be, cognizant. Based on this standard, liability serves to protect the recently declared rights for individuals in the administrative state. Liability is assessed in a judicial forum and is intended to compensate victims of illegal or unconstitutional administrative action. It also serves as a deterrent and creates an incentive to be responsive to the judiciary's interpretations of the Constitution and laws.

Whistle-blowing also places a new emphasis on personal responsibility. The reformist culture viewed it as insubordination and a threat to effective administration. Communication was supposed to flow downward and upward, but not outward. This perspective has clearly and dramatically changed in a way that demonstrates administrative cultures can be rapidly and even radically transformed. As Robert Vaughn concluded in "Statutory Protection of Whistleblowers in the Federal Executive Branch," "The whistleblower provision breaks new ground not only in the protection of whistleblowers but also in legal control of conduct of members of public bureaucracies. The whistleblower provision in many ways is an important experiment dealing with the role of law and the place of personal responsibility in ensuring honest and efficient administration. Less than a decade ago, whistleblowing was a scorned activity often officially punished; today, Congress approves whistleblowing in the strongest terms and protects whistleblowers in several innovative and important ways" (1982:667). Although there may be no specific or clear legal obligation to engage in whistle-blowing, there is certainly an emerging sense that it is morally reprehensible and irresponsible not to do so whenever matters of life, individuals' safety or health, or substantial public concern are at stake. In the future, whistle-blowing may become a major channel through which public administration will be checked and held accountable.

Remarkably, the concept of personal responsibility includes an incipient right to disobey illegal or unconstitutional orders. In *Harley v. Schuylkill County* (1979), a federal district court found such a right to be grounded in the Constitution's "privileges and immunities" clause and to be a corollary of public administrators' qualified immunity (see Vaughn, 1984:chap. 16).

Conclusion: Public Administration Is Governance

The emerging administrative culture, which views public administration as governance, can go a long way toward making public administration in the United States more compatible with the Constitution. The new culture does not consider public administration as limited to executive or businesslike functions. Nor does it treat administration as politics in the sense of partisan advantage or power seeking. Rather, by conceiving of public administration as governance, it augments the reformist culture by bringing legislative and judicial concerns into the center of administrative theory and practice. Rights, representation, participation, checks and balances, and personal responsibility are all fundamental parts of the constitutional scheme. Today, they are becoming ingrained in public administration as well.

The diverse elements of the emerging administrative culture evolved somewhat separately from one another. The development of new constitutional rights for individuals as they come into contact with public administrators was largely associated with the shift from the "Roosevelt Court" to the Warren and Burger courts (Pritchett, 1948; Rosenbloom, 1983; Blasi, 1983). The emphasis on representation flows from the broad delegations of legislative authority to administrative agencies since 1935 and from the civil rights movement's demands for equal opportunity and affirmative action. Public participation is associated with the Great Society's social programs and its restructuring of federalism (Kaplan and Cuciti, 1986). Internal checks and balances in administration seem to be rooted in the emergence of a keener understanding of bureaucratic politics and power (Seidman, 1970). Emphasis on personal responsibility is largely the capstone of the judiciary's response to the contemporary administrative state. All of these elements, however, are fundamentally based on the growing recognition that public administration is governance, rather than neutrally applied, businesslike expertise, and that it must be retrofit into the constitutional order.

The diverse elements also contain a certain internal logic. If public administrators are important governmental actors, then the administrative state ought to be representative of the public, or at least some segments of it. Policy-making should provide for public participation where possible. Administrative power, like all governmental power, should be subject to checks and balances. Individual rights must be protected from administrative encroachment if the essence of the liberal state envisioned by the Constitution is to survive.

The new administrative culture does not replace other means of exercising control over the administrative state in general. It can augment them. It does not do serious damage to the exercise of external political checks, such as legislative oversight or direction by political executives. Nor does it prevent Congress from reducing administrative discretion through more specific statutory standards and more explicit statements of legislative intent. "Juridical democracy" is not foreclosed (Lowi, 1969). Internal hierarchical control remains intact, except when whistle-blowing or disobedience is appropriate. Privatization and other reductions in the scope of the administrative state are substantially unaffected by the emerging culture. Efficiency and economy may be compromised in some ways, but they are promoted in others. A public service that is socially representative, open to public scrutiny and participation, cognizant of individual rights, subject to internal checks and balances, and partly based on a sense of personal responsibility may well be able to overcome effectively the tunnel vision that sometimes accompanies administrative and organizational specialization.

The emerging administrative culture is comfortable with Alexander Hamilton's statement that "the administration of government, in its largest sense, comprehends all the operations of the body politic, whether legislative, executive, or judiciary" (Rossiter, 1961:435). It is constitutional. An appropriate agenda for public administration is to recognize that the public-administration-as-governance culture is already present in embryonic form, to embrace it, and to define, develop, and refine it further.

REFERENCES

Administrative Procedure Act. 1946. 60 Stat. 237; 5 U.S.C.A. 551.

Aleshire, Robert. 1972. "Power to the People: An Assessment of the Community Action and Model Cities Experience." *Public Administration Review* 32:428–43.

Appleby, Paul. 1949. *Policy and Administration.* Tuscaloosa: University of Alabama Press.

Arnold, Peri. 1986. *Making the Managerial Presidency.* Princeton, N.J.: Princeton University Press.

Arnold, R. Douglas. 1979. *Congress and the Bureaucracy.* New Haven, Conn.: Yale University Press.

Barger, Harold. 1984. *The Impossible Presidency.* Glenview, Ill.: Scott, Foresman.

Beer, Samuel. [1978] 1986. "Federalism, Nationalism, and Democracy in America." In *Classic Readings in American Politics,* edited by P. Nivola and D. Rosenbloom. New York: St. Martin's.

Berger, Raoul. 1977. *Government by Judiciary.* Cambridge, Mass.: Harvard University Press.

Berlin, Isaiah. 1969. *Four Essays on Liberty.* London: Oxford University Press.

Blasi, Vincent. 1983. *The Burger Court: The Counter-Revolution that Wasn't.* New Haven, Conn.: Yale University Press.

Boudin, Louis. 1932. *Government by Judiciary.* New York: William Godwin.

Branti v. Finkel. 1980. 445 U.S. 507.

Buckley v. Valeo. 1976. 424 U.S. 1.

Civil Service Reform Act. 1978. 92 Stat. 1111.

Cleveland Board of Education v. Loudermill. 1985. 470 U.S. 532.

Cronin, Thomas E. 1975. *The State of the Presidency.* Boston: Little, Brown.

Dahl, Robert. 1947. "The Science of Administration: Three Problems." *Public Administration Review* 7:1–11.

Davis, Kenneth. 1975. *Administrative Law and Government.* St. Paul, Minn.: West.

Delaware v. Prouse. 1979. 440 U.S. 648.

Dimock, Marshall. 1980. *Law and Dynamic Administration.* New York: Praeger.

Dodd, Lawrence, and Richard Schott. 1979. *Congress and the Administrative State.* New York: John Wiley and Sons.

Economic Opportunity Act. 1964. 78 Stat. 508.

Edwards, George, and Stephen Wayne. 1985. *Presidential Leadership.* New York: St. Martin's.

Federal Advisory Committee Act. 1972. 86 Stat. 770.

Federal Trade Commission v. Ruberoid Co. 1952. 343 U.S. 470.

Fiorina, Morris. 1977. *Congress: Keystone of the Washington Establishment.* New Haven, Conn.: Yale University Press.

Fiss, Owen. 1983. "The Bureaucratization of the Judiciary." *Yale Law Journal* 92:1442–68.

Freedom of Information Act. 1966. 80 Stat. 378; 5 U.S.C.A. 552.

Garcia v. San Antonio Metropolitan Transit Authority. 1984. 469 U.S. 528.

Garrity v. New Jersey. 1967. 385 U.S. 493.

Goodnow, Frank. 1900. *Politics and Administration.* New York: Macmillan.

Gormley, William. 1986. "The Representation Revolution: Reforming State Regulation through Public Representation." *Administration and Society* 18:179–96.

Government in the Sunshine Act. 1976. 5 U.S.C.A. 552b.

Gulick, Luther. [1937] 1978. "Notes on the Theory of Organization." In *Classics of Public Administration,* edited by Jay Shafritz and Albert Hyde. Oak Park, Ill: Moore.

Gulick, Luther, and L. Urwick, eds. 1937. *Papers on the Science of Administration.* New York: Institute of Public Administration.

Harley v. Schuylkill County. 1979. 476 F. Supp. 191.

Hayek, Friedrich. 1944. *The Road to Serfdom.* Chicago: University of Chicago Press.

Heady, Ferrel. 1966. *Public Administration in Comparative Perspective.* Englewood Cliffs, N.J.: Prentice-Hall.

Heffron, Florence. 1983. *The Administrative Regulatory Process.* New York: Longman.

Heidenheimer, Arnold, ed. 1970. *Political Corruption.* New York: Holt, Rinehart and Winston.

Hess, Stephen. 1976. *Organizing the Presidency.* Washington, D.C.: Brookings Institution.

Horowitz, Donald. 1977. *The Courts and Social Policy.* Washington, D.C.: Brookings Institution.

Hummel, Ralph. 1982. *The Bureaucratic Experience.* 2d ed. New York: St. Martin's.

Immigration and Naturalization Service v. Chadha. 1983. 462 U.S. 919.

Jacoby, Henry. 1973. *The Bureaucratization of the World.* Berkeley: University of California Press.

Kaplan, Marshall, and Peggy Cuciti, eds. 1986. *The Great Society and Its Legacy.* Durham, N.C.: Duke University Press.

Kolender v. Lawson. 1983. 461 U.S. 352.

Krislov, Samuel, and David H. Rosenbloom. 1981. *Representative Bureaucracy and the American Political System.* New York: Praeger.

Leonard v. City of Columbus. 1983. 705 F. 2d 1299.

Levine, Charles. 1984. "Citizenship and Service Delivery: The Promise of Coproduction." *Public Administration Review* 44:178–87.

Long, Norton. 1949. "Power and Administration." *Public Administration Review* 9:57–64.

Lowi, Theodore J. 1969. *The End of Liberalism.* New York: W.W. Norton.

Malbin, Michael. 1977. "Congressional Committee Staffs: Who's in Charge Here?" *Public Interest* 47:16–40.

———. 1979. *Unelected Representatives.* New York: Basic Books.

Mayo, Elton. 1933. *The Human Problems of an Industrial Civilization.* New York: Macmillan.

Model Cities Act (Demonstration Cities and Metropolitan Development Act). 1966. 80 Stat. 1255.

Morrow, William. 1975. *Public Administration.* New York: Random House.

Mosher, Frederick. 1968. *Democracy and the Public Service.* New York: Oxford University Press.

Moynihan, Daniel. 1970. *Maximum Feasible Misunderstanding.* New York: Free Press.

Nachmias, David, and David H. Rosenbloom. 1978. *Bureaucratic Culture: Citizens and Administrators in Israel.* New York: St. Martin's.

———. 1980. *Bureaucratic Government, U.S.A.* New York: St. Martin's.

National Environmental Policy Act (1969). 1970. 83 Stat. 852.

Occupational Safety and Health Act. 1970. 29 U.S.C.A. 651.

Pickering v. Board of Education. 1968. 391 U.S. 563.

Pritchett, C. Herman. 1948. *The Roosevelt Court.* New York: Macmillan.

Privacy Act. 1974. 5 U.S.C.A. 552a.

Redford, Emmette. 1969. *Democracy in the Administrative State.* New York: Oxford University Press.

Reich, Charles. 1964. "The New Property." *Yale Law Journal* 73:733–87.

Rieselbach, Leroy. 1986. *Congressional Reform.* Washington, D.C.: Congressional Quarterly Press.

Rohr, John. 1986. *To Run a Constitution.* Lawrence: University of Kansas Press.

Rosenbloom, David H. 1971. *Federal Service and the Constitution.* Ithaca, N.Y.: Cornell University Press.

———. 1977. *Federal Equal Employment Opportunity.* New York: Praeger.

———. 1983. *Public Administration and Law.* New York: Marcel Dekker.

———. 1986a. "The Judicial Response to the Bureaucratic State." In *Bureaucratic Power in National Policy Making,* edited by Francis Rourke. Boston: Little, Brown.

———. 1986b. "The Great Society and the Growth of 'Juridical Federalism'—Protecting Civil Rights and Welfare." In *The Great Society and Its Legacy,* edited by Marshall Kaplan and Peggy Cuciti. Durham, N.C.: Duke University Press.

———. 1987. "Public Administrators and the Judiciary: The 'New Partnership.' " *Public Administration Review* 47:75–83.

Rossiter, Clinton, ed. 1961. *The Federalist Papers.* New York: Mentor.

Seidman, Harold. 1970. *Politics, Position, and Power.* New York: Oxford University Press.

Shapiro, Martin. 1968. *The Supreme Court and Administrative Agencies.* New York: Free Press.

Sharp, Elaine. 1980. "Toward a New Understanding of Urban Services and Citizen Participation: The Coproduction Concept." *Midwest Review of Public Administration* 14:105–18.

Simon, Herbert. 1946. "The Proverbs of Administration." *Public Administration Review* 6:53–67.

Skowronek, Stephen. 1982. *Building a New American State.* New York: Cambridge University Press.

Spady v. Mount Vernon. 1974. 419 U.S. 983.

Steck, Henry. 1984. "Politics and Administration." In *Politics and Administration,* edited by Jack Rabin and James Bowman. New York: Marcel Dekker.

Turner, Robert. 1981. "Governing from the Bench." *Boston Globe Magazine,* November 8.

Uniformed Sanitation Men's Association v. Commissioner. 1968. 392 U.S. 280.

United States Commission on Civil Rights. 1975. *The Federal Civil Rights Enforcement Effort–1974,* vol. 5. Washington, D.C.: Commission on Civil Rights.

United States President's Committee of Administrative Management. [1937] 1976. "Report." In *Basic Documents of American Public Administration, 1776–1950*, edited by Frederick Mosher. Reprint. New York: Holmes and Meier.

United States v. Brignoni-Ponce. 1975. 422 U.S. 873.

United States v. Richardson. 1974. 418 U.S. 166.

Vaughn, Robert. 1982. "Statutory Protection of Whistleblowers in the Federal Executive Branch." *University of Illinois Law Review.* 1982:615–67.

————. 1984. *Merit Systems Protection Board: Rights and Remedies.* New York: Law Journal Seminars Press.

Waldo, Dwight. 1948. *The Administrative State.* New York: Ronald Press.

————. 1980. *The Enterprise of Public Administration.* Novato, Calif.: Chandler and Sharp.

Wayne, Stephen. 1978. *The Legislative Presidency.* New York: Harper and Row.

White, Leonard. 1926. *Introduction to the Study of Administration.* New York: Macmillan.

————. 1948. *The Federalists.* New York: Macmillan.

————. 1951. *The Jeffersonians.* New York: Macmillan.

————. 1954. *The Jacksonians.* New York: Macmillan.

Wilson, Woodrow. [1887] 1941. "The Study of Administration." *Political Science Quarterly* 56:481–506.

Woll, Peter. 1963. *American Bureaucracy.* New York: W.W. Norton.

Woll, Peter, and Rochelle Jones. 1975. "Bureaucratic Defense in Depth." In *Watergate and the American Political Process*, edited by Ronald Pynn. New York: Praeger.

★ 6 ★

Supreme Court Activism and the Constitution

LAWRENCE BAUM

Of all the courts in the world, the U.S. Supreme Court may well be the most important policy maker. Throughout the Court's history, its decisions have helped to reshape the system of government created by the Constitution and to determine the outcome of major national issues. This essay examines the Supreme Court's role as a policy maker and considers how the Constitution has helped create that role by focusing on three related aspects of the Court's development and status.

The first is the Court's level of activism. The term *judicial activism* is ambiguous, because commentators have used it in several different ways (Canon, 1982). I use the term to refer to the extent of the Court's participation in making national policy, with emphasis on its interventions to overturn or modify the policies of the legislative and executive branches.[1] By this definition, the Court's long history of activism dates back at least to its 1803 decision in *Marbury v. Madison*. The Court has been a particularly active policy maker in the past century, and by most measures its involvement in the making of national policy reached an unprecedented level in the last thirty-five years.

The second is the content of the Court's activism. For most of its history, the Court could be characterized in today's terms as a conservative institution, one that gave its most consistent support to business interests and property rights.[2] In the past half-century, however, the Court has paid the greatest attention to the civil liberties of individuals, and its primary ideological direction has been liberal.

The final aspect to be considered is speculative. Supreme Court activism has ebbed and flowed over the past two centuries, but there has been little ebbing since 1954. In light of this recent history, it is possible that the Court has established for itself a more permanent position as a critical policy maker.

An analysis of the Supreme Court's development as an institution could focus on issues other than activism, but activism is particularly useful in exploring the relationship between the Court and the Constitution. By considering the Court's involvement in national policy-making, we can gain a sense of the ways in which the Constitution has shaped its role.

An inquiry into the relationship between the Supreme Court and the Constitution poses some special difficulties. Much more than Congress and the president, the Court regularly takes action that is connected with the Constitution directly and explicitly. Today, about half of its decisions—and a majority of its most important decisions—involve interpreting constitutional provisions. The Constitution and the Court are thus not easily disentangled, and complications beset any efforts to treat the Constitution as an independent variable influencing the Court. Nonetheless, the importance of this question makes the effort worthwhile.

The Constitution and the Supreme Court's Role

Our inquiry can begin with the obvious: the place of the Supreme Court in national policy-making, like that of Congress and the president, is structured by the Constitution. Explicitly and implicitly, provisions of the Constitution have created a system of government within which the Court operates. Three basic characteristics of that constitutional system have shaped the Court's place in government and its activity as a policy maker.

Constitutionalism

The first of these characteristics is constitutionalism itself. The Constitution as the basic document of the new government reflected a commitment to legal restraints on government action. In turn, the existence of those restraints invited the courts to serve as arbiters of constitutional rules. Whether or not *Marbury v. Madison* was consistent with the intent of the framers, its logic has a fundamental appeal to those who accept the idea of constitutional government: only if the courts refuse to validate government policies that go beyond the limits of the Constitution will those limits maintain their force. From this perspective, perhaps it was inevitable that John Marshall and the Court ultimately won the debate over judicial review of legislation.

By winning this debate and thereby holding the constitutional high ground, the Court achieved a basis for active involvement in policy-making and a degree of independence from the other branches. For those who accept the Court's role as interpreter of the Constitution, refusals to follow its decisions have a tinge of illegitimacy, and efforts to attack the Court as an institution have more than a tinge. As Martin Shapiro has argued, the Court's power stems in part "from the fact that its pronouncements are perceived as 'the law' in a nation that believes in obeying the law—and not only 'the law,' but 'the constitutional law' in a nation that believes that the Constitution is a higher and better law" (1978:195).

As manifested in judicial review, constitutionalism gives the Supreme Court a strength that translates into power over other government institutions; the action they can take and their positions in relation to each other depend in part on the Court's rulings. This power is exemplified by the relationship between the federal and state governments. The Constitution leaves the boundaries between the two levels uncertain, and this ambiguity gives the Supreme Court a potentially major role in determining these boundaries. Indeed, throughout its history, the Court has been active in adjudicating disputes over federalism. In doing so, it has helped to determine the relative importance of the national and subnational governments as policy makers. In turn, this power gives the Court some implicit leverage in its dealings with other government institutions.

Powers of the President and Congress

The independence and power that the Supreme Court gained through acceptance of its authority to interpret the Constitution should not be exaggerated. The Court's independence is limited by a second relevant characteristic of the constitutional system: the powers of Congress and the president that counterbalance those of the Court. Those powers are of several types.

One type is related to Alexander Hamilton's oft-cited observation that the judiciary "has no influence over either the sword or the purse" (*Federalist No. 78*). Deference to the Court helps it secure obedience to its decisions, but officials who are responsible for carrying out those decisions often do so less than fully, and some controversial decisions have suffered from serious implementation problems (Johnson and Canon, 1984). When such problems occur, action by Congress and the executive branch may determine whether they can be overcome. This dependence on the other branches was underlined dramatically by the aftermath of *Brown v. Board of Education* (1954). Meaningful desegregation of schools in the Deep South began only when Congress backed the Court with financial sanctions for noncompliance with its ruling and the Johnson administration enforced the sanctions vigorously. Congress and the president can influence the implementation of Court decisions through less dramatic means, such as statements supporting or opposing controversial decisions. In all these ways the other branches help determine the Court's effectiveness as a policy maker.

A second type of power derives from direct controls over the Court that the legislature and executive have. Congress and the president determine the Court's size, its jurisdiction, and its budget. Laws can be written to overturn statutory decisions, and amendments can be proposed to overturn constitutional decisions. The other branches have shown a marked reluctance to utilize most of these powers, in part because of the protection that constitutionalism provides the Court. But even if these powers are used rarely, their mere existence provides an incentive for the justices to avoid or retreat from confrontations with the president and Congress.

Finally, the other branches choose the Court's members. Use of the appointment power to control the Court suffers from significant limits: lifetime terms, the resulting irregularity of vacancies, and the deviation of some justices from their appointers' expectations. Most justices, however, reflect fairly well the views of the presidents who chose them, and appointments provide a powerful mechanism with which to rein in the Court. Robert Dahl has argued that, because of the appointment power, "the policy views dominant on the Court are never for long out of line with the policy views dominant among the lawmaking majorities" (1958:285). Arguably, Dahl overstates this link between the Court and the other branches (Casper, 1976), but his statement seems accurate for the most part.

The powers of the president and Congress serve to limit the Court's independence as a policy maker. The appointment power fosters a similarity between the Court's collective policy views and those of the other branches. The other powers foster judicial caution about taking positions with which the president and congressional majorities strongly disagree, particularly when such positions produce direct confrontations with one of the other branches. But the Court has its own less tangible power, derived primarily from its legitimacy as interpreter of the Constitution. The Court and the other branches of the federal government thus have reasons to make accommodations with each other.

Demand-Activated Policy Making

Article III of the Constitution made the Supreme Court a conventional court, one that responds to legal cases brought by litigants. The Constitution thus created an important link between the Court and the rest of government and society. As a policy maker, the Court is activated by the cases brought to it; unlike the other branches, it cannot intervene in issues at will. In reality, other policy makers may be nearly as dependent on external demands as a spur to action, but the Court's reactive posture creates a particularly direct and unavoidable dependence.

This reactive posture means, of course, that the Supreme Court's work as a policy maker depends on the content of the cases brought to it. The Court could do little to determine the scope of constitutional protection for freedom of expression until substantial numbers of First Amendment cases were brought before it. It also means that the Court's work is tied to the activity of government in at least two ways: first, litigation before the Court is based on legal rights that are established primarily by the other branches; second, that litigation derives most often from challenges to government action. The breadth and depth of government activity thus help determine the number and kinds of cases that come to the Court.[3]

As a conventional court, one that operates within a structured litigation process, the Supreme Court relies heavily on litigants for information as well as opportunities to act. Justices are likely to gauge the importance of an issue, for instance, by the volume of cases coming to the Court on that issue. Litigants are also the Court's primary source of arguments and policy alternatives.[4]

Those interests that are most capable of bringing cases to the Supreme Court and arguing effectively before the Court thus have the greatest opportunity to shape the Court's policies. The federal government itself is particularly adept at bringing and arguing cases, and its success in the Court is impressive.[5] The resources of large business corporations also give them considerable capability as litigants. In contrast, many other private interests cannot afford the costs of effective litigation unless they receive special help.

If the Court's activation by litigants limits what it can do in some respects, that characteristic supports activism in another respect. The Court serves as a point of access for interests that have lost in the other branches or simply see an opportunity to advance their policy goals in the judicial branch. Such interests will provide opportunities for activism by bringing cases that raise significant policy issues. Moreover, if the Court takes an activist course, it encourages interests favored by its policies to bring new cases that provide additional opportunities for policy making; in this sense, the Court's activism is self-reinforcing.

Further, groups wishing to use this point of access will tend to support the Supreme Court's role as a significant policy maker. Of course, an activist Court will receive the strongest support from those interests that its policies favor at any given time. Less favored interests may even seek to restrict the Court's power in order to protect their own positions. If the justices are attentive to the need to maintain support, however, their allies will be more powerful than their opponents. Even those interests that the Court treats unfavorably at a particular time may prefer to continue fighting for victories in the Court rather than weaken an access point in government that might serve them better at a later time.

These three characteristics—constitutionalism, the powers of the president and Congress, and activation by demands—have a powerful impact on the Supreme Court's work as a policy maker. The sections that follow consider the ways in which these aspects of the constitutional system have shaped the Court. They also examine the limits on the impact of these forces and other influences on the Court's development. The result will not be a comprehensive explanation of the Court's role in national policy-making but one partial perspective on the link between the Court and the Constitution.

The Growth of Activism

After a tentative beginning in the 1790s, the Supreme Court under John Marshall's leadership involved itself in many of the major issues of public policy. During the period when Marshall was chief justice (1801–35), the Court asserted its power to overturn federal and state laws on constitutional grounds and did much to draw lines between the proper spheres of national and state activity. Later in that century, the Court involved itself in the issues that arose over slavery—most dramatically, in the *Dred Scott* case in 1857—and the prosecution of the Civil War and Reconstruction. Yet the Court's intervention into policy issues in this period appears relatively limited and episodic from our perspective today. The *Dred Scott* case, for example, was only the second instance in which the Court directly declared a federal statute unconstitutional.[6] Moreover, during this period, as in later periods, the Court seldom ruled that presidential actions were illegal (Schubert, 1957).

During the half-century that ended in 1937, the Court engaged in a more sustained activism. It acted with increasing resolve to place limits on government regulation and management of the economy, and its resolve was reflected in a growing number of decisions declaring regulatory laws in violation of the Constitution. As measured by the number of statutes held to be unconstitutional, the height of the Court's activism came in the 1920s, when it struck down more than 150 federal and state laws—the overwhelming majority of them involving economic regulation. More dramatic was the series of decisions in the 1930s that overturned several major pieces of the New Deal program. Those decisions brought the Court into direct confrontation with President Franklin Roosevelt, a confrontation that ended only when the Court changed course and Roosevelt had the opportunity to make new appointments.

After the Court retreated in 1937, it remained relatively passive for several years. It gradually reasserted itself, and in the past half-century as a whole its activism arguably has been greater than in any previous era (Casper, 1976). Of all the Court's decisions to overturn federal statutes and state and local laws, nearly half of each have come since 1950. The Court has played an integral role in shaping government policy on a wide range of major issues, among them·police procedure, abortion, school segregation, the death penalty, legislative apportionment, and the balance of constitutional power between Congress and the president.

The Court's decisions also have been the primary catalyst for a massive increase in judicial rulings that require positive action by other government institutions—rulings that involve particularly vigorous intervention in the policy-making process (Cooper, 1988). This development began with the Court's school desegregation decisions, under which federal district judges have in effect become administrators of many school districts, and it has continued with a series of district court rulings that required fundamental restructuring of prisons and mental institutions.

This historical growth in activism is striking. Whether the framers intended the Supreme Court to hold the power of judicial review is a matter of debate that has not been, and probably cannot be, resolved. It does seem quite unlikely that the framers envisioned the frequent use of judicial review and the level of judicial activism that have characterized the past century (Hall, 1985:2).

The growth of activism to its present level can be understood largely in relation to the characteristics of the constitutional system that were discussed in the preceding section. Perhaps most important, nineteenth-century justices showed considerable skill in drawing on constitutionalism to assert their authority while limiting the number and severity of their confrontations with the president and Congress. By doing so, they helped to create widespread acceptance of the Court's position as a significant policy maker. Further, by developing that position, they gave the Court a degree of leverage with which to deter attacks by the other branches.

John Marshall was especially sensitive to the need for this kind of strategy (Beveridge, 1919:vols. 3–4; McCloskey, 1960:chaps. 2–3). *Marbury v. Madison* exemplifies his approach: the Court claimed the power of judicial review in a decision that supported the position of the current administration, so President Thomas Jefferson had no basis for a direct conflict with the Court. More broadly, Marshall established something of an alliance between the Court and the other branches of the federal government. His Court struck down only the minor federal law at issue in *Marbury v. Madison* while giving state laws less friendly treatment, and it supported an expansive interpretation of federal powers under Article I.

Although the Taney Court that followed supported federal power less uniformly than the Marshall Court, it generally displayed similar caution. The one glaring exception, of course, was the *Dred Scott* decision. Yet Robert McCloskey has pointed out that reaction to this ruling demonstrated how well the Court had established itself (1960:98–100). The decision aroused intense antipathy toward the Court throughout the North, but the Court as an institution and its power of judicial review were left standing.

The Court continued its careful path during and after the Civil War, engaging in few direct confrontations with the other branches despite the extraordinary and constitutionally dubious measures taken by Abraham Lincoln and then by the Reconstruction-Era Congress. When Congress cut back the Court's jurisdiction in 1868 to prevent review of the Reconstruction program, the Court upheld that action, even though the legislation required it to forego a decision in a case it already had heard (Murphy, 1962:38–40).

Having strengthened its institutional position in this way, the Court possessed the freedom to engage in more concerted activism in the late nineteenth century. The justices who served in and after that period had reason to believe that the Court could safely weather conflicts with the other branches over major elements of national policy. It is likely that this perception encouraged the Court's gradually escalating attacks on government regulation of the economy. The Court's considerable strength was demonstrated when Franklin Roosevelt found himself unable to secure adoption of his Court-packing plan, though the Court did much to protect itself by abruptly changing its interpretation of federal regulatory powers (Leuchtenburg, 1969; Caldeira, 1987).

Particularly in the twentieth century, a growth in litigation also has fostered an increased level of activism. As the number of cases coming to the Court multiplied (Casper and Posner, 1976), the Court gained far more opportunities to intervene in policy issues. In response to this growth in cases, Congress acted several times to increase the Court's control over its docket, so that gradually the Court gained nearly total freedom to grant or deny hearings to litigants.[7] With more cases before it and greater ability to choose cases for decision, the Court has largely been freed from the constraints created by its dependence on litigants to set its agenda (Gressman, 1964).

This growth in litigation appears to have multiple sources. Perhaps most important is the increased volume and breadth of government activity, which produce more legal challenges to government decisions. Congressional action and the Court's own rulings have provided new legal bases for litigation, especially over civil liberties issues. As noted earlier, the Court's activism has been self-reinforcing in that it has encouraged interests with a stake in government policy to turn to the Court—particularly those interests toward which the Court has already shown sympathy.

The greatest leap in the level of activism arose from interaction between a Court that was skeptical about government economic regulation and business groups that challenged regulatory policies. The litigation capabilities of large corporations provided the Court with opportunities to attack regulations of economic activity and influenced the justices' thinking about the constitutional status of regulatory policies (Twiss, 1942). At the same time, the Court's growing propensity to strike down regulatory laws spurred new litigation by business interests. The Court's decisions favoring the corporate sector also provided it with a powerful ally that was in a particularly good position to defend the Court's policies and to help legitimize its activist role.

As this discussion suggests, the constitutional system in which the Supreme Court operates facilitated a growth in its activism. But that growth probably was not an inevitable product of the constitutional system; other factors came into play. The Court's early activism helped to accustom both its audiences and its own members to a significant policy-making role; a more passive Court might have established a pattern of limited involvement in national policy-making. The political skills of John Marshall and others helped limit attacks on the Court during the period in which it asserted its powers most boldly; without such skills, the Court might have suffered serious attacks to its institutional position before it gained the strength to withstand them. Moreover, if the justices of the early twentieth century had been more sympathetic toward government regulation of the economy, an opportunity to raise the level of activism might not have developed.[8]

All this being true, it is still the case that the Supreme Court operated within a constitutional system that structured its development. This system constrained the Court in important ways, but it also created opportunities for activism and the means to develop an integral role in policy-making. In the presence of other favorable conditions, the Court did develop that role.[9]

The Court and Civil Liberties

If the extent of the Supreme Court's current activism has deep historical roots, the same is not true of its content. For most of its history, the Court's policies were primarily conservative by today's standards. Aside from the federal government, their major beneficiaries were businesses and owners of substantial property (Galloway, 1982; Miller, 1968). The Court provided little support for civil liberties as most people would define them today; indeed, in the late nineteenth century it limited the power of the federal government to protect civil liberties.[10] Most striking was the Court's use of the Fourteenth Amendment, intended to protect the civil rights of black citizens, primarily as a means to protect business interests (Collins, 1912).

This pattern in the Court's policy positions remained strong as recently as a half-century ago. In 1941, U.S. Attorney General Robert Jackson wrote that "never in its entire history can the Supreme Court be said to have for a single hour been representative of anything except the relatively conservative forces of its day" (Jackson, 1941:187; see also Commager, 1943:428). Four years earlier, legal scholar Henry Edgerton offered this assessment of judicial review: "In one who identifies the country with the well-to-do minority of its population, enthusiasm for judicial control over Congress is as logical as enthusiasm can be. It is hard to see why, apart from convention, one who does not make that identification should share that enthusiasm" (1937:348).

In the past half-century, the Court has departed dramatically from its traditional stance. Since 1937, the Court has displayed only limited sympathy for the business interests and private property rights that it supported for so long. For most of the post-1937 period, it has instead concentrated primarily on civil liberties cases, and for the most part it has expanded legal protections of civil liberties.

The Court's support for civil liberties over the past few decades is well known, but the scope and extent of that support merit emphasis. The Court has adopted sweeping expansions of due process rights, particularly on behalf of criminal defendants, and of freedom of expression. It gave real meaning to the Fourteenth Amendment as a guarantee of equality for blacks, and it has used the amendment to support equal treatment for women, aliens, and other groups. Although the pre-1937 Court seldom struck down laws as violations of civil liberties, the great majority of the laws struck down in the past half-century have been declared unconstitutional on that basis (Baum, 1989:188).

In effect, the Court has followed the path tentatively suggested by Justice Harlan Stone's famous footnote in *United States v. Carolene Products Co.* (1938), which offered a set of rationales that could be used to justify activism in support of civil liberties even while the Court avoided interference with government economic policies (Cover, 1982).[11] Historian William Leuchtenburg summarized the Court's policies in another way: "Whereas the beneficiaries of the Court before 1937 had been businessmen and other propertied interests, after 1937 they became the less advantaged groups in America" (1969:108).

Although the post-1937 Court has been consistent in its general acceptance of an active government role in economic regulation, its commitment to the protection of civil liberties has risen and fallen. Civil liberties issues came onto the agenda gradually (Pacelle, 1986), and the Court did not take a consistently expansive view of legal protections for civil liberties until the 1960s. Since the end of the Warren Court in 1969, the Court has maintained a primary focus on civil liberties, but its position on the scope of protections for liberties has been mixed. By historical standards, however, even the Burger Court of the 1970s and 1980s was a civil liberties Court. It accepted most of the legacy of the Warren Court, and its own activism was directed primarily at the protection of civil liberties (Blasi, 1983). The Burger Court became more conservative in its second decade, and the Rehnquist Court ultimately may end the era of a Supreme Court commitment to civil liberties. Even so, the existence of such an era is a striking development in the Court's history.

The features of the constitutional system that fostered activism can also help in understanding the Supreme Court's expansion of legal protections for civil liberties. Most fundamentally, the long-standing acceptance of judicial activism in the service of constitutionalism increased the Court's freedom to intervene actively in a new area of policy. Some who disagree with the Court's civil liberties decisions in the current era have challenged their legitimacy, but these challenges came too late; by the time they were asserted, they ran up against a broad consensus on the other side. When U.S. Attorney General Edwin Meese seemed to argue in 1986 that the Supreme Court's legal rulings are not authoritative, he was heavily criticized and was forced to disavow the argument (Taylor, 1986; Kurtz, 1986; Meese, 1986).[12]

Just as important, activism in the current era has taken a form that limited damage to the Court's relationships with the other branches of the national government. Relatively little of this activism has been directed against the national government. For the most part, the major policies that the Court has struck down were essentially exclusive to state and local governments, such as school religious observances and prohibitions on abortions, or were of greater significance to those governments, such as school segregation and police investigative techniques. Since the 1950s, the Court has declared an unprecedented number of federal laws unconstitutional, but only a handful of these laws could be regarded as important—and most of these exceptions were ambiguous.[13] Thus, even when the Court's decisions were quite unpopular with Congress and the president, they seldom created a direct confrontation between the Court and those policy makers. When such a confrontation did develop in the late 1950s, primarily in the national security area, the Court retreated discreetly (Murphy, 1962).

Further, the Court's policies have not been entirely at variance with the views of the other branches; they hardly could be since the president and Senate determine the Court's membership. On federalism, an issue of critical importance to the other branches, the Court has been highly supportive of Congress and the president. It has adhered to very broad interpretations of federal powers and has been willing to support revolutionary federal incursions into the power and autonomy of the states. The outstanding example of this support is *South Carolina v. Katzenbach* (1966), in which the Court upheld the Voting Rights Act provision requiring that the election laws of southern states receive federal approval before they could go into effect. Since 1937, the Court has struck down only one federal law on grounds related to federalism, and that decision was later reversed.[14]

The Court's support for expansive federal powers might have helped reconcile presidents and members of Congress to civil libertarian policies with which they disagreed. But even in civil liberties the Court's positions have been less unpopular than they could have been. The collective preferences of the executive and legislature probably are more favorable to civil liberties now than in any past era.[15] In turn, these preferences reflect a relatively high level of public support for civil liberties, especially those related to equality— the strongest theme in the Court's policies since 1950 (Shapiro, 1978:181–82). Arguably, the Court's efforts on behalf of racial equality also served the interest of the national government by weakening the southern caste system that had become an increasing problem for foreign policy and other national interests.[16]

Largely because of these two factors—the Supreme Court's legitimacy and the relative absence of direct conflict with the other branches—the president and Congress have done surprisingly little to attack the Court and its decisions in the current era. Proposals to limit the Court's jurisdiction have been rejected, even when the Court policies arousing these efforts were as unpopular as approval of school busing and disapproval of school prayer. Despite a number of efforts over the past three decades, Congress has formally proposed no constitutional amendment to limit or overturn the Court's expansions of legal protections for civil liberties.

The Court's commitment to civil liberties also reflects a third factor, changes in the pattern of demands on the Court. Individuals with civil liberties claims ordinarily are quite limited in their capacity to bring cases to the Supreme Court, and this limitation helps account for the general absence of decisions involving such claims for most of the Court's history. In this century, however, organized groups increasingly have sponsored civil liberties cases, enabling those cases to reach the Court. In addition, some of these groups have developed considerable expertise in Supreme Court advocacy, allowing them to match and often to surpass the skills of their opponents.[17]

The most important of these groups is the NAACP Legal Defense Fund, established in 1938, which carried forward and expanded an NAACP litigation program begun early in the century (Kluger, 1976; Wasby, 1983). The Legal Defense Fund's litigation program, like the Supreme Court's concern with racial equality, has extended across a broad range of civil liberties issues. The Legal Defense Fund also has served as a model for similar organizations representing other social groups.

The American Civil Liberties Union has been second in importance (Krislov, Perry, and Peterson, 1988; Markmann, 1965). Although the ACLU has given some emphasis to freedom of expression, its agenda is even broader than that of the NAACP Legal Defense Fund. To a great extent, it represents interests lacking the capacity for effective organization and independent action, such as criminal defendants and individuals who have been sanctioned for their speech.

Organizations such as these have made it possible for the Supreme Court to protect civil liberties by putting appropriate cases before it. Less directly, the litigation they sponsor and support suggests to members of the Court that the issues posed by this litigation deserve to be taken seriously. Petitions for hearings communicate the concerns of social groups to the Court. Moreover, the arguments in these petitions and legal briefs lend strength to the positions that underlie them, and some civil liberties groups have developed a credibility of their own that helps them gain a sympathetic hearing from the Court.

The factors I have discussed help explain the development of a civil libertarian role for the Supreme Court and the form that role has taken, but they do not show this role was inevitable. Indeed, I would argue that the Court's development of a commitment to civil liberties was even less inevitable than its development of significant activism as such.[18] Because attitudes on civil liberties in government and society have been mixed, the Court could have resisted demands to expand constitutional protections for those liberties.

Nor did the liberal appointments culminating in the Warren Court closely reflect societal forces. The crystallizing of a majority committed to civil liberties in the 1960s resulted largely from Dwight Eisenhower's mistaken appointments of William Brennan and Earl Warren himself (Abraham, 1985:263). The Kennedy and Johnson appointments of the 1960s, which strengthened the Court's collective support for civil liberties, can be traced to a 1960 election outcome that rested on narrow victories in a few key states and perhaps on a favorable counting of votes in one of those states. In this sense, chance played a considerable part in making the Supreme Court a protector of civil liberties.[19]

Even so, the constitutional system in which the Court works undoubtedly facilitated the development of its civil liberties role just as it facilitated activism. That system created conditions under which the Court gained freedom to take on a new and activist policy role, and it linked the Court to governmental and societal forces supporting this role. In this sense, as surprising as the Court's policy shift after 1937 may have been, it need not be viewed as an aberration.

The Future of Supreme Court Activism

Over the last two decades, as Supreme Court appointments by Republican presidents cumulated, the question that has most interested Court observers is how long it would remain supportive of civil liberties (O'Brien, 1987; Baum, 1987). The attention given to that question is appropriate; aside from the practical significance of this question, it requires close attention to the forces that shape the Court's policy positions. Less attention has been given to a broader question, one that concerns the Court's activism. Will the Court continue the high level of intervention in the policy process that it has exhibited since the 1950s—and, in a sense, for the last century? In this section I explore this question and its implications.

One conclusion seems clear: without question, the Court will remain a major participant in national policy-making. In no era has the Court entirely avoided involvement in significant policy issues, and we would hardly expect a future Court to do so. Less certain is the level of activism in the future. During the Court's history, the extent of its involvement in national policy has risen and fallen, and perhaps the Court will return once again to a more limited activism. Yet it is also possible that the history of the last century has established a permanently high level of activism for the Court, so that future Courts will maintain that level.

The continuation of concerted activism may be encouraged powerfully by expectations of the Court that past and current activism have produced. Just as strong policy leadership is part of the accepted job description for modern presidents (Rossiter, 1956; Cronin, 1980), so there is evidence that active involvement in public policy-making is expected of the modern Supreme Court.

Most clearly, significant interests in government and society have come to think of the Court as a major source of access to the policy process and a means to gain favorable policy outcomes. The level of interest group activity in Supreme Court litigation has risen dramatically, and a diverse range of groups devote substantial efforts to litigation. Amicus curiae briefs are submitted in most of the cases the Court hears, and a high proportion of major decisions result from litigation sponsored by interest groups (O'Connor and Epstein, 1981–82, 1984).

Moreover, the other branches of government increasingly use the Court to influence public policy. This development was especially apparent during the Reagan administration. The administration itself exerted unusually strong control over the Solicitor General's office, so that it could utilize Supreme Court litigation as an instrument of presidential policy (Caplan, 1987). At the same time, Congress and its members involved themselves in a number of cases to attack such administration policies as the expanded use of the pocket veto and to fight for their preferred interpretations of legislation.

This use of the Court by Congress and the president reflects a related change in expectations: the other branches seem to have accommodated themselves to a highly activist Court. The general inaction of Congress in response to decisions as unpopular as those limiting school religious observances reflects this accommodation. On their face, the attacks on judicial activism by officials in the Reagan administration suggest a continued resistance to an interventionist Court, but these attacks were directed primarily at the liberal content of the activism, and those making such attacks might well be pleased with activism in the service of conservative goals.

None of this means that a future Court will be forced to continue a highly activist posture. It does mean at least that litigants will continue to provide opportunities for such a posture and that external pressures against concerted activism probably will be limited and tolerable. Indeed, in some respects it may be easier for the Court to play an interventionist role in policy-making than to eschew it.

Yet the external forces supporting a high level of activism certainly can be resisted. Thus the goals and expectations of the justices themselves probably are the most important factor. The analogy with the president is especially intriguing in this respect. The modern presidency attracts candidates who are predisposed toward policy leadership; those with limited conceptions of the presidency are unlikely to seek the office. In the same way, activism may have become an integral part of what a prospective Supreme Court justice would expect to do on the Court. Lawyers and judges who want to involve themselves in national policy-making find the Court attractive, while those who prefer not to take that kind of role may be ambivalent about becoming Supreme Court justices. Whatever role conceptions new justices bring to the Court, the recent history of concerted activism and the commitment of most colleagues to that activism undoubtedly structure the ways that these newcomers think about cases and choices.[20]

It may be possible for determined presidents to break this cycle. Future presidents might work to choose people who strongly prefer a limited role for the Court in national policy-making. Such appointments might change the collective role definition of the justices that in turn is reflected in a reduced activism. But even presidents who dislike the Court's activist policies are likely to make appointments that are intended to change the direction of policy instead of appointing justices who may avoid activism altogether. Certainly the Reagan appointments followed this pattern.

Of more fundamental importance, perhaps, is the interaction between justices' policy positions and their opportunities for policy interventions. The Court's history from 1937 to the 1950s is instructive. The Roosevelt appointees quickly reversed the Court's stance of monitoring government economic regulation. Having done so, they maintained a relatively low profile for several years. Only when a bloc favorable to civil liberties activism coalesced and appropriate cases started to reach the Court in large numbers did the level of activism rise again. If a new mode of activism had not been identified, the Court might have maintained a relatively passive role.

The same challenge may appear in the next two decades. Should the Court be dominated by conservatives, for instance, it is not certain whether a majority would agree on a form for conservative activism. Enhanced protection for private property rights against government limitations, a theme in some recent Court decisions and commentary, might gain majority support.[21] But protection of property rights is not a consensual value among conservative judges, and its adoption by a conservative Court is not guaranteed.

At the least, however, the Court's history will facilitate strong activism for a future Court. Despite all the denunciations of interventionist decisions and policies, the Supreme Court has helped create conditions under which it can, with relative safety and considerable encouragement, actively make policy.

Conclusions

The forces shaping an institution such as the Supreme Court are multifarious and complex. This reality cautions against any unicausal explanation of the path an institution has taken, no matter how fundamental the base on which it rests. It certainly would ignore a great deal of reality to assert that the Supreme Court's course over two centuries has followed inevitably from its place in the Constitution. The Constitution left too many matters open, and too many forces have impinged on the Court since then, to support such an interpretation of the Court's history.

It does seem clear that characteristics of the constitutional system in which the Supreme Court operates have structured its participation in national policy-making. Constitutionalism created a basis for the Court to develop and maintain an active policy role. The powers of the president and Congress have constrained the Court and channeled the course of its activism. The Court's operation within a litigation process has linked its policy-making activity with the content of the cases brought to it and, indirectly, with the relative capacities of societal interests to litigate in the Court.

Taken together, these characteristics help account for the Supreme Court's history as a policy maker. They provide a partial explanation for the development of strong activism and the way in which it developed. To a lesser extent, they help account for the Court's evolution into a protector of civil liberties during its second century.

Predicting the Court's future is even more hazardous than explaining its past and present. The level of its activism in the decades to come is highly uncertain. It does seem certain that the Court will continue to be an important policy maker. The extent and content of its involvement in national policy will continue to rest in part on the Constitution and the system it created.

NOTES

I would like to thank Paul Quirk and Peter Nardulli for their comments on earlier drafts of this chapter.

1. One problem in using the term *activism* is that it has a negative connotation for many judges and commentators. People tend to label as activist judicial decisions and policies with which they disagree, while treating decisions they support as nonactivist. Even judges who seem to be engaged in a good deal of activist policy-making tend to eschew that label (but see Wright, 1987). Thus I should emphasize that I am treating activism as a phenomenon that in itself is neither desirable nor undesirable.

2. The identification of liberal and conservative policy positions, of course, has varied over time. Thus it is important to underline the fact that I am using the conception of liberalism and conservatism that is dominant today. Some of the judicial policies of past eras that appear conservative from a current perspective would not have been interpreted in that way at the time the Court adopted them.

3. This was the case even in the Court's early history, when its agenda did not reflect the activities of the other branches as fully as it does today (Roe and Osgood, 1975).

4. The Court's reliance on litigants for information and alternatives should not be exaggerated, because the justices can and do look to other sources for both. A classic illustration is the Court's decision in *Mapp v. Ohio* (1961). Mapp was briefed by the parties and argued before the Court as an obscenity case, but the Court converted it to a landmark decision on the exclusionary rule for illegally seized evidence (Stewart, 1983).

5. The success of the Solicitor General's office in the Justice Department as legal representative of the federal government has been well documented. See Scigliano (1971:chap. 6) and Segal (1988).

6. Data on laws overturned by the Supreme Court are taken from the Congressional Reference Service (1987), as aggregated in Baum (1989:177, 180).

7. Congress increased the Court's control over its agenda in three stages. In 1891 it created the federal courts of appeals as intermediate courts and made some of the Court's jurisdiction discretionary rather than mandatory. In 1925 it made the bulk of the Court's jurisdiction discretionary. In 1988 Congress virtually eliminated the Court's remaining mandatory jurisdiction.

8. It can be argued, however, that the Court's collective skepticism toward economic regulatory policies was the product of systematic forces re-

lated to its membership. Selection as a justice was effectively restricted to attorneys at a time when lawyers were even more likely to come from higher-status backgrounds than they are today, and the members of the bar who had the best chance to be selected as justices had even more elite backgrounds and associations than did the bar as a whole. Such people, of course, were likely to hold conservative economic views (Schmidhauser, 1979:chap. 3).

9. The sources of the Court's activism could be probed further by examining the development of the roles of high courts in the states and in other nations. Such an inquiry is beyond the scope of this essay, but a few comments may be useful.

In the states, the traditional legislative deference to the courts in the "common law" fields, such as torts and contracts, virtually forced major policy roles on state supreme courts. In the constitutional arena, the level of activism historically seems to have varied considerably among states (Field, 1943). There has been a recent growth in constitutional activism in the states, largely in response to the Supreme Court's reduced support for civil liberties (McGraw, 1985); here too, the various state supreme courts have differed fundamentally in their roles (Emmert, 1988; Collins, Galie, and Kincaid, 1986). Comparative historical analysis of state supreme courts may help illuminate the sources of differing levels of activism.

The high courts of many other nations have involved themselves actively in policy-making, sometimes in opposition to important policies of the other branches (Murphy and Tanenhaus, 1977; Ehrmann, 1976; Goodhart, 1964; Mufson, 1987). The power of judicial review over government actions facilitates such activism, as suggested by the impact of the new, judicially enforceable Charter of Rights and Freedoms in Canada (Morton, 1987), but it is certainly not the only factor determining the extent of a court's activism. If the U.S. Supreme Court is the high court that plays the largest role in public policy-making, its standing probably results from several different conditions. As with the American states, comparative analysis of the development of courts' policy roles would help shed light on the impact of various conditions.

10. Having used the term *civil liberties* already, and now focusing on civil liberties in this section, I should clarify what I mean by this highly ambiguous term. I am following the most common usage today, which encompasses fair procedural treatment by the government, equality for disadvantaged groups in both the public and private sectors, and a set of substantive rights that include freedom of expression, freedom of religion, and privacy. Rights related to the protection of property—at least for those who are economically advantaged—tend not to be included in the civil liberties category. Prior to 1937, such property rights were viewed by many as the most fundamental civil liberties.

Two other matters of terminology should be noted. First, by *civil rights* I mean rights to equal treatment for disadvantaged groups. Second, I have identified support for civil liberties as an ideologically liberal position. This does not mean conservative justices are necessarily opposed to legal protection for civil liberties; it simply means they give such protection a lower priority than do liberals, so that in perceived conflicts between civil liberties and other values (e.g., national security or effective law enforcement) they are more likely to rule in favor of those competing values. On this ideological dimension, see Rohde and Spaeth (1976).

11. The footnote reads in part as follows: "It is unnecessary to consider now whether legislation which restricts those political processes which can ordinarily be expected to bring about repeal of undesirable legislation, is to be subjected to more exacting judicial scrutiny under the general prohibitions of the Fourteenth Amendment than are most other types of legislation. . . . Nor need we enquire whether similar considerations enter into the review of statutes directed at particularly religious . . . or national . . . or racial minorities . . . whether prejudice against discrete and insular minorities may be a special condition, which tends seriously to curtail the operation of those political processes ordinarily to be relied upon to protect minorities, and which may call for a correspondingly more searching judicial inquiry" (152, n. 4).

12. Also noteworthy is the aftermath of the Court's 1974 decision (*United States v. Nixon*) requiring in effect that President Richard Nixon provide the evidence that would secure his removal from office. Nixon found himself unable to defy the decision, because such defiance would have been regarded as illegitimate—in effect, unconstitutional—and in itself almost surely would have brought about his impeachment and conviction.

13. The Court struck down provisions of the Subversive Activities Control Act in *Aptheker v. Secretary of State* (1964), *Albertson v. Subversive Activities Control Board* (1965), and *United States v. Robel* (1967); by the time it did so, the act was no longer important. It declared the legislative veto unconstitutional in *Immigration and Naturalization Service v. Chadha* (1983) and struck down a key provision of the Gramm-Rudman-Hollings Deficit Reduction Act in *Bowsher v. Synar* (1986), but it was ruling in favor of the president and against Congress rather than against the federal government as a whole. The one clear example of the Court's overturning major federal policy is *Buckley v. Valeo* (1976), which declared a set of key provisions in the Federal Election Campaign Act unconstitutional.

14. The decisions were *National League of Cities v. Usery* (1976) and *Garcia v. San Antonio Metropolitan Transit Authority* (1985).

15. This conclusion, of course, is impossible to document systematically, but there is some evidence to suggest its validity. Since 1957, Congress has passed significant civil rights legislation for the first time since the Reconstruction Era. It has shown solicitude for freedom of expression with the Freedom of Information Act of 1966 and for the right to privacy with the Privacy Act of 1974 and the 1988 legislation limiting the use of lie-detector tests by employers. In such instances as its 1980 legislation requiring that most searches of news media offices operate through subpoenas and the pro-

vision of the 1982 Voting Rights Act establishing a "results" test for discrimination in election laws, Congress expanded protections of civil liberties in ways that the Court had refused to do. (On news office searches, see *Zurcher v. Stanford Daily* [1978]; on voting rights, see *City of Mobile v. Bolden* [1980].) While Congress has defeated efforts to limit civil liberties through constitutional amendments, it has proposed some amendments to expand civil liberties, most notably the Equal Rights Amendment and the Anti–Poll Tax Amendment.

The position of the executive branch on civil liberties has varied considerably, largely with the ideological position of the president. But most presidents over the past half-century have been at least moderately supportive of civil rights (Morgan, 1970). From the Truman administration through the Carter administration, the executive branch gave fairly strong support to civil rights groups through its own litigation activity in the Supreme Court (Elman, 1987).

16. Joan Roelofs (1982) has argued more broadly, from a Marxist perspective, that in the post–World War II era the Court emphasized the protection of civil liberties to serve the regime's need for legitimation.

17. State and local governments opposing litigants with civil liberties claims in such fields as criminal law are often represented by attorneys with little or no expertise in Supreme Court litigation, and the widespread perception that these government attorneys are outmatched by civil liberties lawyers has led to efforts in the 1980s to improve the quality of their advocacy (Witt, 1987).

The Court itself has acted in several ways to facilitate litigation by individuals and groups with civil liberties claims. One example is its decisions on the right to counsel for indigent criminal defendants at the trial and appellate levels, which have helped bring criminal procedure cases up through the courts (*Gideon v. Wainwright*, 1963; *Douglas v. California*, 1963). Another is its approval of solicitation of potential clients by lawyers who seek to shape judicial policy rather than to profit financially, a decision which has eased the task of groups sponsoring cases (*In re Primus*, 1978). Notably, Congress also has facilitated such litigation, both through its funding of the Legal Services Corporation (though LSC-funded litigation to influence policy has been restricted considerably) and through several statutes that allow successful civil rights litigants to recover attorneys' fees from their opponents.

18. At least two kinds of arguments can be made on the other side. The first could be derived from Roelofs's view that the Court's civil libertarianism served a legitimation function for the regime (see note 16); one might argue that, given the place in the system that Roelofs identifies for the Court, the justices had no choice but to carry out this function. The second can be put in the terms that Samuel Huntington (1981) used to describe broader political developments: the Court was reducing the gap between the ideals reflected in the Bill of Rights and the Fourteenth Amendment and the reality of U.S. institutions in a period when that gap was

increasingly intolerable to the U.S. public as a whole. From this perspective, the potential for a Supreme Court committed to civil liberties was built into the Constitution itself, just waiting for the right conditions for the Court to make that commitment.

19. The chance element in the Court's civil liberties policies is symbolized by *Brown v. Board of Education*, the single decision that appears most inevitable in retrospect (Elman, 1987; Kluger, 1976; Ulmer, 1971). In reality, the Court was closely divided over the *Brown* case during the first year it was considered, and the case was held for reargument because of this deadlock. Chief Justice Fred Vinson was ambivalent about the case and unlikely to lead the Court to a decision squarely overturning school segregation. When Vinson died before reargument in the case, Justice Felix Frankfurter said that "this is the first indication I have ever had that there is a God" (quoted in Kluger, 1976:656). Religious explanations aside, neither Vinson's 1953 death nor the appointment of Earl Warren by a president who apparently favored school segregation are easy to interpret as inevitable.

20. The expectations of justices and their audiences might be interpreted in terms of the concept of an organizational mission. In effect, activism may be accepted as the mission of the Supreme Court, just as some administrative agencies develop and maintain missions that guide their own personnel and that presidents and members of Congress accept even when they would prefer that an agency take a different direction.

The concept of organizational mission is even more relevant to the stability of the Court's support for civil liberties. The absence of a sharper turn away from that support after a series of appointments by Republican presidents might be interpreted in terms of a reluctance of even conservative justices to abandon a role that had become fairly well established. Similarly, one implication of the hearings and vote on Robert Bork's 1987 confirmation to the Supreme Court may be that many members of Congress had come to accept the Court's civil libertarian role and were unwilling to facilitate its abandonment. But we should be careful not to reify this concept, and in any case the recent deregulation movement in the federal government is a reminder that even well-established organizational missions can be changed under some circumstances (Derthick and Quirk, 1985). I am grateful to Paul Quirk for suggesting this line of analysis.

21. The decisions favoring private property rights were *First Lutheran Church v. Los Angeles County* (1987) and *Nollan v. California Coastal Commission* (1987). The Court, however, took a different direction in *Pennell v. City of San Jose* (1988).

REFERENCES

Abraham, Henry J. 1985. *Justices and Presidents.* 2d ed. New York: Oxford University Press.

Albertson v. Subversive Control Board. 1965. 382 U.S. 70.

Aptheker v. Secretary of State. 1964. 378 U.S. 500.

Baum, Lawrence. 1987. "Explaining the Burger Court's Support for Civil Liberties." *P.S.* 20:21–28.

———. 1989. *The Supreme Court.* 3d ed. Washington, D.C.: Congressional Quarterly Press.

Beveridge, Albert J. 1919. *The Life of John Marshall.* 4 vols. Boston: Houghton Mifflin.

Blasi, Vincent, ed. 1982. *The Burger Court: The Counter-Revolution that Wasn't.* New Haven, Conn.: Yale University Press.

Bowsher v. Synar. 1986. 478 U.S. 714.

Brown v. Board of Education. 1954. 347 U.S. 483.

Buckley v. Valeo. 1976. 424 U.S. 1.

Caldeira, Gregory A. 1987. "Public Opinion and the Supreme Court: FDR's Court-packing Plan." *American Political Science Review* 81:1139–53.

Canon, Bradley C. 1982. "A Framework for the Analysis of Judicial Activism." In *Supreme Court Activism and Restraint,* edited by Stephen C. Halpern and Charles M. Lamb. Lexington, Mass.: Lexington Books.

Caplan, Lincoln. 1987. *The Tenth Justice: The Solicitor General and the Rule of Law.* New York: Alfred A. Knopf.

Casper, Gerhard, and Richard A. Posner. 1976. *The Workload of the Supreme Court.* Chicago: American Bar Foundation.

Casper, Jonathan D. 1976. "The Supreme Court and National Policy Making." *American Political Science Review* 70:50–63.

City of Mobile v. Bolden. 1980. 446 U.S. 55.

Collins, Charles Wallace. 1912. *The Fourteenth Amendment and the States.* Boston: Little, Brown.

Collins, Ronald K. L., Peter J. Galie, and John Kincaid. 1986. "State High Courts, State Constitutions, and Individual Rights Litigation since 1980: A Judicial Survey." *Publius* 16:141–61.

Commager, Henry Steele. 1943. "Judicial Review and Democracy." *Virginia Quarterly Review* 19:417–28.

Congressional Reference Service. 1987. *The Constitution of the United States: Analysis and Interpretation.* Washington, D.C.: Government Printing Office.

Cooper, Phillip J. 1988. *Hard Judicial Choices: Federal District Court Judges and State and Local Officials.* New York: Oxford University Press.

Cover, Robert M. 1982. "The Origins of Judicial Activism in the Protection of Minorities." *Yale Law Journal* 91:1287–1316.

Cronin, Thomas E. 1980. *The State of the Presidency.* 2d ed. Boston: Little, Brown.

Dahl, Robert A. 1958. "Decision-Making in a Democracy: The Supreme Court as a National Policy-Maker." *Journal of Public Law* 6:279–95.

Derthick, Martha, and Paul J. Quirk. 1985. *The Politics of Deregulation.* Washington, D.C.: Brookings Institution.

Douglas v. California. 1963. 372 U.S. 353.

Edgerton, Henry W. 1937. "The Incidence of Judicial Control over Congress." *Cornell Law Quarterly* 22:299–348.

Ehrmann, Henry W. 1976. *Comparative Legal Cultures.* Englewood Cliffs, N.J.: Prentice-Hall.

Elman, Philip. 1987. "The Solicitor General's Office, Justice Frankfurter, and Civil Rights Litigation, 1946–1980: An Oral History." *Harvard Law Review* 100:817–52.

Emmert, Craig F. 1988. "Judicial Review in State Supreme Courts: Opportunity and Activism." Paper presented at the meeting of the Midwest Political Science Association, Chicago.

Field, Oliver Peter. 1943. *Judicial Review of Legislation in Ten Selected-States.* Bloomington: Bureau of Government Research, Indiana University.

First Lutheran Church v. Los Angeles County. 1987. 482 U.S. 304.

Galloway, Russell. 1982. *The Rich and the Poor in Supreme Court History, 1790–1982.* Greenbrae, Calif.: Paradigm.

Garcia v. San Antonio Metropolitan Transit Authority. 1985. 469 U.S. 528.

Gideon v. Wainwright. 1963. 372 U.S. 335.

Goodhart, A. L. 1964. "Legal Procedure and Democracy." *Cambridge Law Journal* 51–59.

Gressman, Eugene. 1964. "Much Ado about Certiorari." *Georgetown Law Journal* 52:742–66.

Immigration and Naturalization Service v. Chadha. 1983. 462 U.S. 919.

Hall, Kermit L. 1985. *The Supreme Court and Judicial Review in American History.* Washington, D.C.: American Historical Association.

Huntington, Samuel P. 1981. *American Politics: The Promise of Disharmony.* Cambridge, Mass.: Harvard University Press.

Jackson, Robert H. 1941. *The Struggle for Judicial Supremacy.* New York: Alfred A. Knopf.

Johnson, Charles A., and Bradley C. Canon. 1984. *Judicial Policies: Implementation and Impact.* Washington, D.C.: Congressional Quarterly Press.

Kluger, Richard. 1976. *Simple Justice: The History of Brown v. Board of Education and Black America's Struggle for Equality.* New York: Alfred A. Knopf.

Krislov, Samuel, R. Christopher Perry, and Dennis Peterson. 1988. "The ACLU and Economic Rights: Junctures and Judgments." Paper presented at the meeting of the American Political Science Association, Washington, D.C.

Kurtz, Howard. 1986. "Meese's View on Court Rulings Assailed, Defended." *Washington Post,* October 24.

Leuchtenburg, William. 1969. "Franklin D. Roosevelt's Supreme Court 'Packing' Plan." In *Essays on the New Deal,* edited by Harold M. Hollingsworth and William F. Holmes. Austin: University of Texas Press.

McCloskey, Robert G. 1960. *The American Supreme Court.* Chicago: University of Chicago Press.

McGraw, Bradley D., ed. 1985. *Developments in State Constitutional Law.* St. Paul, Minn.: West.

Mapp v. Ohio. 1961. 367 U.S. 643.

Marbury v. Madison. 1803. 1 Cranch 137.

Markmann, Charles L. 1965. *The Noblest Cry: A History of the American Civil Liberties Union.* New York: St. Martin's.

Meese, Edwin, III. 1986. "The Tulane Speech: What I Meant." *Washington Post,* November 13.

Miller, Arthur Selwyn. 1968. *The Supreme Court and American Capitalism.* New York: Free Press.

Morgan, Ruth P. 1970. *The President and Civil Rights: Policy-Making by Executive Order.* New York: St. Martin's.

Morton, F. L. 1987. "The Political Impact of the Canadian Charter of Rights and Freedoms." *Canadian Journal of Political Science* 20:31–55.

Mufson, Steve. 1987. "South African Judges Flexing Their Muscles." *National Law Journal,* January 12.

Murphy, Walter F. 1962. *Congress and the Court.* Chicago: University of Chicago Press.

Murphy, Walter F., and Joseph Tanenhaus. 1977. *Comparative Constitutional Law: Cases and Commentaries.* New York: St. Martin's.

National League of Cities v. Usery. 1976. 426 U.S. 833.

Nollan v. California Coastal Commission. 1987. 483 U.S. 825.

O'Brien, David. 1987. "The Supreme Court: From Warren to Burger to Rehnquist." *P.S.* 20:12–20.

O'Connor, Karen, and Lee Epstein. 1981–82. "Amicus Curiae Participation in U.S. Supreme Court Litigation: An Appraisal of Hakman's 'Folklore'." *Law and Society Review* 16:311–20.

———. 1984. "The Role of Interest Groups in Supreme Court Policy Formation." In *Public Policy Formation,* edited by Robert Eyestone. Greenwich, Conn.: JAI Press.

Pacelle, Richard L., Jr. 1986. "The Supreme Court Agenda across Time: Toward a Theory of Agenda-Building." Paper presented at the meeting of the Midwest Political Science Association.

Pennell v. City of San Jose. 1988. 485 U.S. 1.

Primus, In re. 1978. 436 U.S. 412.

Roe, David B., and Russell K. Osgood. 1975. "United States Supreme Court February Term 1824." *Yale Law Journal* 84:770–808.

Roelofs, Joan. 1982. "Judicial Activism as Social Engineering: A Marxist Interpretation of the Warren Court." In *Supreme Court Activism and Restraint,* edited by Stephen C. Halpern and Charles M. Lamb. Lexington, Mass.: Lexington Books.

Rohde, David W., and Harold J. Spaeth. 1976. *Supreme Court Decision Making.* San Francisco: W. H. Freeman.

Rossiter, Clinton. 1956. *The American Presidency.* New York: Harcourt, Brace.

Schmidhauser, John R. 1979. *Judges and Justices: The Federal Appellate Judiciary.* Boston: Little, Brown.

Schubert, Glendon A., Jr. 1957. *The Presidency in the Courts.* Minneapolis: University of Minnesota Press.

Scigliano, Robert. 1971. *The Supreme Court and the Presidency.* New York: Free Press.

Scott v. Sanford [Dred Scott case]. 1857. 19 Howard 393.

Segal, Jeffrey A. 1988. "Amicus Curiae Briefs by the Solicitor General during the Warren and Burger Courts." *Western Political Quarterly* 41:135–44.

Shapiro, Martin. 1978. "The Supreme Court: From Warren to Burger." In *The New American Political System,* edited by Anthony King. Washington, D.C.: American Enterprise Institute.

South Carolina v. Katzenbach. 1966. 383 U.S. 301.

Stewart, Potter. 1983. "The Road to *Mapp v. Ohio* and Beyond: The Origins, Development and Future of the Exclusionary Rule in Search and Seizure Cases." *Columbia Law Review* 83:1365–1404.

Taylor, Stuart, Jr. 1986. "Meese Says Court Doesn't Make Law." *New York Times,* October 23.

Twiss, Benjamin. 1942. *Lawyers and the Constitution.* Princeton, N.J.: Princeton University Press.

Ulmer, S. Sidney. 1971. "Earl Warren and the Brown Decision." *Journal of Politics* 32:689–702.

United States v. Carolene Products Co. 1938. 304 U.S. 144.

United States v. Robel. 1967. 389 U.S. 258.

United States v. Nixon. 1974. 418 U.S. 683.

Wasby, Stephen L. 1983. "Interest Groups in Court: Race Relations Litigation." In *Interest Group Politics,* edited by Allan Cigler and Burdett Loomis. Washington, D.C.: Congressional Quarterly Press.

Witt, Elder. 1987. "States and Localities at the Supreme Court: High Stakes, No Appeals." *Governing,* October, 19–25.

Wright, J. Skelly. 1987. "The Judicial Right and the Rhetoric of Restraint: A Defense of Judicial Activism in an Age of Conservative Judges." *Hastings Constitutional Law Quarterly* 14:487–523.

Zurcher v. Stanford Daily. 1978. 436 U.S. 547.

The Constitution and Its Institutional Penumbra

★ 7 ★

The American Constitutional Framework and the Structure of American Political Parties

KENNETH JANDA

When the framers created the U.S. Constitution two hundred years ago, they made no provision for political parties. Since they wrote before the advent of modern parties, that omission may not be surprising. It is surprising that the Constitution does not mention parties in any of its twenty-six amendments, one of which arose from party conflict in the electoral college in the elections of 1796 and 1800. The Twelfth Amendment, which required the electoral college to vote separately for president and vice-president, implicitly recognized that presidential elections would be contested by party candidates nominated for the separate offices but running on the same ballot. Yet the amendment was written without referring to the political organizations that prompted it.

By not mentioning political parties, the U.S. Constitution stands in the minority of the world's constitutions. According to a survey of 142 national constitutions, 65 percent contain provisions regarding political parties (van Maarseveen and van der Tang, 1978:71). About one-third of the constitutions that provide for parties do so in a discriminatory way. In fact, about one-fifth of all constitutions contain provisions that permit only certain parties to operate or that ban certain ones.

Looking at two hundred years of political development, we can clearly see that competitive political parties are essential for the democratic style of government the framers sought to create.[1] Informed by years of practice with party politics in scores of other countries, we can also see that American parties are quite different from those elsewhere.

Political parties have limited functions in the United States. They function well in structuring the voting choice in elections, but they function poorly in coordinating the actions of officials in government. Some scholars argue that parties, as organizations, need to assume a more important role in initiating and enacting coherent public policies (Schattschneider, 1942; Price, 1984:294). Other observers contend there is little hope for changing the structure of American parties to function more cohesively in government because of the constitutional system, which, they say, determines the basic nature of the parties (Kirkpatrick, 1971:976–77). Indeed, both David Brady and Graham Wilson argue this point elsewhere in this book.

Although parties are not mentioned in the Constitution, conventional wisdom holds that U.S. parties are what they are because of major constitutional features. For example, scholars contend the United States has a two-party system primarily because of the importance of the presidency in the political system and the method for selecting the president. Because the presidency can be won only by the single candidate who wins a majority of electoral votes across the entire nation, political groups coalesce into two rival groups large enough to vie for a majority of the electoral votes. David Brady, among other contemporary scholars, discusses in this volume two salient features of the Constitution—federalism and the separation of powers—which help produce the fragmented, highly decentralized nature of our two major parties.

Contemporary scholars did not originate the view that the Constitution has shaped the nature of American parties. This view surfaced long ago in early studies of our political system.[2] Based on his observations on American politics from 1870 to 1894, the British scholar James Bryce observed,

I have kept to the last the feature of the House [of Representatives] which Europeans find the strangest.

It has parties, but they are headless. There is neither Government nor Opposition. There can hardly be said to be leaders, and til 1900 there were no whips. No person holding any Federal office or receiving any Federal Salary can be a member of it. That the majority may be and often is opposed to the President and his cabinet, does not strike Americans as odd, because they proceed on the theory that the legislative ought to be distinct from the executive authority [(1889) 1912, vol. 1:151].

Writing nearly a century ago, Henry Jones Ford, an early president of the American Political Science Association, said succintly, "The peculiarities of American party government are all due to this separation of party management from direct and immediate responsibility from the administration of government" (1898:326). J. Allen Smith, the progressive reformer and critic of the Constitution, concurred: "To understand the peculiar features of the American party system one must bear in mind the constitutional arrangements under which it has developed. . . . It is this lack of power to shape the entire policy of the government which, more than anything else, has given form and character to the party system of the United States" (1907:208–9). Woodrow Wilson, writing as a political scientist before becoming president, severely criticized the "Whig doctrine" of checks and balances and federalism as a mechanical theory of political dynamics that frustrates leadership and control in government ([1908] 1917:54).[3] He maintained, "All the peculiarities of party government in the United States are due to the too literal application of Whig doctrine to the infinite multiplication of elective offices" (210).

Two decades later, but still some fifty years ago, Harold Bruce of Dartmouth cited "our federal type of government" and the existence of strong state party organizations as major factors producing the "elaborate organization" characteristic of American national parties, which are really "loose federations of state and local organizations, held together, in large measure, by the habit of cooperation in presidential elections" (1936:69–71).

An exhaustive analysis of all the constitutional features affecting the organization of American parties is beyond the scope of this work. Instead, it focuses on the Constitution's two most prominent features—federalism and the separation of powers—that are so frequently cited in the early and contemporary literature.

Most previous studies of constitutional influences on American party politics have relied on historical analysis of the U.S. experience, perhaps in comparison with experiences in another country. This essay uses a different methodology. Drawing on a cross-national study of environmental effects on party characteristics (Harmel and Janda, 1982),[4] it relies on a quantitative analysis of the relationship between constitutional structure and party characteristics for seventy-three political parties in twenty-two democratic nations.[5] This approach is not necessarily better than traditional research; however, introducing a comparative dimension and treating the issue in a more theoretical manner may improve our understanding of constitutional effects on party characteristics.

Framework of Analysis

Political parties are, to some extent, products of their context—or so it has been widely assumed. Jean Blondel has argued that "in all cases, the influence of outside elements has played a part in the development or modification of internal [party] structures" (1969:125), and Kay Lawson has noted that "no political institution operates in a vacuum, political parties least of all" (1976:27).

Environmental effects have been given special consideration by students of American parties. William Keefe, for instance, began his book on the American parties with this argument:

Any attempt to unravel the mysteries of American political parties might well begin with the recognition of this fact: The parties are less what they make of themselves than what their environment makes of them. The parties are not free to develop in any fashion that they might like, to take on any organization form that might appear desirable, to pursue any course of action that might seem to be required, or to assume any responsibility that might appear appropriate. The truth of the matter is that the shape of American parties is strongly influenced by the design of the legal-political system, the election system, the political culture, and the heterogeneous quality of American life. To a remarkable extent, the party system owes its form and substance to the impact of external elements [1972:1].

To the extent parties *are* creatures of their environment, there are limits to the extent parties can be changed or "reformed." As Edward Banfield noted,

With respect to the American party system, it seems obvious that the crucial features of the situation are all fixed. The size of our country, the class and cultural heterogeneity of our people, the number and variety of their interests, the constitutionally-given fragmentation of formal authority, the wide distribution of power which follows from it, the inveterate taste of Americans for participation in the day-to-day conduct of government when their interests are directly at stake—these are all unalterable features of the situation. Taken together, they mean that the party system can be reformed only within very narrow limits [1964:26].

Arguing in effect that "we get the parties we deserve," Austin Ranney has said that our governmental system is "designed to inhibit majority rule, and in such a system American parties, decentralized and irresponsible as they are, are entirely appropriate" (1954:160).

Environmental Influences

As diagramed in Figure 1, three broad types of environmental factors can be identified: (1) physical factors, such as the size, shape, and climate of the country; (2) socioeconomic factors, such as the racial and occupational composition of the society, the degree of urbanization, and the educational level of its citizens; and (3) political factors, such as the structure of the legislature, the type of electoral system, and the frequency of elections. For purposes of this inquiry, we are interested only in the last class of factors, the political ones.

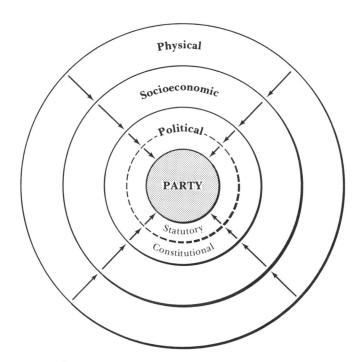

Figure 1. Environmental Influences

Features of the political environment vary in their susceptibility to change. On the relatively immutable side are the constitutional aspects of the governmental system that are either written into fundamental law—as in the United States—or enshrined in tradition—as in Britain. On the more changeable side are the statutory procedures specified by law but not embedded in the constitution or the culture. Again for purposes of this study, we concentrate on the constitutional aspects of the political environment.

By structuring the distribution of political power, constitutions indirectly influence the operation of political parties. Although there are various ways to structure the constitutional distribution of power, this study examines only two structural features, federalism and the separation of powers. Of all the constitutional factors that might impinge on party structure, scholars have identified these as the most important. Lawson succinctly stated the effect of federalism: "Decentralized, federal governments breed decentralized parties; centralized, unitary governments foster parties with power equally concentrated" (1976:79). David Truman elaborated on the theme: "The basic fact of federalism is that it creates self-sustaining centers of power, privilege and profit which may be sought and defended as desirable in themselves, as means of leverage upon elements in the political structure above and below, and as bases from which individuals may move into places of greater influence and prestige in and out of government" (1955:123).

The constitutional separation of powers—especially the division of legislative and executive powers between Congress and the president—is widely viewed as a major factor in the decentralization of the Democratic and Republican parties. Keefe, for instance, has argued, "One of the frequent by-products of this system is the emergence of a truncated party majority—that is, a condition under which one party controls one or both houses of the legislature and the other party controls the executive ... at no time does [this] contribute a particle to the development and maintenance of party responsibility for a program of public policy" (1980:30–31).

An earlier study to isolate the effects of separation of powers and federalism on political parties was undertaken by Leon Epstein (1964). He compared the United States and Canada for effects of different constitutional frameworks on party politics. While both Canada and the United States have federal systems of government, Canada has a parliamentary, rather than a presidential, structure. Although Epstein focused on party cohesion in legislative voting, his study was laced with comments on the centralization of power as a more general phenomenon. After reviewing a variety of environmental factors, he concluded, "Explaining the existence of cohesive legislative parties in Canada, within the scope of the factors outlined here, leads straight to the British parliamentary system as the apparent determining factor. Among the four circumstances postulated as basic at the beginning of the essay, it is only this parliamentary system, as opposed to the separation of powers, that Canada has in common with Britain rather than with the United States" (54).

While Epstein's research spoke directly to party politics in the United States and Canada, it was limited in its scope of explanation. By holding federalism constant, it neutralized the variable's influence and could say nothing about how federalism did or did not affect party organization. Epstein's research also did not establish how much the separation of powers affected party organization. Studying the separation of powers *and* federalism in a larger sample of countries can provide a broader and more accurate explanation of these constitutional effects.

It should be noted that the U.S. Constitution, which specifies federalism and the separation of powers, is again in the minority. By any criteria for measuring federalism, most countries in the world are not federal nations, and most constitutions do not provide for a separation or division of powers among national organs. Only 13 percent of the world's constitutions manifest federalism and only 18 percent separate the executive and legislative powers (van Maarseveen and van der Tang 1978:54). Moreover, less than 10 percent of the world's nations have a federal structure *and* separate organs of government that exercise legislative, executive, and judicial powers. If our parties are truly different from parties elsewhere, it may be because of their peculiar constitutional environment.

Nonenvironmental Influences

Earlier writers who argued for the importance of environmental effects on party politics might have conveyed the impression that the environment alone inexorably determines the nature of our parties. Of course, environmental factors are not the sole causes of party characteristics, and any comprehensive theory of party organization must provide for other causal factors. One advantage of a cross-national comparative analysis of party structure is that it

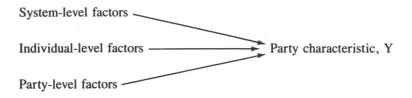

System-level factors

Individual-level factors ⟶ Party characteristic, Y

Party-level factors

Figure 2. Basic Model for Explaining Party Characteristics

encourages a broader and richer theoretical framework. Parties operating in the same environment (i.e., within the same nation) differ in their characteristics due to two other broad types of causes: individual-level factors and party-level factors. Such nonenvironmental factors may work against environmental influences, or they may even work in addition to the environment. This basic theoretical model is diagramed in Figure 2, which portrays all three factors as independent causes of some party characteristic, Y.

Individual-level factors subsume activists' ideas that a party ought to be formed in the first place, party leaders' views of appropriate party strategy, and party dissidents' campaigns for organizational change. For instance, some prominent Democrats (e.g., George McGovern and Donald Fraser) led a movement to revise the party's rules to select delegates to the 1972 nominating convention, which simultaneously produced more openness in the selection process but also gave the National Committee more control of the process. Such individual-level actions can combat environmental effects, and they are an important source of change in party organization over time.

Party-level factors pertain to organizational theory, which predicts that some organizational characteristics affect other ones. Party ideology, for example, can affect party organization according to whether the party is regarded as an agent of social change. In large part, the Democrats reformed their delegate-selection procedures in 1972 to increase the representation of blacks and women. In contrast, the Republicans did not feel compelled to promote equality by requiring state parties to meet quotas in selecting blacks and women as convention delegates. Because of such individual-level and party-level factors, parties in the same country never have identical characteristics. If the environment has the "causal primacy" claimed by writers cited above, then environmental influences should show clearly in explaining party characteristics across nations.

Research Procedures

This study of constitutional effects on party characteristics extends across many nations and parties. The original sample of fifty-three nations was drawn to represent a random sample (stratified by regions) of all nations in which political parties operated for at least half of the time from 1950 to 1962 (Janda, 1980).[6] This study focuses on only twenty-two nations which had competitive political parties operating under governments that were more or less democratic during the latter half of this period, 1957 to 1962. Some nations, most notably Lebanon, would not now qualify for inclusion, but all met the criteria at the time and experienced vigorous party politics, albeit of varying forms.

Parties in each country were selected for the study if they could meet minimum standards of strength and stability, which meant receiving at least 5 percent of the seats in the lower chamber in two successive elections. A total of seventy-three parties qualified for inclusion (see Table 1, which lists the countries and parties included in the sample). Although these data pertain to a period over twenty-five years ago, that should not invalidate testing for constitutional effects on party characteristics. Theories of causal primacy of the environment on political parties are as applicable to the 1960s as they are to the 1980s. Both U.S. parties have changed in important respects since the 1960s, but their changes have been minor when judged against the breadth of party experience worldwide. Essentially, the Democratic and Republican parties are still one of the "odd couples" in the political cotillion of the world.

Measuring Party Decentralization

American parties are ineffective in initiating and enacting public policy, the argument goes, because of their organizational weaknesses, especially their extreme decentralization of power. When power is decentralized within a party, the party may have difficulty getting its members in government (particularly in the legislature) to back its leaders' policies. The belief that American parties are decentralized has been widely shared among parties scholars. Almost fifty years ago, E. E. Schattschneider wrote, "Decentralization of power is by all odds the most important single characteristic of the American major party; more than anything else this trait distinguishes it from all others. Indeed, once this truth is understood, nearly everything else about American parties is greatly

Table 1. Nations and Parties in the Analysis

Regions and Nations	Political Parties in the Study	No. of Parties
ANGLO-AMERICAN		
United States	Democratic, Republican	2
United Kingdom	Labour, Conservative	2
Australia	Labor, Liberal, Country	3
Canada	Progressive Conservative, Liberal, New Democratic, Social Credit	4
New Zealand	National, Labour	2
Ireland	Fianna Fail, Fine Gael, Labour	3
WESTERN EUROPE		
Austria	Peoples, Socialist, Freedom	3
France	MRP, Radical Socialist, Socialist, Gaullist, Communist	5
West Germany	Christian Democratic Union, Social Democratic, Free Democratic	3
Greece	Liberal, National Radical Union, United Democratic Left	3
SCANDINAVIA AND LOWLANDS		
Denmark	Social Democrats, Moderate Liberal, Conservative, Radical Liberal	4
Iceland	Independence, Progressive, Social Democratic, People's Alliance	4
Sweden	Social Democratic, Center, Liberal, Conservative	4
The Netherlands	People's, Labor, Liberal, Anti-Revolutionary, CHU, Communist	6
Luxembourg	Christian Social, Socialist, Democratic, Communist	4
SOUTH AMERICA		
Ecuador	Velaquistas, Conservative, Liberal, Concentration of Popular Forces	4
Peru	Movement of National Union, ARPA, Popular Action, Democratic Movement	4
Uruguay	Colorado, National (Blanco)	2
Venezuela	Republican Democratic Union, COPEI, Democratic Action	3
ASIA		
India	Congress, Communist	2

Table 1. Nations and Parties in the Analysis
(*Continued*)

Regions and Nations	Political Parties in the Study	No. of Parties
MIDDLE EAST		
Turkey	Republican, Democratic	2
Lebanon	Progressive Socialist, Constitutional Union, Phalanges, Nationalist Bloc	4

Note: Total number of countries in the study = 22; total number of parties = 73.

illuminated" (1942:129). Thirty years later, Keefe said, "There is no lively debate among political scientists concerning the dominant characteristic of American political parties. It is, pure and simple, their decentralization" (1972:25). Scholars made such definitive statements, despite the lack of comparative surveys, because the impressionistic evidence seemed overwhelming. Aided now with data on seventy-three parties across the world, we can check out the accuracy of their sharp characterizations.

The term *decentralization of power* refers to the distribution of control over decision making among the levels of party organization. More concretely, it is the extent to which the national level of party organization is free from control by regional and local organs in conducting national party business and is capable of enforcing its decisions on the subnational levels. To measure this complex concept, we can disaggregate the "party's business" into categories and score each party on infringement on national control in each category (see Table 2 for a description of these categories and the scores assigned to the Democrats and Republicans circa 1960).

When summed over all seven indicators of decentralization in the 1960s, the Democratic and Republican parties earned (in different ways) the same total score, 32. When scored for the same seven indicators, the British Labour and Conservative parties' scores summed to 10 (each sum earned again in different ways). Judged against parties in Britain, the two U.S. parties certainly were more decentralized. This finding conforms to conventional wisdom that British parties are far more centralized than U.S. parties, and it illustrates the effect of the environment, which appears to impinge equally on parties *within* each country while differentiating among parties *between* countries.[7]

Table 2. Indicators Used to Score Party Decentralization of Power

	Democrat	Republican
1. *Control over communications:* scored from 0 to 7, with high scores to parties for which regional or local (rather than national) levels of organization controlled mass media or to parties that lacked their own media of communications. Neither party controlled any important means of mass communication.	7	7
2. *Administration of discipline:* scored from 0 to 4, with high scores to parties that administered discipline locally or that lacked effective means of disciplining legislative members. There was virtually no exercise of discipline within either party.	4	4
3. *Selection of legislative candidates:* scored from 1 to 9, with high scores to parties that selected candidates locally. Neither national party had any say in naming candidates for Congress: this was normally done by voters in primary elections.	9	9
4. *Allocation of funds:* scored from 0 to 6, with high scores to parties that collected and allocated funds locally, rather than nationally. National organs in both parties had roles in collecting and disbursing funds, including setting state quotas. Though neither party enjoyed complete success in collecting state quotas, the Republicans did better than the Democrats. (By the 1970s, Republicans began collecting massive funds nationally, which enabled them to reverse the flow and to fund selective state operations.)	4	3
5. *Selections of the national leader:* scored from 0 to 8, with high scores to parties that allowed local officials to help choose the national leader. Both parties selected presidential nominees at national conventions attended by state delegates.	4	4

Table 2. Indicators Used to Score Party Decentralization of Power
(*Continued*)

	Democrat	Republican
6. *Formulation of party policy:* scored from 0 to 7, with high scores to parties letting local officials participate in formulating policy, as in national conventions. Both parties adopted their platforms in conventions in the 1960s. Democrats also used an advisory council.	1	2
7. *Nationalization of structure:* scored from 0 to 6, with high scores to parties that lacked hierarchical structure headed by the national level of organization. Both national committees consisted of delegates from state organizations and had little authority over state parties. (By 1972, the Democrats' structure changed considerably, as the party issued national guidelines forcing state parties to change their procedures for selecting delegates or be denied seating at the convention.)	3	3
Total decentralization scores assigned to each party	32	32

Note: The original source of these data is Janda (1980:205, 210). In the original, however, the scores were reversed so that high scores meant centralization, not decentralization.

For more exacting comparisons with parties in other countries, all the scores were standardized and combined to form a single, composite scale for the decentralization of power. This scale was constructed so that the average score (the mean) centered toward zero.[8] Negative scores were earned by the more centralized parties, whereas the more decentralized parties earned positive scores. The composite scale scores for all seventy-three parties in the study are graphed in Figure 3.

The two U.S. parties are rated as very decentralized according to our scale—just as they are described in the literature. In fact, they were among the four most decentralized parties examined. Only two parties in Uruguay were more decentralized, and some scholars

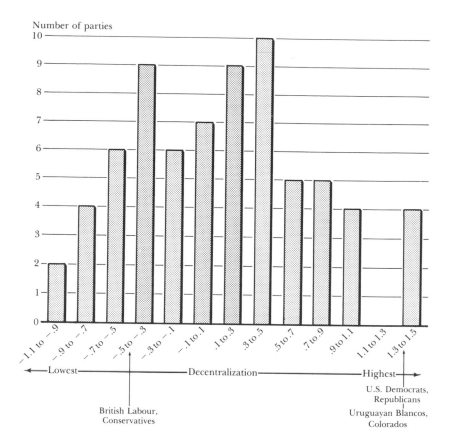

Figure 3. Party Decentralization of Power Scores

argue those parties, the Blancos and Colorados, were not individual parties but coalitions of distinct parties which themselves had different names and were labeled as such on the ballot. These partisan factions coalesced into two larger groups after the election because Uruguay's existing electoral system allowed votes won by factions to be summed to establish control of government. In any event, the two U.S. parties clearly fulfilled their characterization as "extremely decentralized."

Measuring Constitutional Influences

Our cross-national data strongly support scholars who characterize the U.S. parties as decentralized. Do the data also support scholars' reliance on federalism and separation of powers to explain party decentralization? To answer this question, we must first categorize the nations' constitutional systems; then we can analyze the level of decentralization among parties within each category.

Federalism. Federalism in a constitution does not always guarantee federalism in practice, and we need to draw distinctions between federalism and decentralization of power in the government itself. We can conceive of federalism and governmental decentralization as two separate but related concepts, each of which taps a different dimension of a broader concept, the vertical structure of the political system. Written constitutions usually provide for federalism in a formal sense. The U.S. Constitution, for example, recognizes the formal division of powers between the national and state governments in fixing representation in Congress, in electing the president, in providing for jurisdiction of the Supreme Court, in establishing citizens' rights among states, and in ratifying andamending the Constitution itself. The way federalism actually operates, however, depends on the way the nation's constitutional framework is implemented.

Decentralization of governmental power refers to the extent to which policy-making is actually distributed among the levels of government. A system formally designated as federal does not always display decentralization of governmental power. For example, the Soviet Union formally had a federal system, but the government operated in a centralized manner—at least during the years of this study. Even in the United States, the national government has accumulated powers that test the concept of federalism.[9] Despite the expansion of national power at the expense of the states, state governments in the aggregate still employ many more employees and account for more domestic expenditures than does the government in Washington. Moreover, the politics of election to Congress and to the presidency ensure that the formal federalism provided in the Constitution is reflected in a real decentralization of governmental power.

Figure 4 shows the relationship between formal federalism and decentralization of governmental power for the twenty-two nations in our study. Only seven nations were classified as formally federal in constitutional structure. Of these, all but two—Austria and Venezuela—were scored as decentralized in governmental structure.[10] All of the formally unitary states were regarded as centralized.

	Unitary Nations $(N = 15)$	Federal Nations $(N = 7)$
Centralized Nations $(N = 17)$	Denmark Ecuador France Greece Iceland Ireland Lebanon Luxembourg The Netherlands New Zealand Peru Sweden Turkey United Kingdom Uruguay	Austria Venezuela
Decentralized Nations $(N = 5)$		Australia Canada India United States West Germany

Figure 4. Relationship between Federalism and Decentralization of Power

Thus, there is as strong relationship between the constitutional basis of federalism and decentralization of governmental power. Because decentralization of power refers to the actual, rather than the formal, status of the vertical structure of political system, we will use it, rather than federalism, as a predictor of party decentralization. We will examine the empirical relationship between decentralized government and party decentralization after we consider the separation of powers, the other salient feature of the U.S. Constitution.

Separation of powers. One major component of the separation of powers formula, American style, is the separate selection of the president and the legislature. This separation is in marked contrast to the more unified parliamentary system, in which individual members tend to be reelected or defeated according to the party's overall appeal to the voters. In the parliamentary system, there is both a need for central party direction and a willingness to accept it. In a presidential system, where individual legislators and the chief executive are rewarded separately in elections, control by the national party is not only less necessary but actually discouraged by the dynamics of campaigning within different constituencies.

As noted earlier, most national constitutions do not separate legislative and executive powers. Although students in high school and even college in the United States often regard the separation of powers as a requirement of democratic government, many democratic nations get along quite nicely with the legislative and executive powers joined in a parliamentary structure. Moreover, presidentialism alone does not guarantee separation of powers, which assumes that the legislature is an effective body in its own right rather than merely a rubber stamp for the executive. To classify nations according to the separation of powers, we therefore need to consider two factors: whether the government is presidential or parliamentary and whether its legislature is effective or ineffective. Again, the effectiveness of the legislature does not strictly follow from the constitution, but constitutions can be written so that they produce strong or weak legislative bodies. Clearly, the framers of the U.S. Constitution sought to devise a strong Congress, and they anticipated political conflict between Congress and the president. One can assume that framers elsewhere also planned for the powers of the legislature.

Figure 5 shows the distribution of our sample of democratic nations on the two factors, presidential-parliamentary structure and legislative effectiveness. Since an effective legislature is characteristic of democratic government, we should not be surprised that nineteen of our twenty-two democratic nations have one. Because separation of powers is so peculiar to American thought and practice, we should also not be surprised that most nations with presidential forms of government are in North or South America. Of the nations in our sample outside the Western Hemisphere, only France's unique presidential form of government can qualify as a separation of powers, and even then it is not really like the U.S. model.[11] All told, only four nations in our sample manifest some form of separation of powers.[12] Of special note, the United States is the only country in the sample that has a functioning federalism (effectively decentralized government) and separation of powers.

	Presidential Nations (N = 6)	Parliamentary Nations (N = 16)
Partially Effective Legislature (N = 3)	Ecuador Peru	Lebanon
Effective Legislature (N = 19)	France United States Uruguay Venezuela	Australia Austria Canada Denmark Greece Iceland India Ireland Luxembourg The Netherlands New Zealand Sweden Turkey United Kingdom West Germany

Figure 5. Two Factors Involving the Separation of Powers

Effects on Party Decentralization

Before examining the effects of the nation's constitutional framework on party characteristics, we should be reminded of what we could reasonably expect to find or, more specifically, what we should not expect. First, we should not expect to find that the constitutional framework explains all or even most of the variance in party decentralization—despite the strong claims about the U.S. experience. After all, a nation's constitutional framework represents only one set of variables in the class of environmental factors affecting party characteristics. Other environmental factors, such as the size or heterogeneity of the country, would also be expected to affect party decentralization.

Second, we should not expect that all the environmental factors taken together would explain all or even most of the variance in party organiations. How much variance environmental factors can be expected to explain for any type of social organization is an issue in organizational theory. In their review of environmental influences on organizations, H. E. Aldrich and J. Pfeffer (1976) compared the "natural selection" model, which holds that organizations are formed to fit the environment, with the "resource dependence" model (also called the "structural contingency" model), which holds that environmental influences are important but do not determine organizational properties and that organizations seek to, and can, manage their environments within limits. According to the structural contingency model, we cannot hope to explain large amounts of variance in party characteristics without allowing for the party-level and individual-level factors discussed earlier.

Constitutional Effects

In this analysis, nations that had decentralized (federal) systems were scored 1, and those with centralized systems were scored 0, on the federalism feature. On the separation of powers feature, nations with a presidential form of government and an effective legislature (separation of powers) were scored 1; all others, those with parliamentary forms of government or ineffective legislatures, were scored 0. These constitutional features were thus treated as dichotomies in the analysis (commonly called "dummy variables").

As mentioned earlier, the United States is the only country of the twenty-two studied that manifested governmental decentralization along with separation of powers. The correlation between these constitutional traits over all seventy-three parties is virtually zero ($r = -.03$). However, the product moment correlations between each factor (.31 for federalism and .29 for separation of powers) and party decentralization are positive (as hypothesized) and significant at the .05 level. Still, neither factor explains as much as 10 percent of the variance in party decentralization. While these findings tend to support scholars' claims about the constitutional causes of party decentralization in the United States, these bivariate correlations are less than convincing.

A more appropriate test of scholars' claims about constitutional effects on party decentralization comes from combining both variables in a multiple regression model. The results are in Table 3, which shows that the variables together explain almost 20 percent of the variation in party decentralization. In addition, each variable is statistically significant. These results are encouraging for those who hold that constitutional factors affect party decentralization.

Table 3. Multiple Regression Analysis of Federalism and
Separation of Powers on Party Decentralization

	Unstandardized b Coefficients	Standardized Beta Coefficients	Standard Error of b	Significance
Government Decentralization	.51	.32	.18	00
Separation of Powers	.51	.30	.19	.01
Intercept	−.01			

Note: R^2 = .18; adjusted R^2 = .16; N = 73.

However, since these factors explain so little of the variance, how can we be confident they would still retain their effects if other factors were entered into the analysis?

Nonenvironmental Effects

One can really assess the effects of variables on a dependent variable only when the model is properly specified—i.e., when all theoretical linkages are examined. Although we may never know all the causes of any social phenomena, we assume—from the basic model in Figure 2—that party decentralization is also caused by factors other than the environment. Even if we are interested only in assessing environmental causes, we must introduce other causes into the analysis to improve our estimate of environmental effects. We will move toward a more adequately specified model by introducing two party-level variables that are known to relate to party structure. If the explanatory model is valid, the two constitutional factors should retain their effects, the two party-level variables should demonstrate their own effects, and the explanation of party decentralization should improve overall.

To consider all the party-level factors that might affect party decentralization would entangle us in organizational theory.[13] We can, however, gain some additional confidence in our effort to account for the effects of constitutional factors on party decentralization by introducing two major party-level variables—ideology and institutionalization.

Table 4. Multiple Regression Analysis of Federalism, Separation of Powers, Leftism, and Institutionalization on Party Decentralization

	Unstandardized b Coefficients	Standardized Beta Coefficients	Standard Error of b	Significance
Government Decentralization	.41	.25	.16	.01
Separation of Powers	.63	.37	.17	.00
Party Leftist Ideology	−.31	−.34	.09	.00
Party Institutionalization	.27	.26	.10	.01
Intercept	−.19			

Note: $R^2 = .38$; adjusted $R^2 = .34$; $N = 73$.

As mentioned earlier, party ideology can affect party organization. In the literature on comparative political parties, Maurice Duverger theorized many years ago that the centralization of power in political parties was strongly related to party ideology, with leftist parties tending to be more centralized than "bourgeois" parties (1963:xxxiv). Just as Duverger theorized, there is a negative correlation between a measure of "leftism" and decentralization over all the parties in the study.[14] Moreover, the correlation is significant and fairly strong at −.30.

Party decentralization is also likely to be related to party institutionalization, which Samuel Huntington has described as "stable, valued, recurring patterns of behavior" (1965:394). The argument is that newer parties—which are less institutionalized—are more apt to be centralized, because they reflect the organizational forces that created them in the first place. As parties mature, however, they adapt to local bases of power and thus become more decentralized as they become more institutionalized. Supporting this reasoning, the simple correlation between party decentralization and a measure of institutionalization is .36 over all the parties in the study.[15]

As shown in Table 4, when these party-level variables are added to the constitutional factors in regression analysis, the new equa-

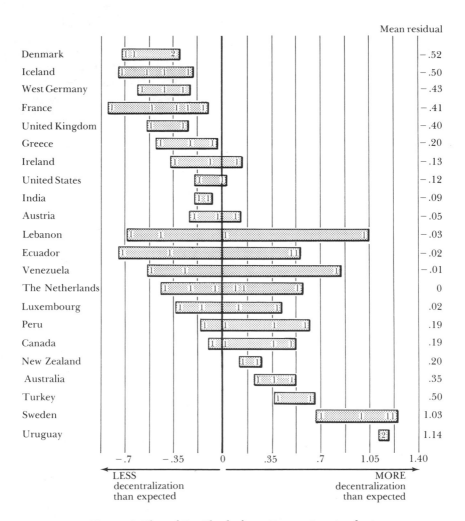

Figure 6. Plot of Residuals from Regression Analysis
Arranged by Country

tion explains 38 percent of the variance while retaining the effect of each constitutional factor. A useful part of regression analysis involves examining the "residuals"—the differences between the score that the equation predicts for each case and the score that was originally assigned. Figure 6 plots the residuals for each party by country, with countries arranged according to mean values of the residuals, from negative to positive. A negative residual reveals that the equation predicted a higher decentralization score than the party actually scored on the decentralization scale. That is, the equation overestimates the party's decentralization. Conversely, positive residuals indicate that the equation underestimates its decentralization.

Figure 6 clearly demonstrates the effects of a country's environment on the structure of political parties across nations. Except in Lebanon, Ecuador, and Venezuela, where parties range widely across the decentralization scale, parties in most other nations cluster around some national "norm." For example, although the regression analysis does a poor job in estimating the decentralization of power among parties in Denmark and Sweden, its prediction goes in different directions: overestimating each of the four Danish parties and underestimating each of the four Swedish ones.

To explain fully why this occurs requires more discussion than can be given now; however, some explanation is needed to clarify the analysis. Because both Sweden and Denmark are unitary states with parliamentary systems, the constitutional variables in the equation predicted that both countries would have centralized, rather than decentralized, parties. In fact, every party in both countries was more centralized than either of the American parties. During our time period, however, the national organs of the Danish parties, compared with the Swedish, were scored as more likely to exercise party discipline and more likely to publish or control newspapers.[16] This gave the Danish parties lower scores for decentralization. Because the parties in both countries did not differ much in institutionalization and were similarly arrayed above the left-right continuum, the two party-level variables had similar effects in Denmark and Sweden. The model thus overestimated party decentralization in Denmark and underestimated it in Sweden. The explanation for why the Danish parties exercised more party discipline at the national level, and also better controlled communications, lies outside the constitutional environment.

Presumably, one could introduce other environmental factors into the analysis—physical, socioeconomic, or statutory—that would explain additional cross-national variance. Such factors, however, would not account for the great differences in decentralization among parties in Lebanon, Ecuador, and Venezuela, shown in Figure 6. Other variables—either party-level or individual-level—are needed to explain why parties in the same country differ so greatly. The four variables in the present model do a poor job estimating party structure in these three countries, where other factors are obviously operating to cause some parties to be highly centralized and others highly decentralized.

The same variables, however, estimate the extreme decentralization of U.S. parties rather well, estimating the Democrats almost exactly and only slightly overestimating the Republicans. On the other hand, the equation greatly underestimates the extreme decentralization of the Blanco and Colorado parties in Uruguay. Apparently, Uruguay's peculiar electoral arrangement—omitted from the equation—operated as an additional environmental factor that spurred party decentralization.

Conclusion

Historically, distinguished scholars have attributed the structure of American parties to salient features in the U.S. Constitution. Specifically, they have attributed the extreme decentralization in the Democratic and Republican parties to the horizontal separation of legislative and executive powers between Congress and the president and to the vertical separation of powers between the national and state governments (federalism). The literature contains much scholarly testimony on this constitutional consequence, and it reports some case studies designed to test the thesis of constitutional causation.

In some ways, this quantitative cross-national study of constitutional effects on party decentralization simply extends Epstein's (1964) work, cited earlier. Whereas Epstein compared two federal nations (the United States and Canada) to assess the influence of separation of powers on party cohesion, this study used statistical analysis to examine the effects of federalism and separation of powers on party organization in twenty-two countries. It is reassuring that our findings are compatible. Constitutional factors—federalism as well as separation of powers—do help shape the distribution of power within a nation's parties.

What lessons do these cross-national findings hold for understanding party politics? First, they validate conventional knowledge that links the nature of American parties to the structure of its political system. In this sense, those who wish to see fundamentally different parties in the United States need to produce a fundamentally different political system, which is unlikely. Second, they give more precision to conventional knowledge by estimating constitutional effects on party characteristics. Third, the findings remind us that single-cause explanations are seldom as powerful as their advocates claim. Party structures are complex phenomena and result from complex causes. While the constitutional environment undoubtedly imposes severe constraints on attempts to change the character of American parties, the cross-national analysis suggests that constitutional factors do not determine party decentralization, as the Danish and Swedish examples clearly show.

Those who favor restructuring American parties to make them stronger can achieve some greater degree of centralization by changing laws and otherwise altering the nonconstitutional environment. Nevertheless, American parties are bound to reflect the decentralizing forces of the U.S. constitutional framework. For good or ill, the Constitution's diffusion of governmental powers between president and Congress, and between nation and state, severely limits the prospects for party government in the United States over the next two hundred years of political development.

NOTES

1. Some scholars vigorously argue that the framers had no intention of creating a truly democratic government. In a landmark study, James Allen Smith, professor of political science at the University of Washington at the turn of the century, wrote, "The framers of the American Constitution, however, succeeded in erecting barriers which democracy has found it more difficult to overcome. For more than a century the constitutional bulwarks which they raised against the rule of the numerical majority have obstructed and retarded the progress of the democratic movement" (1907:207). Smith charged that "American political writers" ignored "the obstacles which the Constitution has placed in the way of majority rule" and laid "the blame for corruption and machine methods upon the people" (212). Smith's (1913) analysis was later cited in Charles Beard's more celebrated indictment of the Constitution's creators for serving their economic interests. More charitable interpretations of the Constitution recognize the great step the framers took toward providing for popular participation in government.

2. For an excellent, annotated guide to writings on political parties in the United States prior to 1915, see New York Public Library (1915).

3. For a colorful diagram of the "Mechanical Representation of the United States under the Constitution" depicting the mechanical theory that Wilson criticized, see Houghton (1884).

4. *Parties and Their Environments: Limits to Reform?* (Harmel and Janda, 1982) sought to determine what constraints, if any, the country's environment imposed on attempts to "reform" American parties—

specifically to change them to conform to the model of "responsible party government." The book concluded that environmental factors did indeed shape the characteristics of a nation's parties, but that the American parties had not yet reached their environmental "limits" and could become somewhat more organized, centralized, and cohesive. Portions of this essay are drawn from that study, but all the data analysis has been redone.

5. The data base for *Parties and Their Environments* was somewhat larger, consisting of ninety-five parties for twenty-eight democratic nations. Given the narrower focus of this essay, several marginally democratic nations (and their parties) were dropped from the analysis.

6. The original data set consisted of approximately 100 variables for 158 parties in fifty-three countries from ten cultural-geographical regions of the world (Janda, 1980).

7. Readers who are more statistically minded may think of analysis of variance as a technique for measuring the variation of party characteristics within and between countries. Harmel and Janda (1982) used analysis of variance extensively to assess the total impact of environmental factors on ninety-five political parties in twenty-eight countries, regardless of the precise source of the environmental impact. We found substantial evidence of "country" effects—ranging from 57 to 68 percent—on decentralization of power, organizational complexity, and legislative cohesion.

8. The scale was constructed by transforming all the indicators into standard scores with means of 0 and standard deviations of 1, summing the standard scores for each party over all its indicators, and dividing by the number of indicators with valid data. The resulting scale has a reliability of .83 as measured by Cronbach's alpha. See Janda (1980:153–54) for the procedure. Note that the scale used herein has dropped one item and contains only seven items rather than the eight items reported for the centralization of power scale in Janda (1980).

9. Whether the United States still has a truly federal form of government or is simply a decentralized unitary state has been hotly debated. Opposing positions are summarized in Advisory Commission on Intergovernmental Relations (1986:1–3).

10. For support of these codings, see Wheare (1964:22). For additional evidence on Austria, see Lane and Ersson (1987: 194–95).

11. See Lane and Ersson (1987) for a discussion of the French form of presidentialism.

12. Uruguay qualifies for inclusion in this analysis under the constitution in effect during the period of study.

13. For an extensive investigation of this topic, see Harmel (1977). For a shorter treatment limited to only environmental factors, see Harmel (1981).

14. The measure of "leftism" is the seven-item Marxism scale described in Janda (1980:147–49). The scale has a reliability of .90, as measured by Cronbach's alpha.

15. The measure of institutionalization is a standardized scale of four variables: party age, competition for leadership, legislative instability, and

electoral instability. The reliability of the scale, as measured by Cronbach's alpha, is .79. See Janda (1980:143–44).

16. At least this is what the few sources had to say about parties in these countries in the late 1950s and early 1960s. There is evidence that these parties would be scored differently in the 1980s. In his comparative analysis of parties in Denmark and Sweden, Sjöblom (1987) reports little differences in party organization between the countries, but he does not address the specific indicators I used to measure decentralization for individual parties. Nevertheless, he concludes that "Swedish party organizations are stronger than the Danish" (194).

REFERENCES

Advisory Commission on Intergovernmental Relations. 1986. *The Transformation in American Politics: Implications for Federalism.* Washington, D.C.: Government Printing Office.

Aldrich, H. E., and J. Pfeffer. 1976. "Environments of Organizations." *Annual Review of Sociology* 2:79–105.

Banfield, Edward. 1964. "In Defense of the American Party System." In *Political Parties, U.S.A.,* edited by Robert A. Goldwin. Chicago: Rand McNally.

Beard, Charles A. 1913. *An Economic Interpretation of the Constitution.* New York: Macmillan.

Blondel, Jean. 1969. *An Introduction to Comparative Government.* New York: Praeger.

Bruce, Harold R. 1936. *American Political Parties and Politics.* New York: Henry Holt.

Bryce, James. [1889] 1912. *The American Commonwealth,* vol. 1. New York: Macmillan.

Duverger, Maurice. 1963. *Political Parties.* New York: John Wiley and Sons.

Epstein, Leon D. 1964. "A Comparative Study of Canadian Parties." *American Political Science Review* 58:46–59.

Ford, Henry Jones. 1898. *The Rise and Growth of American Politics.* New York: Macmillan.

Harmel, Robert. 1977. "Relative Impacts of Contextural and Internal Factors on Party Decentralization: A Cross-National Analysis." Ph.D. dissertation, Northwestern University.

———. 1981. "Environment and Party Decentralization: A Cross-National Analysis." *Comparative Political Studies* 14:75–99.

Harmel, Robert, and Kenneth Janda. 1982. *Parties and Their Environments: Limits to Reform?* New York: Longman.

Houghton, Walter R. 1884. *History of American Politics.* Chicago: Caxton.

Huntington, Samuel. 1965. "Political Development and Political Decay." *World Politics* 17:386–430.

Janda, Kenneth. 1980. *Political Parties: A Cross-National Survey.* New York: Free Press.

Keefe, William. 1972. *Parties, Politics, and Public Policy in America.* New York: Holt, Rinehart and Winston.

————. 1980. *Parties, Politics, and Public Policy.* New York: Dryden.

Kirkpatrick, Evron M. 1971. " 'Toward a More Responsible Two-Party System': Political Science, Policy Science, or Pseudo-Science?" *American Political Science Review* 65:965–90.

Lane, Jan-Erik, and Svante O. Ersson. 1987. *Politics and Society in Western Europe.* London: Sage Publications.

Lawson, Kay, 1976. *The Comparative Study of Political Parties.* New York: St. Martin's.

New York Public Library. 1915. *Political Parties in the United States, 1800–1914: A List of References.* New York: New York Public Library.

Price, David E. 1984. *Bringing Back the Parties.* Washington, D.C.: Congressional Quarterly Press.

Ranney, Austin. 1954. *The Doctrine of Responsible Party Government.* Urbana: University of Illinois Press.

Schattschneider, E. E. 1942. *Party Government.* New York: Henry Holt.

Sjöblom, Gunnar. 1987. "The Role of Political Parties in Denmark and Sweden, 1970–1984." In *Party Governments: European and American Experiences,* edited by Richard S. Katz. New York: Walter de Gruyter.

Smith, J. Allen. 1907. *The Spirit of American Government, a Study of the Constitution: Its Origin, Influence and Relation to Democracy.* New York: Macmillan.

Truman, David. 1955. "Federalism and the Party System." In *Federalism: Mature and Emergent,* edited by Arthur Macmahon. Garden City, N.Y.: Doubleday.

van Maarseveen, Henc, and Ger van der Tang. 1978. *Written Constitutions: A Computerized Comparative Study.* Dobbs Ferry, N.Y.: Oceana.

Wheare, K. C. 1964. *Federal Government.* New York: Oxford University Press.

Wilson, Woodrow. [1908] 1917. *Constitutional Government in the United States.* New York: Columbia University Press.

CHAPTER

⋆ 8 ⋆

Interest Groups and the Constitution

GRAHAM K. WILSON

Two of the central questions long asked about the political system of the United States are, How great is the power of interest groups and which aspects of the system and society promote the power of interest groups? Implicit in these questions was the assumption that interest groups were more important in the United States than elsewhere, as observers of American politics from Alexis de Tocqueville onward have contended. The contribution of interest groups was celebrated by some (Tocqueville, [1840] 1986; Dahl, 1956) and deplored by others (Schattschneider, 1960; Lowi, 1969). The importance of interest groups was accepted by all involved in the argument, however. It did not seem particularly difficult to explain the importance of interest groups. The supposed tendency of Americans to be "natural joiners" of interest groups was noted by Tocqueville, and more recent political scientists provided apparently confirming evidence (Verba and Nie, 1972). Weak political parties allowed scope for interest group activity by, for example, hardly constraining legislators through party discipline. The supposed pragmatism of American politics, better understood as the curtailment of political debate to that narrow part of the political spectrum which falls within the dominant ideology of the country, was unusually well suited to interest group politics, or so the argument went. The size and diversity of the country likewise required a political system that would be responsive to local needs or interests, often best articulated by interest groups.

Finally, and for our purposes most relevant, the Constitution itself has been thought to advantage interest groups. As will be discussed later, the Constitution not only gave interest groups rights and liberties but also provided them with unusual opportunities to influence public policy. In particular, the separation of powers created a multiplicity of points of access to decision making. Interest groups with little leverage in the Senate might fare better in the House of Representatives; groups with little standing in Congress might fare better with the president. Indeed, the whole constitutional design was influenced by an awareness of the need to incorporate within the political system the clash of economic interests that was so famously noted as inevitable in *Federalist No. 10.*[1] A president chosen indirectly through an electoral college of notables, senators drawn in equal numbers from states without regard to population, and a House of Representatives chosen by what was for the late eighteenth century a very extensive white male franchise could be expected to offer a sympathetic hearing to a variety of interest groups. *Mutatis mutandis,* much the same is true today. Different parts of the government continue to provide hospitality for a variety of interests. The House Education and Labor Committee has remained sympathetic to unions, and the agriculture committees favor farmers. The House and Senate respond to different interests on such issues as energy policy and speed limits, while presidents are less likely to be seen as somehow above alliances with interest groups just because they represent "all the people" (Kumar and Grossman, 1984). All branches of government are likely to be involved in reflecting the "different sentiments and views" of interests in American society.

Over the last thirty years, however, developments in political science have raised questions about the relative importance of U.S. interest groups; interest groups may be both less powerful in the United States than assumed and more powerful elsewhere. Such doubts arose in part from the studies of interest groups by Raymond Bauer, Ithiel de Sola Pool, and Lewis Anthony Dexter (1963) and Lester Milbrath (1963). These studies portrayed lobbyists as relatively weak, unable to coerce legislators, and dependent on long-term relationships of trust and cooperation to influence them. In contrast, studies of interest groups in other countries, generally completed somewhat later than their counterparts in the United States, showed that interest group activities, though less visible than in the United States, were arguably more important. Many British interest groups were regularly accorded extensive opportunities by ministers and civil servants to influence policy or legislation before it was presented to Parliament (Finer, 1966; Beer, 1965; Self and Storing, 1963; Eckstein, 1960; Jordan and Richardson, 1987). The belief in the legitimacy of functional representation has allowed economic interest groups regular access to policy makers on terms that would give Common Cause apoplexy. Civil servants and ministers give interest group officials almost constant, off-the-record opportunities to influence policy, with no public scrutiny of the relationship. The profoundly interesting work of such scholars as Gerhard Lehmbruch and Philippe Schmitter showed that in such neocorporatist countries as Sweden, Austria, and The Netherlands, the most important interest groups entered into a partnership with government that obliterated the distinction between government and interest group (Schmitter and Lehmbruch, 1979; Lehmbruch and Schmitter, 1982). Interest groups were partners of government in implementing as well as developing policy; indeed, interest groups often made and implemented policy on behalf, or instead, of government. Much the same was true of the relationship between the main Japanese business organization (the Keidanren) and the government of Japan. In short, as studies of interest group activity in the United States advanced, the importance of interest groups seemed to diminish; as studies of interest groups in other democracies advanced, so did the seeming importance of the interest groups themselves.

The importance of interest groups in other democratic systems threw into question many of the assumptions commonly made in explaining the importance of interest groups in the American polity. Strong interest groups were clearly compatible with strong political parties. The Swedish LO (Landsorganatsionen) and British labor unions, clearly stronger than the American Federation of Labor and Congress of Industrial Organizations (AFL-CIO), existed side by side with the Swedish Social Democratic and British Labour parties, themselves far stronger than any American national party. Powerful interest groups allied with a political party (such as British unions with the Labour party) could expect rapid implementation of their favorite proposals if their party attained a majority in the parliamentary elections; there can be little doubt that had the British Labour party won the 1987 elections, British unions would have made legislative gains on a scale the AFL-CIO could never hope for.

More surprising, parliamentary systems have proven capable of providing for active participation by interest groups not closely allied with the governing party. Party competition for support from such supposedly "floating" interests as farmers helps explain why farmers have been treated generously by governments in many parliamentary systems (Wilson, 1977b, 1978). The enormous difference in power for a party holding 49 percent as opposed to 51 percent of the legislative seats in a parliamentary system has been seen by some writers as making majoritarian parliamentary systems such as Britain's more susceptible than the American to exploitation by supposedly floating interest groups that might supply the crucial few votes to create a majority (Pennock, 1962; Barry, 1971).[2] As the neocorporatist literature notes, however, parliamentary regimes have also been able to achieve institutionalized compromise between a ruling political party (e.g., the Swedish Social Democrats) and interests clearly identified with the opposition party (e.g., business). Indeed, Stein Rokkan's (1966) famed verdict on the relative importance of elections and interest groups in Norwegian politics—"Votes count; resources decide"—serves to remind us that in parliamentary systems interest groups are powerful, even when the party with which an interest group is associated has lost the elections.

In brief, over the last thirty years we have become more skeptical about claims that interest groups are particularly powerful in the United States and more aware of the power of interest groups in parliamentary democracies. Naturally, our awareness of the importance of interest groups in other systems requires us to rethink the degree to which factors specific to the United States, including the Constitution, favor interest groups in the United States. If interest groups are not more powerful in the United States than in other advanced capitalist democracies, it would be perverse to assert that specifically American factors, such as the Constitution, make interest groups unusually powerful. Indeed, it may be desirable to examine more fully the opportunities the Constitution provides interest groups, as well as the limitations it imposes on them.

This essay discusses the opportunities the Constitution affords interest groups for exerting influence and the impact the Constitution has had on the nature of interest groups themselves. We are used to thinking of the legal rights of interest groups and the opportunities interest groups enjoy for influencing governments. We are less accustomed to thinking about the way in which the state consciously, as well as unconsciously, structures the nature of political actors, such as interest groups. Yet as the "new institutionalists" who wish to "bring the state back in" have argued, we should surely pay as much attention to how the state influences society as we do to how society influences the state (Skocpol, 1985). The state is not, as much pluralist analysis assumes, merely the aggregator of pressures from groups in society; it is also an actor and a structure shaping interest groups and their activities.

Opportunities for Interest Groups

We find interest groups in countries other than the Western democracies. Interest groups were detected in the Soviet Union prior to perestroika and in countries such as Chile during the dictatorship, which political scientists such as Jeane Kirkpatrick (1982) describe as moderately authoritarian. Even in authoritarian countries, interest groups continue to provide advice, information, and assistance in the implementation of policy, which governments prize although democracy is absent. Few would doubt that Western democratic systems provide the ideal conditions for interest group activity. The freedoms to assemble, to petition government without fear of major reprisal, to speak one's mind, to publish, to try to influence elections, and to engage in legal but frequently disruptive protest provide interest groups in Western democracies with valuable opportunities, without reducing the value of their services to government. No constitution protects such freedoms better than the American. As those who have watched the British government's suppression of *Spycatcher* know, even stable democracies with long histories of supporting civil liberties can compromise those liberties in a way that would be unimaginable in the United States. The U.S. Constitution's guarantees of the individual's civil liberties are so familiar that they need little discussion here; their value is beyond doubt for all of us who live in the United States.

It is perhaps less well known that these basic rights of individuals have been extended to interest groups in the United States, even when the interest group cannot be seen as a grouping of like-minded individuals (as in the case of corporations). In *Santa Clara County v. Southern Pacific Railway* (1886), the courts held that corporations are persons and are entitled to all the freedoms of the individual under the Constitution. Whether or not the Fourteenth Amendment was partly intended to be a bulwark for corporations has been the subject of much debate. Even in recent decades, however, the Supreme Court has determinedly defended the rights of corporations to function as interest groups enjoying the same rights as individuals. The Supreme Court ruled in *Central Hudson Gas and Electric Corporation v. Public Service Commission of New York* (1980) that even privately owned but publicly regulated monopolies have First Amendment rights to promote their views without restriction.[3] After a period in which the courts retreated from involvement in economic policy, the invocation of constitutional rights has become a frequent tactic used by economic interests challenging not only policy-making processes but also policy outcomes they dislike (Shapiro, 1986). Interest groups in general have also been allowed to use procedural rights once restricted to individuals, particularly standing to sue in civil cases. As Karen Orren has written, "Under the new rules the organization is the typical plaintiff. In the course of a spring tide of group activity in society generally, the liberalized approach has enabled numerous consumer, environmental, consumer historical-preservational and other associations . . . to come before the courts to do battle with such diverse parties as land developers, lumber companies and passenger railroads" (1976:725).

The Constitution provides other important opportunties as well. First, even before the Freedom of Information Act, the Constitution's prescription for the sharing of powers ensured that the U.S. government was one of the governments least able to keep a secret. The simple fact that an unusually large number of people in different institutions need to be involved in most policy areas (with the partial exception of foreign policy) makes secrecy hard to maintain for long. Moreover, many of the people involved have an interest in leaking details of the policy under consideration either to sabotage the policy or simply to gain credits for themselves with the press corps or public. Of course, not all policy is public knowledge. The misdeeds of the CIA in the 1950s and 1960s were kept secret until the 1970s; military aid to Iran was kept secret for months in the 1980s. Yet these examples do not refute the fact that the U.S. government is less able to operate secretively than, for example, the British or the French government, even though it has often wished to do so.

The prime beneficiaries of this lack of secrecy, as well as the Freedom of Information Act, are interest groups. Although we might like to think it is the individual citizen who absorbs the information released by the government, in reality it is interest groups that are more likely to use it. Similarly, although we might hope reduced government secrecy will enable individual citizens to exert influence on public policy, in practice it is interest groups that most readily exploit greater openness in government. Interest group success depends on knowing as soon as possible what government is planning to do and why. The longer an interest group knows about a policy proposal, the longer it has to dissuade government or to campaign against the proposal. The relatively open system of government created by the U.S. Constitution considerably enhances the prospect that interest groups will know about policy proposals in time to mobilize effectively. Compare the announcement by a British Chancellor of the Exchequer of a new tax on Budget Day with the long process leading up to the imposition of a similar tax in the United States.

A second way in which interest groups have benefited from the Constitution has been through the requirements of due process. Substantive due process was of course an effective barrier against legislative "interference" with the rights of capital in the nineteenth century. Procedural due process not only has survived the decline in judicial use of substantive due process but has progressed beyond the courthouse to affect government more generally. The extension of procedural due process from purely judicial to administrative procedures has been a major way in which the practical necessity in modern times to delegate powers from the legislature to executive agencies has been reconciled with constitutional doctrine that prevented or inhibited such delegation. The regulatory agencies are a prime example. The Administrative Procedures Act and numerous statutes creating individual agencies have required agencies to follow quasi-judicial procedures to achieve due process in policy-making. Agencies cannot simply make policy; they must first conduct lengthy hearings on a problem and possible solutions to it. The courts have been very ready to supervise these procedures closely and through them the content of agency decisions (Wilson, 1985). Such procedures obviously advantage interest groups. Interest groups are guaranteed rights to participate in policy-making, and in practice they can slow down the process enormously by submitting lengthy evidence or by challenging the process or decision if they fail to convince the executive branch agency.

A third aspect of the Constitution aiding interest groups are those features that facilitate the creation of iron triangles linking interest groups, agencies, and congressional committees in indissoluble ties of mutual interest. Legislators seek to please politically powerful interests in their districts by using congressional power over executive branch agencies to press those agencies to adopt policies benefiting those interests. Iron triangles in the United States have therefore turned on bipartisan coalitions of legislators pragmatically serving interests in their constituencies to advance their own political careers. Of course, iron triangles are caused in part by nonconstitutional factors, such as the congressional tradition of appointing legislators to the committees overseeing an agency in which their constituents have a vital interest. Yet constitutional factors are basic. Without a legislature as powerful as Congress, iron triangles, as they have been understood in the United States, would not have been possible. If legislators were not elected by geographic units (districts and states) within which interest groups can have greater importance than in the country as a whole, iron triangles would never have existed.

As we have seen, the executive branch in other countries can develop very close ties with interest groups. In neocorporatist systems, the major economic groups expect to have considerable influence over a wide range of government policies, a more extensive range of policies than found in any American iron triangle. By and large, close ties have not resulted in a fragmentation of the executive branch because of competing interest group demands, as supposedly happens in the United States because of iron triangles. The ties binding together the Japanese or British executive branch are stronger than the centrifugal pull of interest groups. There are, however, countries in which a different form of pressure on the executive branch is very important. In Italy, for example, the bureaucracy has been colonized by the political parties, using positions within the bureaucracy to reward their supporters, which can include interest groups (LaPolombara, 1964; Di Palma, 1979). Partisan patronage is also common in the United States, but it should be distinguished from the phenomenon of the iron triangle.

Indeed, one might argue the U.S. executive is especially vulnerable to interest groups. Forces pressing other executive branches toward alliances with interest groups, such as the need for advice, assistance, and support for the governing party, are reinforced by the possibility of iron triangles. It is therefore of great importance to assess how many iron triangles exist. There is certainly room for debate on this point. Theodore Lowi (1969) has suggested iron triangles are endemic, and he rests much of his work on this assumption. I suggested long ago that iron triangles did not exist in areas where they are normally expected to be strongest (Wilson, 1977a, 1977b). Agricultural policy-making, for example, is often presented as the classic example of an iron triangle, but in practice it involves the interaction of interest groups that profoundly disagree about the true interests of the farmer, legislators on congressional committees that are often sharply divided along party lines, and the Agriculture Department, whose policies depend on which party controls the White House. Moreover, iron triangles might have lost whatever importance they might have had because of the growth in the number of interest groups. Since the rise of the consumer and environmental movements, agricultural policy can no longer be confined to an iron triangle based on farmers' organizations. Those of us who have argued that iron triangles are fewer than presumed have emphasized how frequently interest groups and congressional committees are divided into contending factions, thus making classic iron triangles impossible. We contend political scientists have considerably overestimated the number of iron triangles existing in the U.S. government.

Nonetheless, the iron triangle concept captured an aspect of reality. Some iron triangles did exist in U.S. history. The Bureau of Land Management (BLM) in the Interior Department, ranchers, and the interior committees of Congress undoubtedly constituted one such triangle, though the environmental movement broke the triangle in the 1970s. Perhaps similar triangles still exist, living in what is at present enviable obscurity, though a force similar to the environmental movement that overwhelmed the BLM–Interior Committee–rancher triangle may bring them to light in the future. More important, the iron triangle concept reminds us that close ties between an interest group and the majority on the Congressional committees that handle issues of most concern to it can be of enormous value, even if a true iron triangle does not exist because of divisions among legislators or interest groups. The linkages between unions, the congressional labor committees, and the Labor Department do not constitute a classic iron triangle because of the antipathy between many Republicans (in the House committee and Labor Department) and unions. Nonetheless, the Democrats on the House and Senate labor committees, who receive strong political support from the unions, have been an invaluable bulwark for unions in recent years, killing in committee legislative proposals that would have further weakened unions industrially or politically. Had it not been for the protective bulwark provided by a friendly majority on the congressonal committees, the unions would have suffered even more from the policies of the Reagan administration. In short, the iron triangle idea reminds us that in the U.S. political system, as in no other, the legislator, motivated by defending his or her own political position, is potentially a major resource for interest groups important in the legislator's district or state.

A fourth way in which the Constitution has helped interest groups has been through weakening political parties. No doubt, as the example of the Soviet Union—which on paper is also a federation—shows, had political parties been strong enough, the fragmenting tendencies of the Constitution would have been less significant. In fact, political parties in the United States, already weakened by numerous other factors, have continued to be hindered by the Constitution. The impossibility of establishing who is the leader of the Democrats at present is due in large part to the Constitution, which established numerous positions to be claimed at the state or national level. A fragmenting Constitution works its influence on political parties as well as government.

The weakness of political parties frequently advantages interest groups. We have noted earlier that interest groups allied with governing political parties in parliamentary systems are well served by that arrangement. There are relatively few such arrangements in the United States, however, and the few interests closely tied to a political party (e.g., the United Auto Workers and the Democrats) may be disadvantaged by weak party discipline. Most interest groups actually benefit from the weak party system, however. Although most political scientists have concluded that lobbying is not as strong an influence as is popularly supposed (Bauer, Pool, and Dexter, 1972; Kingdon, 1973; Milbrath, 1963), lobbying is more effective than it would be if the United States had strong, disciplined political parties. Local interests do not have to contend with extremely strong countervailing pressure from national party leaders able to discipline rebellious politicians. Similarly, although practitioners and many academic commentators deny legislators sell their votes for PAC contributions, the inability of candidates to run campaigns for Congress on resources provided by political parties creates opportunities for interest groups. Insofar as the Constitution makes the creation of strong political parties more difficult by creating numerous independent leadership positions, it advantages interest groups. As has been widely recognized, strong political parties are an antidote to the dangers of numerous interests having power in discrete policy areas, if not to the power of a wide-ranging interest group tied to a political party. The weak U.S. party system allows a multiplicity of groups to have influence outside, as well as inside, party structures.

The Effect of the Constitution on Interest Groups

As previously noted, the new institutionalists have reminded us that institutions shape society, as well as vice versa. Not only does the state often act autonomous of societal pressures and interests, as Eric Nordlinger (1981) has argued, but the state shapes the character and behavior of social actors through deliberate policies and its own structures. The state is thus a determinant, as well as to some degree a victim, of the interest group system.

We are perhaps more familiar with the role of the state in structuring the interest group system in political systems more unified than the American. Governments in such countries as Britain, France, and Sweden have greater latitude in choosing which groups they should talk to meaningfully, sharing information and seeking ideas while policy proposals are still plastic as opposed to going through the motions of consultation once policy is firmly established. For example, for many years British governments had a deliberate policy of building up the National Farmers' Union by refusing to talk to rivals, such as the Farmers' Union of Wales. French governments also selected and promoted congenial interest groups with which to work, for example, on the modernization of French agriculture.

At first glance, the U.S. government's policy on interest groups is to have no policy at all. Instead of attempting to structure the interest group system as the corporatist or neocorporatist states do, the U.S. government seems to respect and even safeguard the autonomy of interest groups. Alfred Stepan (1978) has noted that most Roman-law countries have traditionally viewed private organizations, including interest groups, as bodies that require chartering or licensing by the state. Private organizations need legitimation from the state. This tradition spills over from legal into administrative culture, affecting the whole approach to interest groups (Stepan, 1978). In contrast, in Anglo-American legal traditions, private organizations, such as interest groups, generally require no state legitimation. The rights of interest groups, like those of individuals, are conventionally seen as "natural" or original, not derived from the state. By and large, the doctrine of an invisible hand guiding competition and conflict to serve the public good has been applied to U.S. interest groups, just as it once was to the economy.

Judicial decisions in recent decades have strengthened the autonomy of U.S. interest groups and their freedom to be actors in the political process. The Supreme Court protected the autonomy of interest groups when it refused to allow southern states to require the National Association for the Advancement of Colored People (NAACP) to publish its membership lists, because publication of the names of members would have made them vulnerable to harassment by officials or the public (*NAACP v. Alabama*, 1958). Interest groups—including public utilities—cannot be obliged either to refrain from comment or to facilitate public debate by circulating opposing views in their mailings (*Consolidated Edison Co. v. Public Service Commission of New York*, 1980).[4] The recent rulings of the Supreme Court allowing political party rules to override state laws on delegate selection extend the doctrine of interest group autonomy and may contain possibilities for further protection (*Democratic Party of the United States v. Wisconsin*, 1981).

The most obvious exception to this concept of interest group autonomy would be those interest groups that allegedly enjoy substantial economic power or are in fiduciary relationships. Labor unions, for example, have been quite extensively regulated, in theory if not always effectively in practice, in terms of their internal political practices since the adoption of the Landrum-Griffin Act in 1959. If the Justice Department had succeeded in placing the Teamsters Union under receivership because of its links to organized crime, it would have been an interesting, perhaps unprecedented, departure from the practice of accepting interest group autonomy. Unions have long been unable to claim unrestricted First Amendment rights because of their alleged economic power. The Supreme Court ruled that union picketing can be regulated beyond the degree permissible for demonstrations because it is an exercise of economic power as well as free speech (*American Federation of Labor v. Swing*, 1941).[5]

More recent Supreme Court decisions, however, have upheld the freedom of interest groups to use the resources at their command to influence policy and politics, unless there is a clear danger of, for example, corruption. *Buckley v. Valeo* (1976), for instance, allowed interest groups to spend without limit on election campaigns so long as their expenditures were not under the direct control of the candidate the organization was supporting. The Supreme Court majority in the case argued that "a restriction on the amount of money a person *or group* can spend on political communication during a campaign necessarily reduces the quantity of expression by reducing the number of issues discussed, the depth of their exploration and the size of the audience reached. . . . *the concept that government may restrict the speech of some elements in society in order to enhance the relative voice of others is wholly foreign to the first amendment*" (48–49, emphasis added). The doctrine of *Buckley v. Valeo* was extended in *First National Bank of Boston v. Bellot* (1978), where groups were given unrestricted rights to spend money to influence the outcome of a referendum. Restrictions on campaign contributions in ordinary elections, the Court argued, could be justified by the need to avoid corruption. Arguing that no such danger could exist in a referendum since there was no candidate, the court ruled there could be no justification for spending-limits. Even in promoting a fair contest, therefore, the state is not to regulate interest group behavior closely. Autonomy should be the watchword.

Yet whatever the safeguards for interest group autonomy, administrations have tried to influence the interest group system. The early labor movement suffered far more state repression or repression supported by the state than did most European labor movements. Contrast the relatively peaceful acceptance of labor unions by the British state with the prolonged support of often violent employer opposition by the American state. Emphasizing freedom of contract rather than freedom of association, the Supreme Court upheld the validity of "yellow dog" contracts (*Allgeyer v. Louisiana*, 1897). The deliberate disruption of anti–Vietnam War groups by the FBI under its COINTELPRO program could also be seen as a drastic attempt by the state to structure the interest group system. Under both the Nixon and Reagan administrations, the Internal Revenue Service attempted to weaken public interest groups by taking a narrow view of the activities consistent with tax-exempt status. The Reagan administration also attempted to "de-fund the left" by reducing the flow of federal grants for activities such as training for interest groups opposed to its policies.

Throughout U.S. history, government help has been extended to interest groups that find official favor. The American Farm Bureau Federation was given government help in part to weaken more radical rivals, and the National Rifle Association was given crucial assistance to create a better supply of soldiers. Industrial unions, such as the steelworkers and the auto workers, would have difficulty in unionizing had it not been for the creation of the National Labor Relations Board, which would conduct ballots to see if workers wanted a union and, if they did, would require the employer to bargain in good faith with it. The Supreme Court has given considerable encouragement to civil rights groups, implying and stating that it has a particular duty to listen to those interests which might lack power elsewhere in the political arena. The Court argued, "Litigation may well be the sole practicable avenue open to a minority" (*NAACP v. Button*, 1963:415; see also *New Orleans v. Dukes*, 1976). Of course, most interest group litigation is conducted by more powerful groups (e.g., business), which are also extensively using other aspects of the political system (Brewer, 1987).

Administrations can also choose to listen more carefully to some interest groups than they do to others. In general, the AFL-CIO receives more attention from Democratic politicians than Republicans. The Moral Majority got a warmer reception from Ronald Reagan (if little action) than it would have from Walter Mondale. No one branch of government, however, can completely implement a policy designed to control an interest group. For example, while Secretary of the Interior James Watt worked effectively to reduce environmentalists' links to the Department of Interior, the beleaguered environmentalists employed as lobbyists such former senators as Gaylord Nelson and retained their links to Congress. The administration could try hard to reduce the influence of environmentalists on the executive branch but had no ability to reduce their influence on Congress.

Yet even if conscious policies aimed at shaping the interest group system are harder to implement in the United States than in other countries because of the fragmentation of government, the state continues to exert its influence on the interest group system. Some of the ways in which the state affects the interest group system are through the unintended consequences of other policies. The antitrust policies of the United States, noticeably tougher than those of most European countries (including Britain), are often credited with weakening trade associations. Certainly American executives fear that using trade associations for purposes common in Europe or Japan would make them liable to prosecution; some trade associations (e.g., in the paper industry) even begin meetings with a reminder of the antitrust laws' implications for what can and cannot be discussed. It is significant that the attempts to stimulate a concerted response to the Japanese threat in semiconductors have included a guarantee against prosecution for the firms and trade associations involved.

The Constitution itself also exerts indirect influence on American interest groups so that their character is distinctly different from those in other countries. One of the most obvious differences between interest groups in the United States and those in other democracies is that American interest groups have continued to make the legislature a major target of their activities long after interest groups in other political systems have focused on the executive. Lobbyists for large corporations whom I recently interviewed commonly put the proportion of their time spent lobbying Congress at 70–75 percent. In no other country would the legislature claim as high a proportion of their time.[6] In parliamentary regimes such as the British, lobbying the legislature remains a minor supplement to lobbying ministers and bureaucrats, though it is more common than in the past. Second, American interest groups are able like no others to use the courts to influence public policy. Third, the U.S. interest group system is much more untidy and disorganized than other systems are.

How do these differences affect U.S. interest groups? In spite of specialization and the growth in the size of congressional staffs, focusing on the legislature instead of the executive branch probably encourages a somewhat less technical approach. In general, interest groups dealing with bureaucracies are well advised to adopt the styles of the bureaucracies and emphasize techical, rather than political, points. In contrast, lobbyists dealing with a legislator are better advised to emphasize political principles and considerations, including policy consequences in the legislator's district. A second consequence of a focus on the legislature is that American interest groups are in the habit of forming coalitions. Legislators pay most attention to interest groups that are strong in their districts and to lobbyists with whom they have built up a long-term relationship of trust.[7] An interest group thus may be better advised to approach a legislator through another interest group instead of making a direct approach. It is therefore understandable that many, if not all, interest groups are drawn into semipermanent coalitions, almost embryonic political parties that link allies on a variety of issues. The National Farmers' Union (NFU), AFL-CIO, and NAACP are members of such a liberal grouping; the National Rifle Association, American Medical Association, and several business groups constitute a conservative counterpart.

It is perhaps their dependence on coalitions that helps explain the astonishing range of issues on which many American interest groups take a stand. The commitment of the American Farm Bureau Federation (AFBF) in the 1970s to securing the expulsion of the United Nations from U.S. soil is not clearly related to issues of agricultural policy; it is more probably linked to the extensive involvement of the AFBF's leaders in right-wing politics. Whether or not I am right in explaining such breadth of interest by the legislative focus of interest groups, it is certainly the case that without a legislative focus, such breadth of interest would be damaging. In a country such as Britain, where the executive is the natural focus of interest group activity, it would be utterly bizarre for a farmers' interest group to have strong views on the location of the United Nations. Indeed, the bureaucrats and ministers in charge of farm policy would be disinclined to take seriously a group with such general and politicized concerns. Yet there are few interest groups in the United States that confine themselves exclusively to their obvious fields of interest; the AFL-CIO and NFU would provide liberal counterparts to the wide-ranging conservatism of the AFBF.

The consequence of the availability of legal action as a way of influencing public policy is also uncertain. Some might fear that the availability of the courts reduces the incentives for interest groups to commit resources to more democratic forms of political activity. To the degree that an interest group succeeds in the courts, it is disinclined to spend money on mass mobilizaton, legislative activity, and other forms of political activity involving the public or their representatives. Moreover, legal strategies, with their dependence on expertise and the pursuit of test cases selected on technical grounds, are not amenable to the democratic control of members of the interest group.

I would suggest, however, that the main consequence of the availability of legal action as a strategy for interest groups is to reduce their willingness to compromise. When power rests with political actors in the last analysis (e.g., ministers in a parliamentary system), interest groups are dependent on persuasion or offering inducements, at least between elections. Most Western governments are willing to pay something for the approval of an interest group in return for information, help in policy formulation, or assistance in policy implementation. On the other hand, the interest group knows that in the last analysis the government can impose its will. Compromise on important details can follow disagreement on the basic principles of policy. The creation of the National Health Service and subsequent negotiations between the British Medical Association and the government is a celebrated example (Eckstein, 1960).

Legal procedures, however, discourage compromise for several reasons. In the first place, interest groups that have lost the battle in Congress or with the executive can hope to win in the courts. In the second place, legal proceedings are inherently adversarial, geared to the statement and adjudication of clear differences rather than compromise. It is not surprising that occupational safety and health policy in Britain, where the courts are rarely involved in policy-making, is made with a good deal of compromise and goodwill between unions and employers, whereas in the United States, where the courts are invariably involved, there has been constant strife between employers and unions on the same issues.[8] Other scholars have reached similar conclusions about the greater frequency of conflict in the United States (though sometimes explained by other factors) in studies comparing U.S. and Swedish policies (Lundquist, 1980; Kelman, 1981) and U.S. and British environmental policy (Vogel, 1986). Recourse to the courts reduces the willingness to compromise.

If any one factor distinguishes the interest group system of the United States from that of other countries it is its apparent untidiness and disorganization. Take the example of business. In many Western democracies, particularly the neocorporatist countries, the links between business and government are very tidily organized. The individual enterprise belongs to the trade association for the industries in which it operates, which in turn belongs to the umbrella organization for business in general, such as the Keidanren in Japan, the Swedish Employers' Organization, or the French *Patronat*. There are fairly clear procedures for handling most issues that might arise. In the United States, the situation is much more complicated. An individual company is much more likely to act individually through its Washington office or hired lobbyists (including Washington law firms) and less likely to rely on trade associations than would counterparts in other countries. Trade associations have a lower status in the United States than elsewhere, and no one organization can claim to be *the* voice of business. Whereas in most Western democracies, there is one preeminent umbrella organization for business, there are at least three in the United States (the National Association of Manufacturers, the Chamber of Commerce, and the Business Roundtable). Instead of forging clear and stable links between established interest groups and government, there is a tendency to create entirely new organizations to serve as temporary, ad hoc coalitions on important issues. The very important tax reform issues of the last few years were handled on behalf of business by entirely new organizations taking opposite sides on the issues rather than by an umbrella organization that could reconcile and aggregate different business interests before submitting its case to the government. The untidiness of business organization has its counterparts in many other areas, such as agriculture and labor.

The disorderliness of the American interest group system is surely related to the basic characteristics of the system created by the Constitution. A fragmented interest group system faces a fragmented system of government. Some of the reasons for this parallel have already been discussed. Government cannot pressure interests into forming one organization to replace several (as the British did when the 1964–70 Labour government secured the creation of the Confederation of British Industries to represent employers); no one branch of government controls access to decision making. The Department of Agriculture might find life easier if it could force the quarreling interest groups claiming to represent the American farmer to unite; in practice it cannot force them to do so by saying that only one organization will have effective access to the policy-making process, as the British have done. Indeed, when control of Congress and the executive branch is in different hands, as is frequently the case, the various institutions created by the Constitution will often encourage different interest groups in the same field. The Farm Bureau will usually receive a warm welcome from the Department of Agriculture when the Republicans control the presidency; at the same time, the rival National Farmers' Union will be warmly received by the Democrats controlling the House (and usually Senate) Agriculture Committee.

A single, monopolistic interest group speaking for an entire sector rarely comes into existence "naturally"; it usually requires the active encouragement of government. Even in the "societal corporatist" systems, to use Schmitter's (1974) term, government has helped bring about and maintain the dominance of a single interest group. Moreover, self-discipline on the part of government is required to maintain this interest group unity. Governments have to be prepared to maintain the standing of interest groups with which they disagree and refrain from encouraging rival or splinter groups. For better or for worse, the fragmented system of government in the United States is incapable of building such unity among interest groups because government itself is too disunited to exert effective leverage.

The Constitution encourages the fragmentation of interest groups in one further way. Conceived as it was in a nation that believed it had overcome tyranny in the recent past, the Constitution set out to limit the power of government. No interest with any degree of political influence need fear it would be severely damaged by government. Indeed, the writers of the original Consitution believed that checks and balances offered such protection against government power that not even a bill of rights was required, though of course one was speedily added to assuage Antifederalist critics. The framers were certainly successful in this regard. Government in the United States has rarely seemed really threatening to established interests. Shouts of rage from the business community, for example, have usually been provoked by "crises" such as the New Deal, which historians have subsequently interpreted as far from threatening to the long-term interests of business. When business felt threatened by the social regulatory agencies in the 1970s, the complex policy-making process provided numerous opportunities for corporations to tie the offending agencies in knots.

If government in the United States is less potentially threatening than in countries with weaker judicial review, then the incentive for established interests to build strong interest group organizations is reduced. The weakness and divisions among business organizations in the United States, for example, are at least partly due to the fact that the need for business to protect itself is less in the United States than in other countries. Most writers classify the United States as a "weak state," one unable to mount a sustained challenge to established interests. Those established interests have therefore had less need to organize than in strong states. The Constitution was intended to achieve just such a result.

Conclusion

It would surely be unreasonable for anyone to assert today without qualification or argument that interest groups play a more important role in American politics than in the politics of other countries. The closeness and importance of the links between business and the state in Japan and France, or business, labor, and the state in neocorporatist countries, should give pause to anyone tempted to make such an assertion. Yet neither would it be plausible to portray the United States as a country with a political system in which the state is so strong that it constantly overwhelms struggling interest groups. It would surely be perverse to explain aspects of public policy, such as the weakness of gun control legislation or the extent of U.S. aid to Israel, without reference to interest groups. For those who have the wealth to pay for it, there are no major barriers to group representation in the system. As the rapid growth in the interest group activities of business since the early 1970s shows, those with the requisite resources can soon assemble the necessary interest group organization to have a significant impact on important aspects of public policy. In brief, the discredited notion that interest groups are far more important in the United States should not be replaced with an argument that the American political system

tions only to weaken interest groups. Rather, we should say the American interest group system, like the American party system, reflects the important aspects of the setting in which it operates, including the Constitution.

Whether one likes or dislikes the characteristics of the resulting interest group system is, of course, a matter of personal preference in striking a balance between its advantages and disadvantages. The divisions and competition characterizing the American interest group system can be welcomed on at least two grounds. First, they improve the representativeness of the interest groups; members of interest groups go elsewhere if they are dissatisfied with the policies or behavior of their group. In Albert O. Hirschman's terminology, the American interest group system often provides the opportunity for exit as well as voice. Second, the divisions within the interest group system provide politicians with a degree of freedom they would otherwise lack. Politicians can find a congenial interest group with which to work in most sectors. On agricultural policy, for example, the free market legislator can work with the Farm Bureau, while the most interventionist legislator can work with the National Farmers' Union. In a period when many commentators have worried about the increasing dependency of politicians on interest groups for campaign finance, it is comforting to remember that the fragmented interest group system provides many sources of finance. The more conservative legislator refused money by the United Auto Workers or the AFL-CIO may still obtain a campaign contribution from the construction unions or the Teamsters.

Yet this interest group system is not without its costs. A fragmented interest group system cannot aid governance as much as a more unified system can. Interest groups that can claim to be the authoritative voice of their sector can fulfill a number of useful functions that disunited groups cannot. First, an authoritative interest group can settle what people in its sector want. Fragmented interest groups leave the politician guessing, unless they all agree, which is rare. Second, authoritative interest groups can aggregate demands for their sector in a way competing groups cannot. Differences of interest between, say, wheat and dairy farmers can be settled by the interest group rather than by politicians. Third, authoritative interest groups are better able to make diplomatic compromises than are competing groups, which may be denounced by their rivals as "soft" if they agree to a reasonable compromise. As Mancur Olson (1982) and Samuel Beer (1982) have noted, each interest group in systems with many competing groups faces a dilemma. If the interest group forgoes a selfish advantage in pursuit of the national interest, it has no guarantee that the numerous other groups will make a comparable sacrifice. In contrast, broad, all-encompassing interest groups will be able to make sacrifices in the long-term interests of all (including themselves), without worrying about the risk that other groups will continue to pursue selfish goals and forge ahead. Fourth, authoritative groups can be given the work of policy implementation, whereas developing implementation to competing groups is obviously difficult. In Britain, the government solved the difficult issues of occupational safety and health by turning the issue over to a body controlled by the Confederation of British Industries (CBI) and Trades Union Congress (TUC). Such a solution depends on the existence of authoritative groups to whom responsibility can be given.

The advantages of more unified interest group systems should not be seen as a compelling argument for a major revision of the Constitution to establish a more orderly interest group system. There can be few enterprises so futile as proposing major changes in the U.S. Constitution. Moreover, the advantages of neocorporatist systems in representing interests seem less certain than they did when Schmitter proclaimed this to be still the century of corporatism. The stability of the neocorporatist political economies so much admired in the 1970s seemed more like *immobilisme* in the 1980s, while the U.S. political economy has fared unusually well in reducing inflation and unemployment. The neocorporatist systems have also seemed less stable than in the past. Even in that exemplar of neocorporatism, Sweden, there have been important challenges to the neocorporatist arrangements that have prevailed for several decades. Many commentators attribute these trends to fragmentation caused by the differential effects of economic crisis and by the decomposition of class allegiances in the wake of increasing prosperity since World War II that has brought those countries to levels equal to or greater than the American standard of living. Ten years ago, the American interest group system seemed curiously outdated. Today, the American interest group system may be a vision of the future for other systems.

NOTES

1. "A landed interest, a manufacturing interest, a mercantile interest with many lesser interests grow up of necessity in civilized nations and di-

vide them into different classes accentuated by different sentiments and views."

2. At the very least, Pennock should have noted the existence of similar tendencies in aspects of American politics (e.g., the quest for support from supposedly floating groups in strategic states in presidential elections).

3. The right of the company to advocate the consumption of electricity during a period of energy shortage was upheld as commerical free speech.

4. The Supreme Court ruled that Consolidated Edison could not be forbidden to include leaflets advocating nuclear power in its bills and that the utility could not be obliged to permit critics of nuclear power to reply.

5. Although this is a longstanding precedent, there have been no major changes in the principles set out in the Court's decision. More recent cases on picketing rights are more concerned with questions about picketing by noneconomic groups, especially when they wish to picket on private property (e.g., shopping malls).

6. Robert Nelson, John P. Heinz, Edward O. Lauman, and Robert Salisbury (1987:table 7) find that the largest proportion of governmental affairs staffs of organizations they surveyed maintained regular contact with both Congress and the executive. But 67 percent of unions' governmental affairs staffs maintained regular contact only with Congress. Even for business officials, the number of representatives contacting only the executive regularly was minuscule whereas almost a quarter contacted only Congress.

7. Lester Milbrath (1963) was one of the first to argue this.

8. See Wilson (1985) for a lengthy discussion of this point.

REFERENCES

Allgeyer v. Louisiana. 1987. 165 U.S. 578.

American Federation of Labor v. Swing. 1941. 312 U.S. 321.

Barry, Brian. 1971. "Comments on 'The Pork Barrel and Majority Rule.'" Journal of Politics 33:530–31.

Bauer, Raymond, Ithiel de Sola Pool, and Lewis Anthony Dexter. 1963. American Business and Public Policy. Chicago: Atherton.

―――. 1972. American Business and Public Policy. 2d ed. Chicago: Aldine-Atherton.

Beer, Samuel. 1965. Modern British Politics: A Study of Parties and Pressure Groups. London: Faber and Faber.

―――. 1982. Britain against Itself: The Political Contradictions of Collectivism. New York: W. W. Norton.

Brewer, Patrick. 1987. "Interest Group Litigation." Ph.D. dissertation, University of Wisconsin–Madison.

Buckley v. Valeo. 1976. 424 U.S. 1.

Central Hudson Gas and Electric Corporation v. Public Service Commission of New York. 1980. 447 U.S. 557.

Consolidated Edison Co. v. Public Service Commission of New York. 1980. 447 U.S. 530.

Dahl, Robert. 1956. *A Preface to Democratic Theory.* Chicago: University of Chicago Press.

Democratic Party of the United States v. Wisconsin. 1981. 450 U.S. 107.

Di Palma, Giuseppi. 1979. "The Available State: Problems of Reform." *West European Politics* 2:149–65.

Eckstein, Harry. 1960. *Pressure Group Politics: The Case of the British Medical Association.* Stanford: Stanford University Press.

Finer, S. E. 1966. *Anonymous Empire: A Study of the Lobby in Great Britain.* 2d ed. London: Pall Mall.

First National Bank of Boston v. Bellot. 1978. 435 U.S. 765.

Hirschman, Albert O. 1970. *Exit, Voice, and Loyalty: Responses to Decline in Firms, Organizations, and States.* Cambridge, Mass.: Harvard University Press.

Jordan, Grant, and J. J. Richardson. 1987. *Government and Pressure Groups in Britain.* Oxford: Oxford University Press.

Kelman, Steven. 1981. *Regulating America, Regulating Sweden: A Comparative Study of Occupational Safety and Health Administration.* Cambridge, Mass.: MIT Press.

Kingdon, John. 1973. *Congressmen's Voting Decisions.* New York: Harper and Row.

Kirkpatrick, Jeane J. 1982. *Dictatorship and Double Standards: Nationalism and Reason in Politics.* New York: Simon and Schuster.

Kumar, Martha Joynt, and Michael Baruch Grossman. 1984. "The Presidency and Interest Groups." In *The Presidency and the Political System,* edited by Michael Nelson. Washington, D.C.: Congressional Quarterly Press.

LaPalombara, Joseph. 1964. *Interest Groups in Italian Politics.* Princeton, N.J.: Princeton University Press.

Lehmbruch, Gerhard, and Phillipe C. Schmitter. 1982. *Patterns of Corporatist Policymaking.* Beverly Hills, Calif.: Sage Publications.

Lowi, Theodore J. 1969. *The End of Liberalism: Ideology, Policy, and the Crisis of Public Authority.* New York: W. W. Norton.

Lundquist, Lennart. 1980. *The Hare and the Tortoise: Clean Air Policies in the United States and Sweden.* Ann Arbor: University of Michigan Press.

Madison, James, Alexander Hamilton, and John Jay. 1961. *Federalist Papers,* edited by Clinton Rossiter. New York: Mentor Books.

Milbrath, Lester. 1963. *Washington Lobbyists.* Chicago: Rand McNally.

NAACP v. Alabama. 1958. 357 U.S. 449.

NAACP v. Button. 1963. 371 U.S. 415.

Nelson, Robert, John P. Heinz, Edward O. Lauman, and Robert Salisbury. 1987. "Private Representation in Washington: Surveying the Structure of Influence." *American Bar Foundation Research Journal* 1:141–202.

New Orleans v. Dukes. 1976. 427 U.S. 297.

Nordlinger, Eric. 1981. *On the Autonomy of the Democratic State.* Cambridge, Mass.: Harvard University Press.

Olson, Mancur. 1982. *The Rise and Decline of Nations: Economic Growth, Stagflation and Social Rigidities.* New Haven, Conn.: Yale University Press.

Orren, Karen. 1976. "Standing to Sue: Interest Group Conflict in the Federal Court." *American Political Science Review* 70:723–41.

Pennock, Roland J. 1962. " 'Responsible Government,' Separated Powers and Special Interests: Agricultural Subsidies in Great Britain and America." *American Political Science Review* 56:621–33.

Rokkan, Stein. 1966. "Norway: Numerical Democracy and Corporate Pluralism." In *Political Oppositions in Western Democracies,* edited by Robert Dahl. New Haven, Conn.: Yale University Press.

Santa Clara County v. Southern Pacific Railway. 118 U.S. 394.

Schattschneider, Elmer E. 1960. *The Semi-Sovereign People.* New York: Holt, Rinehart and Winston.

Schmitter, Philippe C. 1974. "Still the Century of Corporatism?" *Review of Politics* 36:85–131.

Schmitter, Philippe C., and Gerhard Lehmbruch, eds. 1979. *Trends towards Corporatist Intermediation.* Beverly Hills, Calif.: Sage Publications.

Schmitter, Philippe C., and Wolfgang Streeck, eds. 1985. *Private Interest Government beyond Market and State.* Beverly Hills: Sage Publications.

Self, Peter, and Herbert J. Storing. 1963. *The State and the Farmer: British Agricultural Policies and Politics.* Berkeley: University of California Press.

Shapiro, Martin. 1986. "The Supreme Court's 'Return' to Economic Regulation." *Studies in American Political Development* 1:91–141.

Skocpol, Theda. 1985. *Bringing the State Back In,* edited by Peter Evans and Dietrich Rueschemeyer. Cambridge: Cambridge University Press.

Stepan, Alfred. 1978. *The State and Society: Peru in Comparative Perspective.* Princeton, N.J.: Princeton University Press.

Tocqueville, Alexis de. [1840] 1986. *De la Democratic en Amerique* [Democracy in America], edited by H. G. Nicholas. London: Macmillan.

Verba, Sidney, and Norman Nie. 1972. *Participation in America: Political Democracy and Social Equality.* New York: Harper and Row.

Vogel, David. 1986. *National Styles of Regulation: Environmental Policy in Great Britain and the United States.* Ithaca, New York: Cornell University Press.

Wilson, Graham K. 1977a. "Department Secretaries: Are They Really a President's 'Natural Enemies'? " *British Journal of Political Science* 7:273–99.

———. 1977b. *Special Interests and Policymaking: Agricultural Policies and Politics in Britain and the United States of America.* New York: John Wiley and Sons.

————. 1978. "Farmers' Organizations in Advanced Economics." In *International Perspectives in Rural Sociology,* edited by Howard Newby. New York: John Wiley and Sons.

————. 1985. *Politics of Safety and Health: Occupational Safety and Health in the United States and Britain.* Oxford: Clarendon Press.

The Constitution and the Federal System

★ 9 ★

The Irony of the Federal Constitution's Genius: State Constitutional Development

KERMIT L. HALL

In 1857 the English historian Thomas Babington Macaulay described the U.S. Constitution as "all sail and no anchor" (quoted in Bartlett, 1955:494). Macaulay believed that centrifugal social demands, most notably slavery, would ultimately rip the fabric of America's ruling document. In the short run, he was prescient; little more than four years later the nation exploded in its greatest constitutional crisis, the Civil War. Over the long haul, however, the forces of sail and anchor balanced one another far more effectively than Macaulay imagined. No other nation has had a longer history of government under a written constitution, a development that scholars attribute to the framers' foresight, the structure of the Constitution itself, or both (Kelly, Harbison, and Belz, 1983:86–106).[1] The difficult amending process in Article V, for example, has shielded the Constitution from abrupt change, while the Supreme Court, sitting as a kind of continuing constitutional convention, has invoked judicial review to forge broad changes in public life through appeal to the rule of law (Hall, 1985). Sir William Gladstone, another nineteenth-century Englishman, concluded that the resulting combination of stability and adaptability formed the "genius" of the Constitution. He described the document as "the most remarkable work . . . to have been produced by the human intellect, at a single stroke . . . " (quoted in Bartlett, 1955:534).

Much present-day scholarship echoes this Gladstonean analysis by interpreting the nation's constitutional history and public law as the unfolding majesty of the federal document (Scheiber, 1981). State constitutions, on the other hand, have received short shrift, even though they were the "first" American constitutions by more than a decade, even though they provided the crucial working models for the framers in Philadelphia, and even though they have historically provided much of the grist for the nation's rich constitutional politics. The Massachusetts Constitution of 1780, for example, is the world's oldest written frame of government in use (Reardon, 1982). Despite this inheritance, state constitutions have not claimed the scholarly attention or public prestige that the federal document has. Law schools, where such matters should be taken seriously, devote far more attention to federal constitutional law than to the public law of the states (Williams, 1985). Scholars from other disciplines have been only slightly more attentive.[2]

An analysis of state constitutions promises to shed new light on the extent to which the "genius"—the ability to be both anchor and sail—of the federal Constitution has been shared by its state counterparts and what, if anything, the federal document has contributed to their development. Both the federal Constitution and state constitutions (and the constitutional systems they have established) have resonated to social and economic demands (Hall, 1989:480–85). But to say that state constitutions tended to mirror social demands, like the assertion that they have been neglected, is only the beginning of wisdom.

This essay explores some of the implications of the federal and state documents for each other and for the political process they have shaped. It first examines some state constitutional developments that are related to specific provisions in the federal document and probes the ways in which state constitutional provisions served to "fill in" the blank pages intentionally left incomplete by the framers in Philadelphia.[3] It then charts the consequences of the states' filling in these blank pages by examining the history of state constitutional traditions. The essay concludes that in some ways the "genius" of the Constitution backfired as far as state constitutions were concerned. Populist and majoritarian impulses in the states produced documents of ever greater length that were more like codes than fundamental laws. They constrained the operations of state governments and prompted social and economic minorities to secure federal constitutional authority to regulate the consequences of industrialization and to fulfill the rising expectations for social equality. Stronger central government was the ironic consequence of the propensity of state constitutions to become more anchor than sail.

The Relationship between the Federal
and State Constitutions

On first impression, the impact of the federal Constitution on the state documents would seem huge, so great that the former would seem to swallow up the latter. The federal Constitution is, as Article VI proclaims, supreme; the states cannot without impunity violate its explicit mandates. While the Constitution is subordinate only to the people of the United States, the state constitutions are subordinate to the national Constitution in substantial ways, as well as to the people of the states. Even accepting that the federal document is one of enumerated powers (considerably expanded by the "necessary and proper" clause in Article I), the fact remains that the framers of state constitutions have crafted their constitutional identities within this national framework (Elazar, 1982a; Hall, Hyman, and Sigal, 1981).

The original text and amendments to the Constitution comprise a mix of restrictions and guarantees that have defined the boundaries of state constitutions. Today, for example, the federal document prohibits states from abridging individual rights, granting titles of nobility, coining money, conducting foreign policy, engaging in war, laying duties on tonnage, maintaining troops and a navy, making compacts with other states, and collecting poll taxes in federal elections.[4] These prohibitions are real limitations on the discretion of state constitution makers. Perhaps the most vivid evidence of the federal Constitution's shaping influence appeared during Reconstruction in the states of the former Confederacy. To gain readmittance to the Union, these states had to abjure the "right" of secession and embrace the broad commands of the Fourteenth Amendment. As the North Carolina Constitution of 1868 proclaimed: "every citizen of this State owes paramount allegiance to the Constitution and Government of the United States . . . " (Article I, Section 4). In more recent times, passage of the Sixteenth Amendment, authorizing a federal income tax, has produced a series of "federalized" amendments to state constitutions authorizing the definition or computation of income for state tax purposes by reference to federal law (Sturm, 1982).

The text of the federal Constitution also provides certain guarantees to the states that tailor their fundamental laws just as much as the prohibitions do. Article IV, for example, guarantees every state a republican form of government and the privilege of calling on the federal government to protect it from internal domestic upheaval. It also directs the federal government to protect the states from foreign invasion and ensure equality for a citizen of one state in another state. Section 2 of the Fourteenth Amendment guarantees that apportionment in the national Congress shall be based on population in the states.

The federal Constitution has a symbiotic relationship with state constitutions. Many of the provisions of the federal Constitution were shaped by the framers' initial experience with state constitution making. As Willi Paul Adams (1980) has shown, the framers in Philadelphia borrowed heavily from their experience with such matters as separation of powers, popular sovereignty, and an independent judiciary. As a growing and restless American population spread across the face of the continent, the states of the ever-moving West mimicked their eastern counterparts, but they also copied, in form and spirit, the broad principles of constitutionalism embodied in the federal document. A sort of cult of the Constitution appeared almost immediately, and the framers of subsequent state constitutions believed that their documents reflected the same spirit of republican government that had informed events in Philadelphia (Kammen, 1986:22–23).

The federal courts and Congress have translated federal constitutional provisions into meaningful, if often hotly disputed, guidelines for state constitution makers. The Thirteenth, Fourteenth, and Fifteenth amendments, for example, clothed federal judges with substantial authority, if they wished to invoke it, to alter state constitutional practices dealing with race relations and the distribution of political power. In the last part of the nineteenth century, constitution makers in the South fashioned fundamental frames of government that aimed to preserve white supremacy. Racial segregation became a matter of fundamental law, and the Supreme Court countenanced it as such. As early as 1870, the Tennessee Constitution provided that no school aided by the state "shall allow white and negro children to be received as scholars together" (Article XI, Section 12). Segregation and disfranchisement went hand in hand. The Mississippi Constitution of 1890 set up a poll tax of two dollars and imposed reading requirements on all electors. The federal courts tested many of these provisions, finding a few wanting but sustaining most. In *Williams v. Mississippi* (1898) the Supreme Court approved both the literacy and poll-tax provisions of the Mississippi Constitution. On the other hand, it ruled unconstitutional the so-called grandfather clauses in several southern state constitutions that excused the sons and grandsons of Civil War white voters from having to meet educational and property qualifications (*Gunn v. the United States*, 1915). In the mid-twentieth century, the Court reversed its direction, and in *Brown v. Board of Education* (1954), it wiped out entire sections of southern state constitutional law.[5]

Congress, too, has frequently shaped state constitutional development. After the creation of the Union by the original thirteen states, the process of admitting new states became a function wholly controlled by the national government, specifically Congress. Article IV, Section 4, of the U.S. Constitution required the federal government to guarantee that each new state had a "republican form of government."[6] Since the vastness of the continent created anxiety over the coherence and stability of a nation of individual republics, Congress took care to ensure that the people of the new states would understand themselves to be citizens of the larger nation, sharing not only a commitment to republican rights and liberties but also an allegiance to the larger polity based on those principles. One consequence was an extraordinary degree of mimesis by state constitution makers. After all, their chief objective was to gain admission to the Union, and they paved the road to statehood by adopting the constitutional provisions of existing states (Hurst, 1950:336).

The constitutional authority of Congress to set terms of admission of new states, when combined with the "guarantee" clause, shaped substantive state policies. Public education was a notable example. The federal government supported under the "guarantee" clause the working assumption that public education was an "essential feature of a republican government based upon the will of the people" (Tyak, James, and Benavot, 1987: 20). Congress in the nineteenth century, building on the Northwest Ordinance of 1787, supported this goal through grants of public lands to the states, stipulating that the states would devote part of the public domain to foster public education. Nineteenth-century state constitution makers responded by devising ever more elaborate provisions guaranteeing public education and mandating bureaucratic structures in detailed constitutional provisions. The federal document, through congressional initiative, thus pressed upon the states specific requirements for institution building.

The inherent superiority of the federal Constitution belies the considerable discretion enjoyed by the states, both in chartering their constitutional course and, as the experience with the Civil War and Reconstruction amendments suggests, in diluting the force of federal pronouncements. Moreover, the federal Constitution, while it mentions the states some fifty times, does not specify anything about the operation of state government, except that it should be republican in character. The federal Constitution, as Donald Lutz reminds us, was *"by design* an incomplete document" (1982:38), meaning that the Constitution did not describe fully the operation of government and politics throughout the nation. The framers purposefully left that task to state constitution makers, a responsibility that meant that the states forged the main lines of the American political process and provided for day-to-day governance on a host of social and economic matters.

Much of the constitutional history of the states (as well as the nation) can be understood as a working out of the implications of the incomplete nature of the federal document. Succeeding generations of Americans have adapted their organic laws to changing social and economic circumstances. The proximity of the states to these pressures meant that constitutional experimentation became much more brisk there than at the federal level. These innovations included, among others, popular election of judges, woman suffrage, equal rights for women, black suffrage, the income tax, and prohibition. Proposed amendments to today's federal Constitution calling for a balanced federal budget and the line-item veto merely confirm an existing pattern of the nation's borrowing from the states (Hall, Hyman, and Sigal, 1981).[7]

The states have been the world's oldest and most active laboratories of constitutional experimentation. Despite social, geographical, and economic differences, they have had remarkably similar experiences. All state constitutions have organized the polity, the relations between the state and its people, and the responsibilities of its officers. They also have been documents of constitutional law that embrace such concepts as sovereignty, individual rights, separation of powers, and judicial review. Each has provided for a legislature (and all of them today except Nebraska are bicameral), an elected chief executive, and a judiciary. In these respects, they have mirrored the federal Constitution, and their provisions underscore that even the incomplete nature of that higher law did not make state constitutional development a free-for-all. Moreover, like the federal document, state constitutions have rested governmental authority on popular consent (Elazar, 1982a).

State constitutions derive from several historical epochs. Although most can be dated from the nineteenth century, the heyday of state constitutional development, eighteen were either created or totally rewritten in the twentieth century. Three documents—Massachusetts (1780), New Hampshire (1784), and Vermont (1793)—are products of the eighteenth century. Fifteen state constitutions were formulated during the last quarter of the nineteenth century, eleven date from the period 1860–74, and three from the first half of the nineteenth century.[8]

Most state constitutions have also been remarkably pliable, a quality essential to their function of filling the vacant spaces of the federal document. Revision of the federal Constitution has proceeded gradually and incrementally. There has never been a second federal constitutional convention. The state experience has been the opposite; states have easily shed one organic law for an entirely new one. There have been 239 separate constitutional conventions, and since the beginning of the republic there has never been a three-year period in which at least one state constitutional convention or, more recently, a constitutional revision commission has not met. Since 1776 the fifty states have operated under no fewer than 146 constitutions, and thirty-one of the fifty states have had two or more constitutions. Eighteen states have had four or more constitutions, with Louisiana topping the list with eleven. On average each state constitution has been amended four times more frequently than the federal document. Through 1985 more than 8,000 amendments to state constitutions were proposed and more than 5,000 of these were adopted (Sturm, 1982).[9]

All of this activity suggests a key feature of state constitutions: they have increasingly become codes rather than fundamental frames of government. Today the federal Constitution is composed of approximately 7,300 words; only the Vermont Constitution among the states is shorter, at an estimated 6,600 words. In 1776 the average length of state constitutions was 7,150 words; by 1985 it ballooned to approximately 26,150 words.[10] The present Alabama Constitution, at approximately 250,000 words, is now the nation's longest, a distinction that the quarter-million-word Louisiana Constitution claimed until it was drastically shortened in 1974 (Sturm, 1982).

State constitutions, unlike the federal document, have evolved into lengthy documents of modest age that have been repeatedly amended and frequently re-created entirely. As stable representations of fundamental principles and timeless structures they pale before the federal Constitution. The federal character of the national document encouraged this development by granting the states significant discretion in shaping their own constitutions (Elazar, 1982b).

Patterns of State Constitutional Development

As documents essential to the functioning of the incomplete federal constitution and as subordinate entities to it, state constitutions reflected distinctive regional traditions or patterns of development. Each of these reveals the way in which state constitution makers at a particular time adapted fundamental law to constituent social and economic pressures, prevailing ideological assumptions about the nature of government, and the dictates as well as the opportunities created by the incomplete federal Constitution.

The Genesis of State Constitutional Development

The first of these constitutional traditions emerged from the same matrix of colonial precedent, English political dissent, and revolution that fostered the federal Constitution (Adrian, 1968; Nevins, 1924:114–40; Lutz, 1979).[11] The *Whig-Republican tradition* appeared between 1776 and 1800, and it mixed notions of republicanism, popular sovereignty, distrust of executive authority, and communitarianism through social contract theory (Elazar, 1982b). It set standards for representation that abetted political inequality as we understand it today, since it excluded women and blacks from political participation and often required a modest freehold to vote and hold office. The legislative branch had great authority to determine community goals and enforce compliance. The state took precedence over the individual, but these documents also made the protection of rights one of the primary purposes of government. By about 1800, formal bills of rights, which limited state interference with individuals (and which had not been part of many of the first state constitutions), became common (Lutz, 1979).

The Whig-Republican tradition incorporated such concepts as small electoral districts, short tenure in office, many elective offices, sharp separation of powers (including an independent judiciary), and constituent instruction of representatives. These brief documents, like the federal Constitution that was so extensively based on them, broadly stated the first principles of government and left to subsequent generations the task of adapting them to the exigencies of social and economic change (Lutz, 1980).[12] Over time, of course, the federal judiciary (and Congress) performed this task at the national level, while in the states more formal modes of direct constitutional change—constitutional conventions, amendments, and direct popular control through the initiative and referendum—eventually took hold.

The *federalist tradition* was established by Federalist delegates to the Philadelphia Convention in 1787 who challenged many features of this Whig-Republican tradition. The dominant group, led by James Madison of Virginia, crafted provisions in the federal document designed to stem radical majoritarianism in the states and to enhance the authority of the new national Union. These Federalists, like spokesmen for the Whig-Republican tradition in the states, embraced the idea that all powers of government derived from the people, but they purposefully curbed the direct impact of popular sovereignty on the national government. They did so by asserting the supremacy of the federal Constitution and then balancing individual and group interests by means of larger electoral districts, longer tenures of office, an independent judiciary (which held office during good behavior), limited numbers of elective offices, and a system of separated institutional sharing of powers (Elazar, 1982b).

A second group of Federalists, led by Alexander Hamilton, believed in an even more comprehensive expansion of national powers. Their goal was to enhance the wealth of the nation by protecting property holders and promoting the nation's commercial interests through government action. They were even more critical than the Madisonians of what they perceived to be the great authority exercised by state legislatures. They succeeded in strengthening the executive at the expense of the legislative branch in the federal Constitution, a development that also became common in the states by about 1800. These Federalists embraced what Daniel Elazar has called the *"managerial tradition"* (1982b:13, emphasis added). Principles of commerce were central to this conception of constitutionalism, since the purpose of the polity was to support the commercial classes. Hamilton accepted that popular will should be the basis of sovereign authority, but he also believed that the wishes of the people should be virtually rather than actually represented. A strong chief executive, whether president or governor, was supposed to rationally administer public affairs free from political and popular influence. The growing wealth of the American commercial empire would redound eventually to the benefit of all citizens. Of course, the Antifederalists who opposed the Constitution rejected just this view of representation and executive authority, but the managerial tradition composed an important challenge to the much more democratic and localistic Whig-Republican tradition (Lutz, 1980).

The Whig-Republican tradition took firmest root in New England, where it remains important today (Sturm, 1982:60–63), but modifications, as the federalist and managerial patterns suggest, quickly appeared. State political leaders adapted their fundamental laws to correspond to particular social and economic interests. These early constitutions, of course, were conceptual documents that, like the federal Constitution, broadly stated their objectives; however, they were shaped as much by interests as by abstract ideas. State constitutions in almost every instance, save for New England where the Whig-Republican tradition persisted, became increasingly specific and lengthy, reflecting in their mounting detail not only changing conceptions of the role of government but also the consequences of moving from an eighteenth-century agrarian society to the postindustrial present.

Nineteenth-Century Patterns of Development

This process of adaptation, given the various sociopolitical cultures and economies in the different regions of the nation, produced several other constitutional patterns. Each of these was a variation or an amalgamation of the Whig-Republican, federalist, and managerial models (Elazar, 1982b:20).[13]

The Whig-Republican tradition underwent the least modification in New England, a region that has historically had the briefest constitutions and the ones least responsive to governmental fads. These documents embraced a distinctively American principle, that of the commonwealth. These documents, despite their brevity, did more than sketch a basic framework of government and provide for individual rights. They also nourished legislative activism, with a veiw to harnessing a state's resources to release the creative potential of its people (Hurst, 1956:2). The "commonwealth idea," Leonard W. Levy has written, "was essentially a quasi-mercantilism conception of the state within a democractic framework." In Europe, where the state was not responsible to the people and was the product of remote historical forces, mercantilism served the ruling classes who contolled the state (1957:305). In America, under the commonwealth theory of constitutional government, the state became intensely real and immediate. The state was the "common wealth" of all the people, and government was responsible for effecting it.

Massachusetts became the model of this *commonwealth tradition*. There, for example, the state legislature drew on the extensive police powers granted it in the Constitution to regulate weights and measures, provide standard measures for commodities, establish rules for packaging, and provide for inspection to ensure that laws are followed. Typical was the remarkably detailed regulation of the nail-making industry in Massachusetts. In a series of statutes, the General Court (the legislature of the state) set exacting standards for the number, size, and weight of iron nails to be packed in casks (Handlin and Handlin, 1947:66–67).

This commonwealth principle strongly influenced the antebellum, free northern states, but in at least eight of them a variant pattern appeared, *commercial republicanism.* The commercial-republican tradition spread into the Trans-Appalachian West and beyond as migrants from New England and the Middle States adapted their learned constitutional traditions to new surroundings. Throughout the nineteenth century these documents embodied compromises resulting from conflict among rival ethnic and economic interests and the overlapping tension generated between the growing commercial cities and the still-influential agricultural regions within each state. The constitutions of the commercial-republican tradition grew in length, in part because compromising these tensions required more, rather than fewer, words and in part because their framers pursued a mercantilist policy designed to promote commercial economic development through these constitutions. The pursuit of commercial wealth shaped such provisions as the organization of local government, public education, and public welfare, as can be seen in the Illinois Constitution of 1848 (Elazar, 1970). Like the constitutions of the commonwealth tradition, the new commercial-republican documents relied on promotion and regulation to enhance the economy, but they differed from the commonwealth constitutions in that they also sought compromise among contending economic groups (farmers and merchants) and rival ethnic groups.

At the same time, the slave states of the South, which were much more sympathetic to the federalist model, fashioned a southern *contractual pattern* (Elazar, 1982b: 21). The organic laws of the South also had mercantilist objectives, and they too grew in length compared with the simple documents of the Whig-Republican tradition. Their framers had the additional burden of perpetuating a social and economic system rooted first in slavery and later in segregation. Constitution makers in these states, especially after Reconstruction, increasingly sought to maintain the social order by adding provisions involving race and economic matters that were left to legislative discretion in most other regions of the country. This southern contractual tradition was typified by a diffusion of authority among many offices to accommodate the swings between "oligarchy and factionalism characteristic of Southern state politics" (Elazar, 1982b:21). Because of the fluctuating balance of factions in many southern states, the framers of their constitutions included materials typically the subject of ordinary legislation outside the section.[14]

The rise of mass political parties in the mid-1830s contributed to the diffusion of constitutional traditions, the increasing detail that filled most fundamental frames of government outside New England, and the negative tone of these documents. As Morton Keller has observed, state constitutions of this era became "deeply mired in party politics and changing social and economic interests" (1981: 71). In state constitutional conventions, which heretofore had usually witnessed benign factionalism and deferential politics, Whigs and Jacksonian Democrats struggled to legitimate their partisan goals through recourse to constitutional authority. They politicized constitution making along partisan lines and developed the practice of constitutional legislation (i.e., writing into constitutions specific provisions that could not be won through the usual legislative processes). The less troublesome, but nonetheless contentious, issues involved free public education, state support for the indigent, and an end to religious tests for political participation. In the South constitution makers formally recognized the institution of slavery, and in almost every state they extended the franchise to adult white males (Hurst, 1950:237–40). The notion of state constitutions as fundamental frames of government waned, and constitutional legislation appeared with greater frequency.[15]

The states' roles in economic development provoked the most serious partisan wrangling. Notwithstanding the formal division of sovereignty in American federalism, the states exercised the most influence over public policy before the Civil War. Using police powers, concurrent power over interstate commerce, and the power of eminent domain, state lawmakers formulated mercantilist policies. They broadly construed their constitutional authority to promote banking, internal improvements, and transportation. State appellate courts lent their support as well by embracing an instrumental conception of the common law that rewarded risk taking and freed the creative energies of individuals in the marketplace (Handlin and Handlin, 1947; Hurst, 1956).

The political aftershocks of the Panic of 1837, however, sparked many state constitution makers to curb mercantilist policies and spendthrift legislatures. The delegates to the Ohio constitutional convention of 1850–51, for example, had soured on the legislature's enthusiasm for public promotion of canals and railroads. They placed language in the new constitution that restricted the power of the state legislature to authorize theretofore popular "loans of credit" to local governments (Gold, 1985).

This reaction to the Panic of 1837 had two important long-term consequences. First, state constitutions departed from the republican model by limiting the power of legislative bodies. These documents increasingly became a litany of restrictions—of thou-shalt-nots. These prohibitions, which aimed to reduce the influence of special interests on state government, dramatically increased the length of constitutions. The Ohio Constitution of 1851, for example, was almost twice as long as its predecessor. Constitutional revision increasingly became the conduct of legislation—or of politics—through other means, and the documents themselves resembled statutory codes rather than organic laws (Keller, 1981).

Second, judicial and executive authority grew apace as state government evolved even more into a shared exercise of power among the three branches. The judiciary became popularly elected for limited terms of office, a reform that simultaneously made judges more accountable to public needs while granting them a popular base from which to scrutinize legislative enactments. Long-suffering chief executives received additional authority to veto legislation, to exercise the pardoning power, and to make appointments (Hall, 1983).

Except in New England, where the commonwealth variant of the Whig-Republican tradition persisted, state constitutions reflected a deep suspicion of government, itself a reaction to the growing influence of parties in American life. The quest for more democratic government during these years was nothing less than a search for greater popular accountability in government. The Mississippi Constitution of 1832 merged increased openness in government with antigovernmentalism, a pattern that became commonplace later in the nineteenth century. Mississippi, at the cutting edge of the expanding southern frontier, provided for universal white manhood suffrage, the election of all state officers, the replacement of county courts by elected boards of police as county governing boards, and the election of all judges (Keller, 1981).

Persistent antigovernmentalism also surfaced in the increasingly difficult provisions made for constitutional amendment and in the acceptance of the idea that the work of constitutional conventions had to be submitted to the public for ratification. Having subdued legislative authority, mid-nineteenth-century constitution makers were loath to have their work easily undone. Constitutional conventions became all the more important and further politicized constitutional development (Hurst, 1950:207–8). Under such circumstances, constitutional conventions became arenas for working out particular, ongoing conflicts rather than restating fundamental principles (Keller, 1981). Issues that proved intractable in the regular legislative process could be resolved only through constitutional conventions, and more often than not the solution was to limit the power of the state.

This populist approach to state constitutions rejected the older Whig-Republican notion of communitarianism and substituted an essentially negative, antigovernmental conception that sought to balance diverse social and geographical interests within the states through public law. Like the national document, state constitutions exemplified the deep distrust with which state residents viewed their governments and their representatives. Unlike the national document, however, these populistic state constitutions were far more susceptible to majority control (Elazar, 1982b).

State constitutions began to lose the creative energy—the sail-like quality—of earlier decades at about the same time the expensive qualities of federal fundamental law became apparent. The pre–Civil War generation had enormous confidence in its ability to shape events through state constitutions, but these increasingly wordy frames of government offered, as their framers intended, limited interpretive possibilities. For example, the incidence of state appellate courts' overturning legislative enactments rose dramatically in the 1850s because the judiciary had to apply the many restrictive provisions in state constitutions and because state appellate judges were typically elected and, therefore, poorly situated to expand significantly the active role of government (Hall, 1984b). At the same time, their more independent federal counterparts, led by Chief Justice John Marshall, creatively applied the open provisions of the federal document in adapting constitutional law to the exigencies of social and economic change (Friedman, 1985:355–57).[16] James Bryce in 1880 reported how far this process had gone: "We find a great deal of matter [in state constitutions] which is in no distinctive sense constitutional law, but of general law. . . . We find minute provisions regarding the management and liabilities of banking companies, or railways, or of corporations generally." Bryce went on to observe that "the framers of these more recent constitutions have in fact neither wished nor cared to draw a line of distinction between what is proper for a constitution and what ought to be left to be dealt with by the State legislature" ([1889] 1959:116).

Bryce also concluded that as a result of these changes the states had begun to lose authority to the federal government. He argued that in the original "partitionment of government functions between the nation and the States, [the] State got the most but the nation the highest, so the balance between the two [was] preserved," but following the Civil War a transformation occurred in which state constitutions gradually lost not only the power to mold conclusively the course of public policy in areas they once exclusively dominated but also their prestige in relation to the federal Constitution ([1889] 1959:425).

The decline of state constitutions after the Civil War was partly the result of federal constitutional developments, but the growing rigidity of many state documents contributed to this development. Bryce was certainly right that the antigovernmental, populist, and lengthy character of these documents made them codes rather than organic laws, but he did not fully appreciate that this enhanced the authority of the national government. For example, the justices of the Supreme Court employed the equal protection and due process clauses of the Fourteenth Amendment to interfere in the states' attempts to regulate social and economic policies through their police powers. From the 1880s through the 1930s the justices invoked the doctrine of substantive due process to bolster property rights and to limit state regulation of the economy. When the agenda of the Court later switched to matters of civil liberties and civil rights, the justices relied on the same amendment to supervise race relations and criminal justice, areas previously the domain of state government (Hall, 1985:37–49).

State constitutional development after the Civil War, as in earlier periods, responded to social demands (Mauer, 1983:1–6). In the southern states, for example, the contract model had to be modified to permit the seceded states to reenter the Union, to define the legal condition of millions of former slaves, and to take account of the enormous burden of public indebtedness incurred during the war (Orth, 1986:120–32). Throughout the nation, moreover, state governments had to adapt to an emerging industrial market economy, urbanization, and the political corruption that accompanied both.

With the practice of partisan interference in state constitution making firmly established in the pre–Civil War era, competing social and economic interests in the 1870s and later aggressively competed to control state fundamental law, usually at the expense of legislative discretion. Many social reformers, workers, and farmers complained that state legislatures were vulnerable to big business, especially railroads. Merchants in growing urban areas were equally concerned that they were suffering at the hands of out-of-state railroad operators, who were seemingly free to set freight rates. The framers of the Illinois Constitution of 1870, for example, revamped the judiciary, strengthened the chief executive, and clamped twenty-three explicit prohibitions on the legislature (Article IV, Section 22). A special article dealt in seven long sections with the regulation of grain elevators and warehouses. In still another section the constitution commanded the legislature to "correct abuses and prevent unjust discrimination in the rates of freight and passenger tariffs on the different railroads in this State" (Article XI, Section 15).[17]

The constitutions of the new western states were much the same, although their distance from the settled East and their small and relatively homogenous populations encouraged the development of another distinct constitutional tradition—the *frame of government*. The constitutions of these states embraced the republican and democratic impulses of the late nineteenth century, but they stressed the structure of state government and the distribution of powers within it more than their eastern and southern counterparts did (Elazar, 1982b).[18] Special constitutional legislation and clear restraints on government also pervaded even these documents. The Washington Constitution of 1889 outlawed free railroad passes and admonished the legislature to "pass laws establishing reasonable maximum rates of charge for the transportation of passengers and freight and to correct abuses" (Article XII, Section 18 and 22). The Colorado Constitution of 1876 and the Idaho document of 1889 provided specific protections for miners and prohibited the use of children in underground mining (Article XVI, Section 2; Article XIII, Section 4, respectively). Still other western constitutions established merit-selection plans for civil servants, ordered the preservation of natural resources, and granted women the right to vote (Friedman, 1985:351).

Whereas the states had earlier pursued a promotional role in economic development, they now engaged in regulatory activity based on their police powers. The framers of state constitutions cast a wary eye over railroads and other business corporations, and they expected independent regulatory commissions to blunt the influence of big business. Framers of the California Constitution of 1879, for example, sought to frustrate railroad magnate Collis P. Huntington's control over the state assembly by establishing an independent railroad commission to regulate passenger and freight rates within the state (Article XI, Section 4).[19] Administrative bureaucracy and antigovernmentalism were reciprocal and reinforcing concepts in late nineteenth-century America, although by the mid-twentieth century advocates of limited government made government bureaucracy itself an object of criticism (Sturm, 1982).[20]

This antigovernmental bias surfaced in other ways. For example, long-standing agitation over state courts culminated in elaborate judiciary articles that specified the jurisdiction and organization of these courts. Governors gained additional authority, most notably through longer terms of office and the line-item veto. They also lost some administrative control to the new regulatory agencies and some political power in civil service reforms (Nelson, 1982:49).

Antigovernmentalism went hand in hand with localism. Rapid urbanization after the Civil War created new centers of local power. Between 1865 and 1875, local governments went on a borrowing binge to fund services for their rapidly growing populations and to provide an adequate infrastructure for economic development. The depression of 1873–77 ruined local and state credit ratings and fueled measures, even more far-reaching than those following the Panic of 1837, that clamped strict controls on public borrowing.

The framers of state constitutions added teeth to earlier limits on local borrowing and state liability in case of defalcation. At the same time, they granted home rule to local towns and cities, a process begun in the Missouri Constitution of 1876. Home rule allowed communities to organize into corporations free to conduct their affairs so long as they abided by the applicable constitutional provisions. Although they were not sovereign entities, local governments further accentuated the trend in state government to balance and share powers (Swindler, 1958).

These state constitutions also had important social functions, especially in the South with its strong contractual tradition of limited government. There, constitution makers, who were skeptical of invoking state constitutional authority to empower government in fiscal and economic matters, were anxious to write racial policies into public law. A distinctively southern pattern emerged (Mauer, 1983).[21] Immediately after the Civil War, the former Confederate states experienced a decade-long orgy of federally imposed constitution making. The radical state constitutions of the South disrupted the old centers of social and political power and created in their place new ones based on black votes. A decade later, Bourbon leaders redeemed the old centers by writing white supremacy into state constitutions. These documents, and the legislation they authorized, prohibited intermarriage between the races, provided for segregation of schools, and imposed race-based suffrage requirements. After the 1870s and 1880s when some southern states experimented with less restrictive documents in economic and fiscal matters, the region as a whole clambered aboard the antigovernmental bandwagon (Kousser, 1974).

By the end of the century, state constitutions were substantial, if cumbersome, facts of public life. They were very different from their federal counterpart. Over the previous century, state constitutions had evolved into diffuse, overly long, negative documents that on the whole prevented the positive exercise of public authority, especially in fiscal and economic matters. As Woodrow Wilson observed in 1887, "It is getting harder to *run* a constitution than to frame one" (quoted in Keller, 1981).

Progressive Constitutionalism in the First Half of the Twentieth Century

The most recent state constitutional tradition emerged at the beginning of the twentieth century. The *Progressive model* echoed many of the principles of Hamilton's managerial scheme, but it also incorporated features drawn from the frame-of-government tradition. Progressive constitutionalism, while strongest in the Midwest and the West, was the first truly national approach to state constitutions, because it permeated every section and had a vigorous national spokesman in Senator Robert M. La Follette of Wisconsin (Elazar, 1982b).[22] The Progressive tradition rejected corruption and partisanship in politics and urged greater efficiency through rational methods of bureaucratic administration and strong executive leadership.

Progressives proposed to destroy the antigovernmental bias in state constitutions by making government at once more bureaucratic and democratic but less partisan. The result was an awkward mix of bureaucracy, democracy, and a commitment to rational administration of government on a scientific, rather than partisan, basis. Progressives, for example, urged adoption of the initiative, referendum, and recall, measures that opened state constitutions to direct popular revision and state officials to close public scrutiny. They also, however, sponsored constitutional provisions that required voters to register, prescribed secret ballots, formed at-large electoral districts, and made some elective offices nonpartisan. The emphasis on rational state government based on professional expertise surfaced in the nonpartisan election of judges and later even the less democratic Missouri plan of judical recruitment. All of these measures depressed the level of voters' participation (Sturm, 1982; Hall, 1984b). The new documents also reorganized governmental services into a limited number of departments, created independent boards and commissioners, gave the governor authority to appoint a single department head, and mandated executive budgets (Buck, 1938:7–8, 11; Adrian, 1968).

The Progressive constitutional tradition had important theoretical implications for the character of state government, but as a practical matter it had limited impact. State constitutions continued to swell, and most documents remained essentially negative in character. Change most often came on a piecemeal basis. Of the more than 2,500 amendments proposed during the first thirty-five years of the century, the voters ratified only 60 percent. A significant portion of the public apparently remained attached to documents it knew, whatever their defects, and it regularly rejected significant constitutional innovations that threatened established bases of power. Restricted state government had—and continues to have—a significant public following. Between 1900 and 1950, voters adopted twelve new constitutions (one each in four new states, two in Louisiana, and one each in six existing states), but they also rejected the same number (Keller, 1981).

Post-Progressive Developments: The Resurgence of the Managerial Tradition

Hamilton's managerial tradition, refracted in many cases through Progressive ideals, has received renewed attention since around 1950. Between then and 1981, twenty states undertook to revise their fundamental documents, with the bulk of this activity coming in the 1960s and 1970s. The pressure for change came from several sources. Proponents of constitutional revision stressed the need for more efficient government and constitutions that better fit the realities of the mid-twentieth century. They pointed especially, but not exclusively, to the U.S. Supreme Court decision in *Brown v. Board of Education* (1954), striking down traditional state practices of racial segregation and legislative malapportionment. The malleable quality of federal constitutional law, with its power to protect minority rights from local majorities, generated strong demands in the states to rewrite constitutions in ways that would keep them consonant with the federal document.

There were other sources of change. Inefficiency and inequality became the new code words in national efforts to encourage reform of these state documents. The federally created Kestenbaum Commission on Intergovernmental Relations in 1955 offered a scathing indictment of state government that pinned its inadequacies on outmoded constitutions. "Many State constitutions," the commissioners reported to President Dwight D. Eisenhower, "restrict the scope, effectiveness and adaptability of State and local action.... The Commission believes that most states would benefit from a fundamental review and revision of their constitutions to make sure that they provide for vigorous and responsible government, not forbid it" (Kestenbaum Commission on Intergovernmental Relations, 1955: 37, 56). The commission's report stressed that state constitutions were too long, too detailed, and almost wholly negative. Under such circumstances, the commission argued, the federal government had encroached on areas of governmental responsibility traditionally the province of the states.

The reports rang true. The struggle over apportionment of state legislatures vividly dramatized the unresponsibe and unrepresentative character of state government. Most state legislatures had not accommodated themselves to the twentieth-century population shift from rural to urban areas. As a result, rural and agricultural interests were dramatically overrepresented. The United States Supreme Court's decision in *Baker v. Carr* (1962) opened fresh opportunities for constitutional revision by reapportioning legislatures in ways that gave greater voice to urban and suburban voters. The new crop of state legislators pressed for constitutional modernization based on the Progressive-managerial model.

Efforts to streamline state government through constitutional revision have met with mixed success. Twenty states engaged in significant reform during these years, and the products of their labors reflected the broad outlines of the model state constitution first proposed by the National Municipal League in the 1920s and updated many times since. Many of these state documents also underscore the growing realization that for state constitutions to succeed they must embody some of the sail-like qualities of the federal document. Many new state constitutions, such as those in Illinois and Michigan, contain provisions mandating that on a regular basis (usually ten years) the public will be able to vote on whether to call a constitutional convention or revision commission. The recent history of the constitutional initiative in California and elsewhere shows how susceptible state documents are to popular pressures.

Antigovernmentalism and negative constitutional legislation remain persistent themes in American public life. The citizenry continues to balk at modernization of these documents; voters have rejected about half of all constitutions put forward since 1950. A combination of special interests worried about losing favored positions under existing documents and public suspicion of the ability of government to tax and spend frustrated many reform efforts (Sturm, 1982). In present-day Mississippi, for example, black political leaders, who have found their power enhanced as a result of the federal constitutional revolution in race relations since 1954, balk at proposals by white business reformers who want to revamp the state's 1890 constitution, one of the most racist state constitutions in the nation (Brammer and Winkle, 1986:15–16).

The present-day appeal by conservatives and liberals to state constitutions underscores that the political process continues to shape state constitutional law. State constitutional law remains alive and well, even if the documents on which it rests command less respect than they did two centuries ago. Conservative critics, who believe the federal government has exceeded its authority, urge amendments to the federal Constitution that would emulate provisions in state constitutions restricting the taxing power, mandating a balanced budget, and equipping the chief executive with a line-item veto. Liberals have also laid claim to state constitutions. Proponents of enhanced civil liberties and civil rights, faced with a Supreme Court unwilling to proceed at the pace of the Warren Court, insist that the bills of rights gracing these state documents can be interpreted to raise the ceiling of rights well above the floor established by the federal Constitution (Abrahamson, 1985:306–35; Swindler, 1984). Today, as was true centuries ago, political vision and constitutional legitimacy remain reciprocal and reinforcing.

Conclusion: The Irony of State Constitutions and the Incomplete Federal Constitution

State constitutions since the mid-nineteenth century have reflected the persistent localism and antigovernmentalism underlying much of American political culture. Because of these pressures, and because the framers of the federal Constitution left to the states the task of describing the substantive function of government, the state documents and the federal Constitution have evolved in quite different ways. Instead of growing as flexible, organic laws readily susceptible to judicial modification, state constitutions have, with the notable exception of those in New England, become code-like documents filled with prohibitions against governmental action.

This historical development is filled with irony. The genius of the federal Constitution so ably captured by Macaulay and Gladstone backfired insofar as state constitutions were concerned. Local majorities often filled the blank pages of the incomplete federal document with populistic codes that constrained the operations of state government. This development generated pressures on the federal government to fill the vacuum created by the inability of state governments to respond fully to the transformation of American society and economy that accompanied the Industrial Revolution. The result was a central government more powerful than most of the framers, save for Hamilton and his allies, would have wanted. The growing centralization of national decision making in our day appears as part of a larger historical trend that was itself one of the consequences of the framing of the Constitution more than two centuries ago.

The success of the federal Constitution and the relative unimportance of state constitutions have not been accidental. They have earned their reputations. Unless we are prepared to overhaul the federal system in fundamental ways (which seems unlikely), the political process will be increasingly molded by the adaptive qualities of the federal Constitution rather than the code-like populism and antigovernmentalism of most state constitutions. From time to time the states have been creative laboratories of constitutional change that have foretold future developments in federal public law, but more often than not they have been mostly anchor and little sail.

NOTES

1. For a discussion of the relevant literature, see pp. 779–82.

2. For a listing of the relevant historical literature, see Hall (1984a, vol. 1:506–22). For the literature in other disciplines, see Sturm (1970) and Williams (1985).

3. The concept of the "incomplete" federal Constitution is discussed further below. See also Lutz (1982:38).

4. For a complete listing of the various restraints and guarantees, see Elazar (1972:38–39).

5. For a discussion of how the *Brown* decision undermined existing racial guidelines in southern state constitutions, see Kluger (1976).

6. On the historical development of the "guarantee" clause, see Wiecek (1972).

7. On the balanced budget and line-item veto measures, see Shultz (1935) and Patterson (1986:275–92).

8. For a fuller discussion of these trends and a listing of the beginning dates of the state constitutions, see Sturm and May (1986).

9. For the period 1980–85, see Sturm and May (1986:7).

10. The 1985 figure does not include the numerous local amendings to the Georgia Constitution.

11. Only Rhode Island and Connecticut retained their original colonial charters as organic laws. These early state constitutions did not rest directly on popular consent, as did the nineteenth-century documents of the populist tradition, since they were framed and adopted by the legislatures. This is one instance where the experience of the federal convention carried into the states.

12. On the general problem of original intent in both federal and state constitutions, see Powell (1985).

13. Twenty new states were admitted before the Civil War, and another fifteen existing states rewrote their constitutions in ways that fitted one of these traditions.

14. The civil law inheritance of Louisiana fostered a distinctive constitutional tradition and ultimately produced, at about one-quarter of a million words, the longest state constitution in the nation's history.

15. On the early nineteenth-century state constitutions, see Peterson (1966:3–17, 125–42, 271–85) and Green (1966:285–86).

16. For the example of one state appellate court, see Nelson (1947). On the changing role of state supreme courts in this period, see Kagan, Cartwright, Friedman, and Wheeler (1977).

17. For fuller discussion of these developments, see Friedman (1985:349).

18. These traditions, of course, tend to overlap. Oklahoma, for example, is a state with a small population but, because of its southern antecedents, the one with the longest constitution of the late nineteenth- and early twentieth-century western states.

19. Of course, many constitutions left the responsibility for creating these commissions to the legislature. The Nebraska Constitution of 1875, like other state constitutions, mandated that the legislature had to establish "maximum rates of charges," but the state's Board of Transportation was to make recommendations (Article XI, Section 4). These matters are discussed more fully in Hendrick (1900).

20. On the competing forces of morality and efficiency that gave rise to the administrative state, see Nelson (1982).

21. For a general discussion of the reformulation of post–Civil War southern constitutions, see Mauer (1983). For developments in the North before the Civil War, see Parkinson (1972:83, 116–117, 148–51, 168).

22. The Whig-Republican tradition continued to persist in New England, although even there the Progressive tradition made inroads.

REFERENCES

Abrahamson, Shirley. 1984. "Homegrown Justice: The State Contributors." In *Developments in State Constitutional Law: The Williamsburg Conference*, edited by Bradley McGraw. St. Paul, Minn.: West.

Adams, Willi Paul. 1980. *The First American Constitutions: Republican Ideology and the Making of the State Constitutions in the Revolutionary Era*. Chapel Hill: University of North Carolina Press.

Adrian, Charles R. 1968. "Trends in State Constitutions." *Harvard Journal of Legislation* 5:311–411.

Baker v. Carr. 1962. 369 U.S. 186.

Bartlett, John, ed. 1955. *Familiar Quotations*. 13th ed. Boston: Little, Brown.

Brammer, Dana B., and John W. Winkle, III, eds. 1986. *Contemporary Analysis of Mississippi's Constitutional Government*. University: Bureau of Governmental Research, University of Mississippi.

Brown v. Board of Education. 1954. 347 U.S. 483.

Bryce, James. [1889] 1959. *The American Commonwealth*, edited by Louis Hacker. New York: G. P. Putnam's Sons.

Buck, Arthur E. 1938. *The Reorganization of State Governments in the United States*. New York: Columbia University Press.

Elazar, Daniel J. 1970. *Cities of the Prairie: The Metropolitan Frontier and American Politics*. New York: Basic Books.

———. 1972. *American Federalism: A View from the States*. 2d ed. New York: Harper and Row.

———. 1982a. "State Constitutional Design in the United States and Other Federal Systems." *Publius* 12:1–10.

———. 1982b. "The Principles and Traditions Underlying State Constitutions." *Publius* 12:11–25.

Friedman, Lawrence M. 1985. *A History of American Law*. 2d ed. New York: Simon and Schuster.

Gold, David M. 1985. "Public Aid to Private Enterprise under the Ohio Constitution: Sections 4, 6, and 13 of Article VIII in Historical Perspective." *University of Toledo Law Review* 16:405–64.

Green, Fletcher M. 1966. *Constitutional Development in the South Atlantic States, 1776–1860*. Rev. ed. New York: W. W. Norton.

Gunn v. the United States. 1915. 238 U.S. 347.

Hall, Kermit L. 1983. "The Judiciary on Trial: State Constitutional Reform and the Rise of an Elected Judiciary, 1846–1860." *The Historian* 45:337–54.

Hall, Kermit L., ed. 1984a. *A Comprehensive Bibliography of American Constitutional and Legal History, 1896–1979*. 5 vols. Milwood, N.Y.: Kraus International Publications.

Hall, Kermit L. 1984b. "Progressive Reform and the Decline of Democratic Accountability: The Popular Election of State Supreme Court Judges, 1850–1920." *American Bar Foundation Research Journal* 2:345–70.

———. 1985. *The Supreme Court and Judicial Review in American History.* Washington, D.C.: American Historical Association.

———. 1989. *The Magic Mirror: Law in American History.* New York: Oxford University Press.

Hall, Kermit L., Harold M. Hyman, and Leon V. Sigal, eds. 1981. "Discussion of 'The Politics of State Constitutional Revision, 1820–1930.' " In *The Constitutional Convention as an Amending Device*, edited by Kermit L. Hall, Harold M. Hyman, and Leon V. Sigal. Washington, D.C.: American Historical Association and the American Political Science Association.

Handlin, Oscar, and Mary F. Handlin. 1947. *Commonwealth: A Study of the Role of Government in the American Economy: Massachusetts, 1774–1861.* New York: New York University Press.

Hendrick, Frank. 1900. *Railroad Control by Commission.* New York: G. P. Putnam's Sons.

Hurst, James Willard. 1950. *The Growth of American Law: The Law Makers.* Boston: Little, Brown.

———. 1956. *Law and the Conditions of Freedom in the Nineteenth-Century United States.* Madison: University of Wisconsin Press.

Kagan, Robert A., Bliss Cartwright, Laurence M. Friedman, and Stanton Wheeler. 1977. "The Business of State Supreme Courts, 1870–1970." *Stanford Law Review* 30:121–56.

Kammen, Michael. 1986. *A Machine that Would Go of Itself: The Constitution in American Culture.* New York: Alfred A. Knopf.

Keller, Morton. 1981. "The Politics of State Constitutional Revision, 1820–1930." In *The Constitutional Convention as an Amending Device*, edited by Kermit L. Hall, Harold M. Hyman, and Leon V. Sigal. Washington, D.C.: American Historical Association and the American Political Science Association.

Kelly, Alfred H., Winfred A. Harbison, and Herman J. Belz. 1983. *The American Constitution: Its Origins and Development.* 6th ed. New York: W. W. Norton.

Kestenbaum Commission on Intergovernmental Relations. 1955. *A Report to the President for Transmittal to Congress.* Washington, D.C.: Government Printing Office.

Kluger, Richard. 1976. *Simple Justice: The History of Brown v. Board of Education and Black America's Struggle for Equality.* New York: Alfred A. Knopf.

Kousser, J. Morgan. 1974. *The Shaping of Southern Politics: Suffrage Restriction and the Establishment of the One-Party South, 1880–1910.* New Haven, Conn.: Yale University Press.

Levy, Leonard W. 1957. *Law of the Commonwealth and Chief Justice Shaw.* Cambridge, Mass.: Harvard University Press.

Lutz, Donald S. 1979. "A Theory of Consent in Early State Constitutions." *Publius* 9:11–42.

———. 1980. *Popular Consent and Popular Control: Whig Political Theory in Early State Constitutions.* Baton Rouge: Louisiana State University Press.

———. 1982. "The Purposes of American State Constitutions." *Publius* 12:27–44.

Mauer, John W. 1983. "Southern State Constitutions in the 1870s: A Case Study of Texas." Ph.D. dissertation, Rice University.

Nelson, Margaret V. 1947. *A Study of Judicial Revision in Virginia, 1789–1928.* New York: Columbia University Press.

Nelson, William E. 1982. *The Roots of American Bureaucracy, 1830–1900.* Cambridge, Mass.: Harvard University Press.

Nevins, Allan. 1924. *The American States during and after the Revolution, 1775–1789.* New York: Macmillan.

Orth, John V. 1986. *The Judicial Power of the United States: The Eleventh Amendment in American History.* New York: Oxford University Press.

Parkinson, George Phillips. 1972. "Antebellum State Constitution-Making: Retention, Circumvention, Revision." Ph.D. dissertation, University of Wisconsin.

Patterson, Samuel C. 1968. "The Political Culture of the American States." In *Public Opinion and Public Policy: Models of Political Linkage,* edited by Norman R. Luttbeg. Homewood, Ill.: Dorsey.

Peterson, Merrill D. 1966. *Democracy, Liberty, and Property: The State Constitutions of the 1820s.* Indianapolis: Bobbs-Merrill.

Powell, H. J. 1985. "The Original Understanding of Original Intent." *Harvard Law Review* 98:885–948.

Reardon, Paul C. 1982. "The Massachusetts Constitution Marks a Milestone." *Publius* 12:45–55.

Scheiber, Harry N. 1981. "American Constitutional History and the New Legal History: Complementary Themes in Two Modes." *Journal of American History* 68:337–50.

Shultz, William J. 1935. "Limitations on State and Local Borrowing Power." *Annals of the American Academy of Political and Social Sciences* 181:118–42.

Sturm, Albert L. 1970. *Thirty Years of State Constitution-Making: 1938–1968.* New York: National Municipal League.

———. 1982. "The Development of American State Constitutions." *Publius* 12:57–98.

Sturm, Albert L., and Janice C. May. 1986. "State Constitutions and Constitutional Revision: 1984–1985." In *Book of the States,* Vol. 26. Lexington, Ky.: Council of State Governments.

Swindler, William. 1958. "Missouri Constitutions: History, Theory, and Practice." *Missouri Law Review* 23:32–61.

———. 1984. "Minimum Standards of Constitutional Justice: Federal Floor and State Ceiling." *Missouri Law Review* 49:1–15.

Tyak, David, Thomas James, and Aaron Benavot. 1987. *Law and the Shaping of Public Education, 1785–1954*. Madison: University of Wisconsin Press.

Wiecek, William M. 1972. *The Guarantee Clause of the U.S. Constiution*. Ithaca, N.Y.: Cornell University.

William, Robert F. 1985. "Introduction: State Constitutional Law in Ohio and the Nation." *University of Toledo Law Review* 16:391–404.

Williams v. Mississippi. 1898. 170 U.S. 213.

★ 10 ★

The Constitution, Institutionalization, and the Evolution of Federalism

JOHN E. CHUBB

Among the institutions established by the U.S. Constitution, the federal system would not appear to be one of the strongest. Its foundation, laid down in constitutional law, has been repeatedly disturbed by reinterpretations and revisions, which Congress, the executive, and the judiciary have been subjected to much less frequently. The federal structure, utterly transformed from decentralized to centralized, has proven more malleable than that of the other major institutions. As if in recognition, scholars have come to conceptualize the contemporary federal system in terms that lack the stability, order, and power of substantial institutions—a marble cake, an arena for implementation games, a complex of intergovernmental relations (Grodzins, 1966; Bardach, 1977; Wright, 1979). To be sure, the system exhibited considerable rigidity in the nineteenth century, and in the twentieth it has helped sustain subnational diversity in policy and politics (Sundquist, 1986b). But if strong institutions are ones that shape, rather than get shaped by, the pressures that bear upon them, the federal system would not seem to be a strong institution, especially in recent decades.

It is partly because of this apparent weakness that changes in the federal system during the 1980s have been so controversial. Beginning at the end of the Carter administration and escalating during the presidency of Ronald Reagan, the federal system underwent a process of decentralization that continues today. The national government's main sources of influence over state and local governments—spending, grant programs, and, to a lesser extent, regulation—were significantly constricted (Chubb, 1985a; Eads and Fix, 1984; Nathan and Doolittle, 1987). State and local governments acquired more responsibility and discretion than they had enjoyed in perhaps two decades, judging by the number of federal grant-in-aid programs and the level of real expenditures for them. The 1980s appear to mark an historic turning point in the federal system's development.

Reactions have been proportionate. Opponents warn that the changes will undermine the nation's support for equality, not only by dividing responsibility for it among the various states but also by devolving it to levels that may have disincentives to pursue it (Goldwin and Schambra, 1987; Gramlich, 1985; Palmer and Sawhill, 1982; Houseman, 1986). Proponents promise major gains in efficiency, a product of better matches between the supply and demand for public services, reduced costs of administration, and increased incentives for experimentation and innovation (Bowman and Kearney, 1986; Walker, 1981; Gramlich, 1985; for the economic literature on fiscal federalism, see Tiebout, 1956; Oates, 1972). Both opponents and proponents see a historically weak institution with great potential for change.

Both are likely to be wrong. The federal system may be a significantly stronger institution than the historical experience suggests. The interests and values the federal system came to promote during nearly two centuries of centralization may now be well protected by political and administrative institutions not only at the national level but at the state level as well. To an unexpected extent, the structures and functions of the federal system may be institutionalized in a way uniquely shaped by the structure of the constitutional system. Recent efforts at the national level to change the performance of the federal system—whether to increase its efficiency or to decrease its generosity—should therefore be substantially moderated by the institutions that now compose the system. Historically, the institutions of the federal system would not have provided such resistance to decentralization. Today they well may.

To appreciate the strengthening of the federal system, it is useful to take a somewhat different look at the system's development, a look that focuses on institutions and their role within the constitutional order. Until recently such a perspective was not customarily taken. Political scientists, at least since the postwar behavioral revolution, have deemphasized institutions in general and the institutions of federalism in particular. Over the last decade, however, there has been an impressive resurgence of interest (labeled "new institutionalism" by March and Olsen, 1984; see also Shepsle, 1986). Scholars increasingly recognize that political and administrative structures can have a powerful influence on political outcomes.

Many scholars have therefore begun to investigate how these structures develop and precisely how their influence operates.

This essay takes such an approach. It begins with a review of the constitutional foundations of federalism and how those foundations have evolved over time. Next, it considers changes in the scope and orientation of national political institutions, focusing on the different forces fostering the centralization in public goods, services, and policies. It details the emergence of categorical grants as "equilibrium institutions" that satisfied diverse interests inherent in the constitutionally structured system of competing power centers, as well as the current threats to the federal system of grants. Finally, it analyzes the reactions of two crucial federal institutions—the vertically integrated bureaucratic network and state political institutions—to changes in this equilibrium.

The Constitutional Foundation

The U.S. Constitution lays the foundation upon which all American governing institutions are built. It also sets the ground rules that constrain the behavior of the individuals who occupy and organize those institutions. The leaders of Congress, for example, might like to increase party discipline to deal more effectively with national issues, but a system of separation of powers is ultimately unsupportive of cohesive political parties (Sundquist, 1986a). In analogous ways the structures of other governing institutions tend to reflect their constitutional foundations. This constitutionally imposed constraint does not mean that structures cannot change without changes in the Constitution or its interpretation. As the interests or occupants of institutions change, individuals will often work to restructure their organizations, subject to the limit of what their constitutional foundation will support. Congress changed from an institution organized by relatively strong parties to one in which parties played a more nominal organizing role as members found it in their electoral interest to eliminate or weaken party controls. Still, as different as the contemporary Congress and those of the latter nineteenth century may be, their structures can be understood with reference to a common foundation.

The structure of the federal system can also be understood in terms of its foundation, with one important difference. Unlike the foundation of the Congress—and of the other major institutions of government—the foundation of the federal system was long unsettled and almost constantly shifting. Changes in the federal structure occurred not only when members of the various parts of the federal system sought to reorganize subject to constitutional ground rules but also when the rules themselves were changed. Indeed, during the course of much of the federal system's development, rule changes were integral to political strategies to restructure the system's authority. It was therefore especially difficult for the system to build real institutional integrity.

The source of this instability can easily be traced to the Constitution itself, but its roots actually go much deeper. Instability ultimately derives from the issue of centralized versus decentralized authority that has divided the nation for more than two hundred years. At the Constitutional Convention of 1787, no issue was more vexing than the allocation of power between the national government and the states. The delegates agreed that the Articles of Confederation had failed and that the national government needed to be stronger than the states, but they disagreed on just how much stronger it should be. The Convention is renowned for reaching the Great Compromise that provided all states—large and small—two seats in the U.S. Senate and thereby reduced state opposition to a national government with constitutionally superior authority. But if the Constitution was effective in relieving the tensions between the forces for and against centralization, it also embodied them.

The principles of federal organization set forth in the Constitution reflect much of the disagreement about just what the federal structure should be. The national government is granted sovereignty and supremacy, its authority derived from "the people" and its legislative acts declared the "supreme law of the land." Yet these grants were not to be final until the states, which were instructed to organize popular conventions to consider them, ratified the Constitution. Article 1 assigns Congress an enumerated set of powers, and the Tenth Amendment grants the states those powers not "delegated to the United States by the Constitution." But what powers are the states effectively granted when Congress is also given the authority to "provide for the ... general welfare" and "to make all laws which shall be necessary and proper" to do so? The Constitutional Convention was worried that self-interested states might take actions that would have disastrous consequences for the nation, so it clearly prohibited the states from coining money, levying tariffs, and negotiating treaties. Despite the Convention's abiding concern about excessive central authority, it also penned a preamble outlining expansive national powers.

The Constitution's provisions for federalism are rife with the conflicts of its time. To be sure, the Constitution can be construed as requiring only a relatively nominal federal structure (Jeffrey, 1987), but that interprets the document too literally. Read in light of conditions during its drafting, the Constitution takes on truer meaning, its vague and somewhat incongruous principles dictating, in the artful language of political compromise, a federal structure with genuine balance (Elazar, 1987). Exactly what balance is another question, one that the Constitution left to those who would restructure the federal system.

The construction of the institutions of federalism has been disturbed by periodic tremors and changes in the constitutional foundation (Tribe, 1978). During the decades immediately following the Constitution's ratification, these disturbances severely shook government structures. To protect slavery and the socioeconomic system of which it was a part, state governments in the South found it necessary to challenge the very supremacy of the national government. While the Civil War finally settled that most important principle of federal organization, state and even national institutions had to be reconstructed from considerable political debris. One of these institutions, the body of rules protecting civil rights and liberties, was built by extending the constitutional foundation. In a process that took one hundred years, the courts used the authority of the Fourteenth Amendment to apply the Bill of Rights incrementally to state governments.[1]

In other realms of the federal system, however, the foundation was not so long unsettled. After the shock of the Civil War and the solidification of the principle of national supremacy, conflicts over the allocation of government authority centered on issues of economic regulation. During the mid-1800s, the courts had held that the Constitution established what later became known as dual federalism, a system in which the state and national governments, though the latter was supreme, exercised authority over separate spheres of interest. As the nineteenth century drew to a close, that doctrine slowly became a greater political and technical problem.

Industrialization, which was well underway at this time, was beginning to exacerbate problems (e.g. monopolies and depressions) that the public increasingly demanded the government alleviate. The state governments, which by constitutional tradition were authorized to provide relief, did not do so. The national government, which according to the prevailing constitutional interpretation was only permitted to regulate industry involved in "interstate commerce," could not provide relief. With the development of an integrated national economy, though, it became more difficult for the courts to draw a clear boundary between interstate and intrastate commerce, and the courts began to open the impasse to government regulation. Finally, under the extraordinary political pressure of the Great Depression, the courts cleared the remaining obstacles limiting national government involvement in economic activity.[2] The constitutional foundation was thereby established for the national government to build the institutions of social welfare and economic management that the public was demanding and state governments were not supplying.

With the Supreme Court's decisions of the 1930s, the foundation for the contemporary federal system was laid, except for the realm of civil rights and liberties. Only once after the 1930s did the Supreme Court decide the powers of the national government were limited, at least in a significant way, relative to the states, and the Court soon overturned that decision.[3] For the last half-century, then, the federal system has been able to build on more or less fixed principles providing for broad national authority in the federal system. Until those principles were firmly established, the construction of strong institutions was indeed problematic; however, from the late 1930s onward, the federal system had a solid foundation on which to build its now centralized edifice. Understanding that process therefore requires a look above the foundation at the modern federal structure and the institutions that make up the federal system.

National Political Institutions

The Saga of Centralization

Although the transformation of the federal system that began during the New Deal has several important facets (e.g., the nationalization of domestic policy and regulation of the states), the most important to understand is the expansion of federal grants-in-aid (Chubb, 1985a; Kettl, 1983). At its peak in 1979, the grant system contained more than five hundred programs, representing nearly 4 percent of the GNP and 33 percent of the federal domestic budget. It also provided nearly 30 percent of annual state and local revenue. Through its economic incentives, spending regulations, and sheer magnitude, it enabled Washington to exert its greatest influence on state and local governments.

How this system—the very infrastructure of centralized federalism—came to be is a story that has been written many times. The action took place in Congress and the White House, and the plot, though played out in a different setting, read much like that followed in the Supreme Court's nationalization of the Constitution. With economic and technological development, the states proved increasingly incapable of meeting new needs and fulfilling traditional responsibilities. Political pressure steadily built for innovative action, and in a burst of historic policy-making the national government accepted the challenge. Strong presidents, especially Franklin Roosevelt and Lyndon Johnson, and congressional leaders played the major roles in this saga. The legislative triumphs of the New Deal and the Great Society were its climaxes.

The story of centralization is not all high drama, however. Only about a third of the federal grant programs extant in 1979, and an even lower proportion of the growth in grant expenditures, can be traced to the heydays of nationalization, the 1930s and the mid-1960s. The fact is, centralization involved a great deal of "low politics." The federal grant system underwent most of its expansion from the late 1950s to the late 1970s, usually without the benefit of strong presidential leadership or decisive party victories in Congress. During that extended period, grant programs were created at the rate of twenty per year, national influence increased in every area of state and local policy-making—not just those of concern in the Great Society—and grant expenditures rose much faster than the rest of the federal budget, which itself grew more rapidly than the GNP. In the absence of mundane political concerns that increasingly encouraged logrolling and pork-barreling during that period, the full extent of centralization is impossible to understand.

To be sure, national politics was genuinely concerned about the capacity of subnational governments to alleviate problems in a number of areas, but federal influence grew rapidly in every area of intergovernmental assistance. For example, by the late 1970s no more than seventy of the more than five hundred programs providing aid to state and local governments targeted the poor or poverty. In fact, the lion's share of the system's growth, both in numbers and in dollars, occurred in nonredistributive areas—areas where state and local effort is usually deemed most adequate—and in grants to subnational institutions. At least until the late 1970s, entitlements and grants for payments to individuals (e.g., Aid to Families with Dependent Children) contributed relatively little to the system's explosive development. If this process were anchored only in high politics, in genuine concern about the capacity of subnational governments to handle domestic problems, it would not have had this timing or character.

Those things would appear to be better explained by reference to the institutionally driven political concerns of the U.S. Congress. Those concerns go a long way toward explaining why all of the problems of this period were addressed in the same way—with specialized categorical grant programs—and how those programs proliferated and grew. Although it is not possible to present detailed evidence here, the explanation is quite clear: categorical grants were favored by Congress because they helped its members get reelected (Chubb, 1985a; Advisory Commission on Intergovernmental Relations, 1981). Categorical grants provided legislators countless opportunities to claim credit for producing discrete benefits for their districts and to help constituents with red tape and other problems that interfered with the delivery of those benefits. These forms of district aid were especially important during the 1960s and 1970s, when members of Congress were finding it increasingly necessary to rely on their own devices, instead of their parties, to get reelected. Grants were also among the easiest programs to legislate. As Congress decentralized its institutional apparatus to give more members control over policies (and their own electoral fates), it became more hospitable to such programs as categorical grants, which were narrow, divisible, and plentiful.

In a theoretical sense, categorical grants were emerging during this period as an "equilibrium institution" (Shepsle, 1986). They were gradually being shaped into instruments that could simultaneously satisfy a number of contending interests and permit progress on public problems that veto groups had long impeded. Liberals favored categorical grants because they provided some assurance that needs identified by Washington, rather than by state and local politicians, would be addressed. Conservatives approved of categoricals, though sometimes grudgingly, because they established accountability for federal expenditures. State and local governments accepted categoricals, despite their bothersome strings, because they were given primary responsibility for implementing them, not to mention a handsome subsidy. Beneficiaries endorsed categoricals as an improvement over the status quo, namely, insuffient state and local services. Most important, members of Congress of all stripes coveted categoricals because these grant programs enhanced their political fortunes and eased their legislative lives.

In time, these virtues encouraged not only the proliferation of grant programs but their institutionalization as well. Executive proposals to consolidate grants into less centralized forms of aid were resolutely opposed by Congress (Conlan, 1988). Until the 1970s, decades of criticism of categorical grants by presidential commissions and academics fell on deaf congressional ears. However burdensome or distorting these grants might have been for recipients, they were too politically valuable for Congress to relinquish control over their allocation and utilization. President Richard Nixon finally broke through this institutional barrier with successful proposals for block grants and revenue sharing. The block grants that were created did not represent an acceptance of the principle of decentralization, however. They owed their existence to the generally acknowledged failure of the categorical grants out of which they were formed—and to the generous additional funding for the block grants. Even general revenue sharing, the ultimate in no-strings assistance, represented a Pyrrhic victory over categorical assistance. Not a single targeted program was terminated to make room for this new form of aid, and total intergovernmental spending was increased. Moreover, during the remainder of the 1970s, Congress added strings to the block grants, converting them into veritable categoricals. By the end of the decade, the centralized mechanism of assistance had confirmed its institutional resilience.

The Coming of Decentralization

The pressures the grant system endured during its long period of growth and institutionalization were nothing compared with those it experienced in the 1980s. Between a budget deficit of unprecedented proportions and an anticentralization president of unusual popularity, the grant system came under severe and sustained pressure to decentralize. As a result, the system in fact decentralized. From the late 1970s to the late 1980s, grant programs were reduced in number and in real value by one-fourth. Nevertheless, the manner in which this change occurred indicates that centralization, rooted in the institutional incentives of Congress, is still pretty firmly entrenched.

First of all, most of the retrenchment in the grant system can be traced to two unique sources: President Reagan's twin fiscal policy triumphs of 1981, the Omnibus Budget and Reconciliation Act (OBRA) and the Economic Recovery Tax Act. Although real grant expenditures began to be restrained in the final years of the Carter administration, the first absolute reductions were contained in OBRA, a historic act of comprehensive spending reform made possible by the Reagan landslide, the Republican capture of the Senate, and the festering popular frustration with inflation and economic stagnation. After that, however, administration proposals for similar radical cuts were unsuccessful. The real retrenchment that occurred after 1982 was primarily due to sustained pressure to curb all federal spending, stemming from the deficit crisis for which the 1981 Tax Act was partially responsible. The majority of grant expenditures were particularly vulnerable to budget cutting, owing to their annual appropriations. Were it not for the deficit, the grant system would probably have resumed a process of slow growth and expansion after its unusual setback in 1981.

These financial losses notwithstanding, the grant system weathered the changes in its economic and political environment in the 1980s without transforming its basic structure. Centralized assistance remained a favorite among members of Congress on both sides of the political aisle. Categorical grants increased their share of federal grant expenditures, while less politically valuable block grants leveled off and revenue sharing, which was terminated in 1986, disappeared. Congress also found ways to tie strings to the new block grants—President Reagan helped establish nine—which frustrated much of the consolidation. Ambitious reform proposals, such as President Reagan's New Federalism, got nowhere. Congress (and the states) so criticized his proposed "swap" with the states—sixty-one categorical programs, Aid to Families with Dependent Children, food stamps, and several federal tax sources in exchange for Medicaid—that it never got out of the White House. Indeed, the congressional strategy for dealing with a burgeoning deficit and administrations philosophically opposed to centralization was to defend the categorical structure at whatever cost, spreading losses equitably among its parts. At this juncture, the categorical grant has proven itself to be an equilibrium institution.

How much longer the categorical system will remain an equilibrium institution is another question. As the deficit crisis drags on and its real or perceived consequences—the October 1987 stock market crash, for example—become clearer, the pressure to continue cutting grant expenditures builds steadily. Alternative means of deficit reduction, such as tax increases or social security reform, are at least as unattractive politically and more difficult legislatively. Even without President Reagan's and President George Bush's commitment to a strong defense, it is hard to construct a plausible scenario in which deficits on the order of 3 percent of GNP are reduced while federal grant-in-aid expenditures are increased or even spared further reduction. Notwithstanding the undeniable reelection value of the district benefits and constituency service that categorical grants provide, members of Congress are not free to maximize these advantages of incumbency without being subject to constraints—and they never were. It just happens that today those constraints are unusually severe. Voters care about such diffuse costs as higher taxes and larger deficits and such broad-purpose expenditures as defense and social security. Members believe that those cares affect their prospects for reelection. Until these constraints are relaxed, they are likely to try to retain the categorical grants but reduce the overall level of federal spending on them.

If these political pressures continue, and the economic value of grant-in-aid programs declines sharply, the forces that have been held in equilibrium by categorical grants may threaten the stability of the centralized structure of assistance. In Congress, logrolling could give way to genuine competition. Members could begin looking for opportunities to build smaller coalitions around select programs to save them from the atrophy that would threaten all programs if cutbacks were apportioned equally. Members might also consider more selective allocations of money within individual programs (e.g., via strict means-testing) to prevent the dissipation of program impacts. At some point in the process of reducing grant expenditures, these strategies should become tempting. The certain benefits of observing the principle of universal distribution, upon which categorical spending rests, will no longer outweigh the risks and prospective benefits of not cooperating (Shepsle and Weingast, 1981). Outside of Congress quiescent forces could also become restive, as will be discussed more fully later. Federal bureaucrats could grow less cooperative as the erosion of their financial leverage over grant recipients undermines their implementation responsibilities. State and local governments could become problems if the benefits of categorical assistance fall below the costs of federal intrusion. At some point, categorical grants would no longer provide a solution to federalism's cooperation problem or an optimal response to Congress's institutional incentives. It would cease to be an equilibrium institution.

To be sure, this scenario need not be followed. Institutional incentives rooted in Congress and the U.S. Constitution—reelection, constituency service, and chamber organization—will continue to shape the national government's role in the federal system and could, under more favorable conditions, restore the traditional equilibrium. But the institutionalized roots of centralization, at least those in the Congress, are not so deep that the centralized structure growing out of them cannot be altered by political and economic change. Currently, the prospects for such an alteration are growing.

Budget cutting in the late 1980s reduced the value of federal aid to a level where the incentives that support its centralized structure may not be enough to sustain it, and national politics mounted two new assaults on it. One was the Balanced Budget Act of 1985, better known as the Gramm-Rudman-Hollings bill. The other was federal income tax reform. Notwithstanding some slippage in its time-tables resulting from 1987 amendments, Gramm-Rudman-Hollings, and the budget-cutting resolve that it represents, signaled a new stage in the national government's efforts to reduce the budget deficit. It gave budget reduction highest priority on the agenda of national concerns, regardless of where it was on the agendas of particular politicians. The battle with the deficit increased the already formidable pressure for the federal grant system to be substantially reformed—or face gradual extinction through annual, across-the-board cuts. The presidential-congressional budget agreement of 1990 guaranteed that domestic spending cuts, many focused on categorical grants, would continue for at least five more years.

Tax reform applied different but no less important pressure. By limiting sales tax deductions in federally taxable income, tax reform increased the difficulties subnational governments face in raising revenue to support their own services, not to mention those encouraged and underwritten by federal aid. By placing state and local tax deduction on the agenda, tax reform also put those benefits at risk in future rounds of tax writing. As a result, Congress is likely to face increased pressure from subnational governments to maintain current levels of federal aid for those programs that the lower governments are least able or willing to support themselves. Like deficit reduction, tax reform increased the probability of restructuring federal aid. Although the centralized structure of aid has certainly bent with the changes in its political and economic environment heretofore, current developments are pushing it much closer to a breaking point.

Only time will tell where these developments will lead, but there is good reason to believe that the values and interests the centralized system of federalism have come to serve will continue to be protected. One reason is that structure of the federal system, so deeply rooted in the institutional incentives of Congress, remains essentially intact. As if waiting to test the "fat cell theory" of budget cutting, the now lean federal grant system could easily regain its former bulk if the current budget constraint's were relaxed. True, the days of fiscal surpluses appear to be permanently behind us, but categorical assistance might already have survived its toughest times. Grant programs may never swell, like fat cells, to their previous size, but they may be able to avoid the sort of radical surgery that would eliminate some of them altogether. The federal government may then go on influencing state and local governments through the institutional apparatus of categorical assistance while rewarding them less generously.

If for aforementioned reasons that proves impossible, however, the result may still prove supportive of the status quo. Congress has begun to acknowledge that some interests protected by centralized federalism may need more protection than others do. The Balanced Budget Act and its 1987 amendments exclude a number of grant programs serving the poor from automatic expenditure reductions. If Congress and the president cannot agree on an annual budget that reduces the deficit by amounts specified in law, the resulting across-the-board cuts in defense and domestic programs exempt Aid to Families with Dependent Children, Medicaid, the Special Supplemental Food Program, child nutrition programs, and a number of small health-care-assistance programs. The problem areas states have traditionally had the most difficulty serving are now guaranteed service by the federal government—unless Congress and the president come to annual budget accords that temporarily void those guarantees. Forced by budgetary constraints to reevaluate the system of categorical assistance, Congress decided it was better to spare some programs at the greater expense of others than to allow all programs to be pared back steadily but equally. Political incentives aside, some federal grant programs owe their existence to the inadequacies of subnational governments more than others do, and the Budget Act in effect certified that. So too does the 1990 budget agreement.

Should it continue to be necessary, then, further decentralization of domestic program responsibility may concentrate on problem areas other than the health and financial welfare of the poor. These other areas are still enormous. They take in half of all federal grant expenditures and include such vital public concerns as economic development, education, and transportation. But there are fewer worries about subnational incapacity in these areas. They are also areas in which state governments have indicated a willingness to take complete responsibility if their current obligations for income security were taken over by the federal government. This was the essence of a proposed swap of program responsibilities, the Evans-Robb initiative, debated by Congress and endorsed by the National Governor's Association in the mid-1980s. None of this guarantees that decentralization will not undermine some interests now protected by centralization, but it certainly reduces the risk of that.

Bureaucratic Institutions

Bureaucracy and Centralization

As the categorical system of aid became institutionalized in Congress, it developed an institutional presence throughout the federal system. Federal agencies and offices were established to allocate formula grants, award project grants, and ensure that all grants were used for congressionally intended purposes. State and local agencies were created or expanded to request, receive, implement, and account for those grants. From the top of the federal system to the bottom, agencies were tied together by planning, reporting and accounting systems. In the process, an intergovernmental bureaucracy was established, giving centralization two additional sources of support: a hierarchical structure for commanding and coaxing state and local cooperation in achieving national domestic policy goals and, potentially more important, an institutional voice for previously underrepresented interests in state and local politics.

In most accounts of categorical grant implementation, this administrative hierarchy is overwhelmed by political conflict (Bardach, 1977). Policy outcomes seem to depend on the idiosyncracies of political circumstance. The only predictable consequence of grant implementation is conflict—at and between all levels of government. Yet there is evidence that with time such conflict settles down (Peterson, Rabe, and Wong, 1986). It can also be argued that behind the diminution of conflict is an intergovernmental bureaucracy that helps settle implementation problems quite systematically.

Consider the problem from the perspective of Congress. After working assiduously to direct funds to specific constituencies for specific purposes, Congress finds itself in serious difficulty. In establishing hundreds of programs involving thousands of individual grants, Congress has exceeded its capacity to supervise carefully the agencies responsible for implementing them. With Congress overburdened, these agencies are then free to do whatever makes their administrative and political life easiest. In the case of grant implementation, it is easiest to follow the wishes of state and local governments that have their own plans for federal money. Congress's problem entails more than gaining the cooperation of federal agents, however. Congress recognizes that its bureaucratic agents have similar problems getting state and local governments to cooperate with them. Only by expensive, time-consuming, and conflict-inducing processes of regulation and monitoring can federal agencies ensure that congressional edicts are being followed.

Congress faces a classic "principal-agent" problem (Chubb, 1985b). As the principal in an organized enterprise, it needs to find some way to counter the interests and advantages of its agents without burdening the enterprise with central control and supervision. The basic way to accomplish this is to select or convert administrative agents who will see cooperation with the federal government as in their best interest. One way this strategy can work is for federal principals to nurture the development of state and local bureaucracies that view federal programs rather than state and local government to be their primary concern. If this can be done, the goals of congressional principals will be supported by self-interested bureaucratic agents in the lower levels of government. Subnational bureaucrats concerned with survival have powerful incentives to see that their programs receive full federal funding, maintain maximum levels of potential state and local funding, and became important to some private clientele. They can also serve as effective implementation monitors. They know, better than any outside auditor, when funds are being diverted or when unintended beneficiaries are being served. They can also be useful enforcers, threatening uncooperative behavior with the sanction of federal auditing and evaluation.

It is difficult to say exactly how successfully the government in Washington recruited these bureaucratic allies. There is no doubt that federal bureaucrats cultivated them, maintaining more communication with subnational bureaucrats than their respective governments did and encouraging their professionalization (Wright, 1979). It is also clear that subnational bureaucrats in certain prominent grant programs were instrumental in achieving congressional goals (Peterson, Rabe, and Wong, 1986). But the more general evidence, however suggestive, is only circumstantial. For example, during the very period that federal categorical grants were exploding in number and dollars, a rather surprising pattern of growth was occurring in public employment: the federal bureaucracy was scarcely growing, while the state and local bureaucracies were growing enormously. By 1982, after growing only 4.8 percent during the preceding three decades, the federal civilian bureaucracy was the smallest of the three levels, behind state bureaucracy, which had grown 222 percent, and local bureaucracy, which, by then three times the size of the federal bureaucracy, had grown 154 percent. Since federal expenditures, often allocated through intergovernmental grants, grew by an amount four times greater than state and local expenditures, Washington obviously fueled some of the lower-level bureaucratic explosion, but it is unclear how much, relative to forces from state and local political economies. This needs to be clarified if the influence of centralization is to be better appreciated and if the consequences of decentralization are to be more accurately anticipated.

Bureaucracy and Decentralization

The subnational bureaucracy will play an important role in any decentralization process. Obviously, it will bear an increasing administrative burden. Assuming state and local governments maintain programs curtailed by the federal government, subnational agencies will be called to deliver services with less central assistance. Traditionally, independent subnational service provision would have been a cause for great concern, but there is now reason to believe that the subnational bureaucracy has the administrative capacity— the organizational and professional competence—to handle this responsibility effectively. For a quarter-century and longer, it has been delivering services of every description for the federal government. In the process, it has developed administrative practices and procedures that are increasingly perfected and routinized (Bowman and Kearney, 1986). This is not to say that this development will prove sufficient for servicing all future demands. Such a projection is exceedingly difficult to make and well beyond the scope of this essay. In any event, increased administrative capacity may not be the key bureaucratic development to result from centralization.

The more important result may be the institutionalization of national interests and values in subnational politics. As federal funds diminish and federal regulations regarding their use ease up, state and local bureaucrats may become the strongest lobbyists at the lower levels for full subnational replacement of federal funding. In part this is because program bureaucrats have professional commitments to federal policies. It is also because the jobs of subnational bureaucrats depend on their success as program advocates. If state and local politicians are inclined to allow programs to diminish in size or even to disappear (though for reasons to be discussed subsequently, they seldom will be), subnational bureaucrats can be expected to be among the politicians' fiercest opponents. These bureaucrats are typically organized in public employee unions, and not infrequently these unions—teachers' associations being the best example—represent the largest coherent blocks of votes in state and local elections. In addition, these bureaucrats can count on the support of the clienteles or beneficiaries receiving the services they provide. So organized, subnational bureaucrats should have considerable leverage on the general issue of whether subnational funds should be found to replace federal cutbacks—and thereby avoid state and local layoffs.

Subnational bureaucrats should also have considerable influence over the disposal of particular programs. If the subnational bureaucracy is to keep its clientele support, and thereby bolster its current size, it must work to maintain the distinctions among the many services it provides. Program consolidations, radical reorganizations, and other organizational innovations, which might be favored by state and local politicians interested in sustaining current services but at lower costs or with greater effectiveness, threaten the bureaucracy. Reforms such as these can weaken ties to easily identified clienteles, which are often organized around program categories (e.g., the beneficiaries of educational aid for the handicapped or disadvantaged), and undermine the justifications for many agencies' existence. Such reforms may also go against the professional convictions of dedicated service providers. For these reasons state and local bureaucracy may become more than a source of support for replacing federal expenditures with subnational ones; it may also become a source of support for federal rules and regulations that decentralization might otherwise relax.

A product, then, of the centralized federal structure is a subnational bureaucracy with the potential to exert real force in support of the status quo. Still, the question remains whether that bureaucracy will realize this potential. If the subnational bureaucracy is deeply rooted in the centralized system of federalism that structured and to some extent supported its growth, it probably will. The subnational bureaucracy will provide an important source of support for all that the federal government has long assisted. If the subnational bureaucracy is not securely anchored in that system and is more closely tied to state and local government and politics, it may favor federally mandated or initiated arrangements, but it will hardly throw up a roadblock to other subnational forces for change.

It is far beyond the scope of this essay to adduce sufficient evidence about the roots of the subnational bureaucracy to begin to resolve this question. Existing work does not support a strong conclusion one way or another (Stein, 1984). Some ongoing work supports the hypothesis of centralized influence.[4] Moreover, if the institutional logic developed in this essay is correct, it is likely that subnational bureaucrats, usually supported by a mixture of national and subnational funds, will not be easily eliminated. Instead, they will remain after the money from Washington disappears to protect many of the goals, programs, and practices established by the national government and to moderate the potential consequences of decentralization.

State Political Institutions

The centralized federal system that the national government established, nurtured, and provided with institutional roots also owes its existence to the subnational political context into which it was introduced. When federal aid began to grow in the 1930s and 1940s, state political institutions, through which most of the money was fed, were generally weak. State executive branches were headed by governors who were often restricted to single terms and frequently held office for only two years. The governor presided over executive branches in which many, if not most, of the departments and agencies were headed by elected executives. These conditions conspired to inhibit strong central control of state executive branches and to encourage fragmentation, a condition most hospitable to categorical aid. State legislatures were also weak. They were in session for relatively short periods of time, were convened in many states only biennially, were staffed by few full-time professionals, and were composed of poorly paid amateurs who seldom stood for reelection more than a time or two. Whatever their interests were in controlling or influencing the use of federal aid, they were poorly equipped to control state bureaucracies supported by strong clienteles, independent executives, and the federal government.

Over the last couple of decades, of course, these institutional conditions have been changing. Governorships have been strengthened by lengthening terms, permitting self-succession, shifting elections to nonpresidential years when national forces are presumably weaker, and reducing somewhat the number of elected state executives. Legislatures have been strengthened by more frequent and longer sessions, additions to committee staff, personal staff, and ancillary agencies, and hikes in legislator compensation (Bowman and Kearney, 1986).

Institutional Development and State Policy-making

What effect will all of these developments have on state policy-making, especially if the decentralization of policy responsibilities continues? Obviously, state political institutions are more competent and, in most states, have the skill and capacity to reshape government services. Competence, however, is not typically a driving force in political decision making. Increased competence does not necessarily lead to a restructuring of government services, an increase or decrease in their level, or a reordering of the priorities among them. Ultimately, the politicians' interests are more pertinent than institutional competence is in state policy-making.

Politicians naturally have a diversity of interests, and that diversity confounds the development of clear expectations about political behavior. Yet among all these political interests, two very basic ones are often thought to influence the behavior of state policy makers universally. One is the interest in reelection or, perhaps more appropriately, the lack of such an interest; the other is the pervasive concern for the health of the state economy. Both of these interests can have important implications for political decision making at the state level.

Politicians who are interested in maintaining their positions behave differently from those who are not. Reelection-minded politicians are more sensitive to the demands of constituents and interest groups than are political amateurs, who may be more sensitive to personal principles. Career politicians are more likely to take an interest in the ongoing provision of government services, urging that programs valued by constituents are generously funded and ensuring that services are properly provided. They are also more likely, in a legislative context, to encourage the development of procedures, rules, and norms, embodied, for example, in committee and seniority systems, that facilitate the distribution of public goods and services. Over time, career politicians are more likely to bring about the institutionalization of policies and practices. All of this makes it very useful to ask whether, or to what extent, politicians are electorally motivated.

Traditionally, state politicians were not very interested in reelection. Governors were often prohibited from seeking it, and legislators were so poorly compensated and so little occupied by the position that they had little incentive to value it. This lack of interest in reelection was often said to incapacitate state political institutions (Wahlke et al., 1962; Polsby, 1968). It kept governors from developing the kind of political base necessary to exert strong leadership over the forces (often bureaucratic) that pulled state government apart, and it slowed the institutional development of state legislatures, undermining their competence and their representativeness. Weak governorships and poorly institutionalized legislatures are key reasons why the capacity of state governments was routinely regarded, until only recently, as inferior to that of the national government, and why decentralization is viewed so skeptically. The question now, of course, is how much that desire for reelection among state politicians has increased, and, in turn, how much that increase has stimulated the process of institutionalization.

The process of institutionalization is important because it stands to influence the state response to decentralization. State legislators interested in reelection can be expected to try to protect themselves from adverse electoral conditions— partisan tides, unusual levels of voter turnout, economic slumps—through a variety of methods: pork-barreling, credit-claiming, casework, and, of course, fund-raising (Mayhew, 1974; Fiorina, 1977; Jewell and Olson, 1982). These strategies have been used with great success in the U.S. Congress, and there is no reason to believe they are not used, albeit on a smaller scale, in the states. All of these strategies are facilitated by connections between legislators and the state bureaucrats who control the programs that constituents and campaign contributors want legislators to influence. Ultimately, reelection is facilitated by legislators' embedding themselves, usually via legislative committees, in well-defined subsystems of policy-making and administration—"iron triangles" of legislators, bureaucrats, and interest groups. On the administrative side, subsystems have long been developing, with assistance from federal grants. This is important because it implies that as state legislators seek political profit by supplementing, elaborating, and otherwise becoming involved in the production of goods and services at the state level, they become part of subsystems that the federal government has been integrally involved with itself. State politicians interested in reelection may therefore develop substantial stakes in the programs the federal government has directly or indirectly assisted, and they may become major defenders of them, particularly if they continue to have the opportunity to reshape the programs.

Interest in reelection could, however, lead state politicians in a different direction. This is suggested by the second basic interest state politicians are frequently said to hold, interest in the health of the state economy. Interpretations of state elections regularly point to state economic conditions as a significant issue. In 1986, for example, the governors of Texas and Iowa were said to be in electoral difficulty because of the recessions in their respective energy- and farming-dependent economies. Conceptualizations of state policy-making also place great emphasis on economic conditions. Policy makers are commonly seen as participants in an interstate competition to attract and retain businesses and taxpayers (Tiebout, 1956; Oates, 1972; Gramlich, 1982; Peterson, 1981). According to this view, shrewd policy makers will produce packages of taxes and benefits that are not steeply progressive or aggressively redistributive, in an effort to encourage economically productive firms and individuals to remain in their state and to discourage unproductive ones from migrating to it. Such policies should also stimulate the state economy. These politicians are likely to respond to the opportunities presented by decentralization in a very different way than do politicians rooted in the status quo: all things being equal, they are more likely to cut taxes (or at least rely less on "ability-to-pay" taxation), reduce programs of income redistribution and other services for the poor and disadvantaged, and boost economic development and infrastructure expenditures.

In one form or another, this expectation has become something of the conventional wisdom about decentralization. Yet there is good reason to doubt its validity (Beam, 1988). For one thing, the most straightforward proposition, state policy-making responds to interstate economic competition, has not been extensively tested. For another, less direct tests of the competition perspective—do business-location decisions or indigent-migration patterns respond to state policy?—have turned up mixed results (Ladd and Doolittle, 1982; Gramlich and Laren, 1984; Helms, 1985). It is also unknown whether state elections really are influenced by the state economy and, by extension, whether state politicians have real incentives to emphasize programs of benefit to businesses and taxpayers in making policy. This is unfortunate because the thesis of interstate economic competition leads directly to expectations about the performance of state political institutions that are at odds with expectations based on the equally plausible thesis of institutionalization, one rooted in the primacy of state legislators' desire for reelection.

Institutions, Elections, and Decentralization

Which thesis should be accepted? Has the apparent increase in concern for reelection at the state level reinforced the status quo and made the states "safe for decentralization" (i.e., not prone to major disruption), or has that concern made the states even more aggressive competitors in an economic marketplace? At this point, the weight of evidence derived from ongoing work supports the former: state electoral politics are becoming institutionalized and are not dramatically affected by state economic conditions (Chubb, 1988). State politicians have little control over state economic conditions and would be foolish to stake their careers on economic promises. Moreover, the evidence suggests that voters do not hold them substantially accountable for the relative performance of state economies.

This finding is important because it suggests state politicians have less to fear from the voters than many observers have assumed. At least state politicians do not need to legislate in grave fear that, should their policies appear to strain their state economies, they will be thrown out of office. All things being equal, policies that can adversely affect state economic performance (e.g., increases in taxes or welfare expenditures) need not be avoided by politicians concerned with remaining in office. Their elections do not turn on state economic performance; they turn on such things as the coattails of candidates for higher office, voter turnout, and national economic conditions.

Moreover, state elections increasingly seem to turn on things over which politicians do have control. State election outcomes are becoming more stable. The parties are retaining larger shares of their legislative seats from one election to the next, and swings in gubernatorial voting are lessening. This is especially pronounced in state legislatures where, since 1968, the rate at which seats are retained has tripled and, equally significant, the overall effect of outside forces has been more than halved. The only exception to this pattern is the influence of the national economy on state legislative elections, which has nearly doubled. In total, though, state elections are becoming insulated against adverse forces beyond the control of state politicians. Why this is happening is not fully understood; however, it is revealing that it is occurring most frequently in states where legislative salaries and staffs have been increased the most—in states where political institutions have been most professionalized. State politicians with the financial incentives and resources to hold on to their positions are evidently working to do so by exploiting the advantages of incumbency—the ability to maintain contacts with and provide goods and services to constituents—that members of the U.S. Congress have long exploited so well.

The increasing advantage of incumbency is at least as important as the relative independence of state elections from state economic performance because it confirms that state governments are becoming institutionalized. The states are building political institutions with the permanence that is necessary to broaden representation, foster compromise, develop expertise, and otherwise provide the capacity to serve state citizens democratically and effectively. It has long been thought that state governments lacked this capacity, even as states grew more professionalized. Now it appears that the politicians in many of these governments are achieving what politicians in mature institutions typically pursue, namely, careers free from enormous electoral uncertainty. It also appears that most of those governments that have not yet reached political and institutional maturity are well on the road to achieving it.

The process of institutional maturation is crucial as we look to a future in which state governments have more authority and responsibility. Political institutions reach maturity as their members establish stakes in the structures and routines that define the institution. State politicians who have succeeded in protecting themselves from political and electoral tides have apparently done so by supporting and taking advantage of the programs, often facilitated by the federal government, that their constituents value. These politicians are becoming, or have already become, integral parts of the system. This provides them with strong incentives to try to maintain the status quo as the federal government reduces its support for it. State political institutions thus are not likely to respond to decentralization by reordering priorities or reforming practices substantially. To the contrary, they are likely to be important sources of stability.

The Future of Federalism

At the Constitutional Convention in 1787 the framers struggled mightily with an issue that was to occupy American politics for two centuries: the proper balance between national and state power. The compromise written into the Constitution only temporarily resolved the issue of balance, and the institution that the Constitution outlined proved to be too fragile to withstand periodic political pressures for a change in the balance. A nation that at its founding had been deeply suspicious of the arbitrariness of centralized power eventually became frustrated with the ineffectiveness and inequities of decentralized power and demanded changes that ultimately rocked the federal system at its very foundation. Constitutional principles needed to be reinterpreted so that the federal system could be restructured. In time, the supremacy of national authority became firmly established, and the structure of the system became centralized. The issue of proper balance was not resolved, however.

Today, the system is being pressured to reverse its historical course of development. Complaints about the inefficiencies of federal grant programs and the clumsiness of federal regulations applied to subnational governments have become frequent. The costs of centralization have been judged excessive, especially in the context of deficit politics. Important steps toward increasing the responsibilities of state and local governments have been taken. It appears that the federal system, restructured so many times in the past, is undergoing another significant transformation. Values protected by a system found politically wanting will be displaced by ones that a new system is better designed to protect. That has been the institutional history of federalism. The system periodically gives way to permit the satisfaction of new interests, demonstrating time and again the flexibility—or weakness—of the constitutional design.

That has not, however, been the system's complete history. Notwithstanding the system's transformation from a decentralized to a centralized system, federalism has also been undergoing a process of institutionalization. The process was slow in getting started, because shifts in the system's constitutional foundation shook existing structures. But once the full extent of national authority was established in the 1930s, the ground was set for more orderly institution building. Beginning at the national level but then reaching rapidly into state bureaucracy and ultimately into state politics, legislators and bureaucrats began to benefit from centralization and to promote its expansion. They also offered it protection. That, it's strongest source of institutional stability, is a key to the future of federalism.

To be sure, the federal system will continue to be buffeted by forces for more and for less centralization, but in the future the federal system will be better protected against them. Institutions from the nation's capital to the state capitals, and probably beyond, protect centralization. The evidence presented in this essay scarcely begins to answer the question of how substantial this protection is, but the essay was not intended to answer this question. The purpose of the essay was to examine the federal system's development from the perspective of its unsettled Constitutional foundation and to suggest an institutional logic for the system's centralization. An important implication of that logic is institutionalization, and it is fair to conclude that both the opponents and proponents of the current wave of decentralization have underestimated it.

NOTES

1. Included in the extension are rights provided by the Bill of Rights (e.g., speech and assembly, immunity from unreasonable search and seizure, and protection from cruel and unusual punishment), rights inferred from various penumbrae of the Bill of Rights (e.g., privacy), and guarantees of equal protection (e.g., prohibitions against racial discrimination).

2. After declaring unconstitutional the New Deal's National Industrial Recovery Act, its first Agricultural Adjustment Act, and its Bituminous Coal Conservation Act on grounds that they overstepped the limits on federal authority over economic activity that did not directly involve interstate commerce, the Supreme Court upheld the National Labor Relations Act and the Social Security Act in 1937, effectively eliminating a separate sphere of state economic jurisdiction.

3. In 1976 a bare majority of the Supreme Court held in *National League of Cities v. Usery* that the Tenth Amendment precluded the federal government from applying the Fair Labor Standards Act to state employees engaged in traditional state functions; however, in 1985 in *Garcia v. San Antonio Metropolitan Transit Authority* one member of the majority, Justice Harry A. Blackmun, changed his mind and argued that it was unworkable to try to distinguish traditional areas of state responsibility.

4. Modeling aggregate state employment across the fifty states for the period of greatest bureaucratic growth, 1965–79, I found that federal aid is one of the most important determinants of the level of state public employment (Chubb, 1985a:296–97).

This impact is important for it suggests that the subnational bureaucracy, owing its origin in large measure to the national government, may support the interests and values long promoted by the national government if the federal system should further decentralize. To be sure, some state and local agencies, especially those most dependent on federal money, might be eliminated if federal money dries up. There have already been bureaucratic casualties in select programs in certain cities (Peterson and Lewis, 1986). To see whether bureaucratic retrenchment is a more systematic consequence of decentralization, I am updating the public employment analysis to include the years 1980–89 and disaggregating the analysis to examine different types of agencies. Still, there is qualitative evidence that subnational bureaucracies have remained intact and worked successfully in the 1980s to preserve the status quo ante in major federal programs (Kennedy, Jung, and Orland, 1986; Nathan and Doolittle, 1987).

REFERENCES

Advisory Commission on Intergovernmental Relations. 1981. *An Agenda for American Federalism: Restoring Confidence and Competence.* Washington, D.C.: Government Printing Office.

Bardach, Eugene. 1977. *The Implementation Game.* Cambridge, Mass.: MIT Press.

Beam, David R. 1988. "Reinventing Federalism: State-Local Government Rules in the New Economic Order." Presented at the annual meeting of the American Political Science Association, Washington, D.C..

Bowman, Ann O. M., and Richard C. Kearney. 1986. *The Resurgence of the States.* Englewood Cliffs, N.J.: Prentice-Hall.

Chubb, John E. 1985a. "Federalism and the Bias for Centralization." In *The New Direction in American Politics,* edited by John E. Chubb and Paul E. Peterson. Washington, D.C.: Brookings Institution.

———. 1985b. "The Political Economy of Federalism." *American Political Science Review* 79:994–1015.

———. 1988. "Institutions, the Economy and the Dynamics of State Elections." *American Political Science Review* 82:133–54.

Conlan, Timothy J. 1988. *The New Federalism.* Washington, D.C.: Brookings Institution.

Eads, George, and Michael Fix. 1984. *Relief or Reform: Reagan's Regulatory Dilemma.* Washington, D.C.: Urban Institute.

Elazar, Daniel J. 1987. "Our Thoroughly Federal Constitution." In *How Federal Is the Constitution?* edited by Robert A. Goldwin and William A. Shambra. Washington, D.C.: American Enterprise Institute.

Fiorina, Morris P. 1977. *Congress: Keystone of the Washington Establishment.* New Haven, Conn.: Yale University Press.

Garcia v. San Antonio Metropolitan Transit Authority. 1985. 469 U.S. 528.

Goldwin, Robert A., and William A. Schambra, eds. 1987. *How Federal Is the Constitution?* Washington, D.C.: American Enterprise Institute.

Gramlich, Edward M. 1982. "An Econometric Examination of the New Federalism." Brookings Papers on Economic Activity.

————. 1985. "Reforming U.S. Federal Fiscal Arrangements." In *American Domestic Priorities,* edited by John M. Quigley and Daniel L. Rubinfeld. Berkeley: University of California Press.

Gramlich, Edward M., and Deborah S. Laren. 1984. "Migration and Income Redistribution Responsibilities." *Journal of Human Resources* 19:489-511.

Grodzins, Morton. 1966. *The American System: A New View of Government in the United States,* edited by Daniel J. Elazar. Chicago: Rand McNally.

Helms, L. Jay. 1985. "The Effect of State and Local Taxes on Economic Growth: A Time Series–Cross Section Approach." *Review of Economics and Statistics* 67:574–82.

Houseman, Gerald L. 1986. *State and Local Government: The New Battleground.* Englewood Cliffs, N.J.: Prentice-Hall.

Jeffrey, William, Jr. 1987. "The Constitution: 'A Firm National Government.' " In *How Federal Is the Constitution?* edited by Robert A. Goldwin and William A. Schambra. Washington, D.C.: American Enterprise Institute.

Jewell, Malcolm E., and David M. Olson. 1982 *American State Political Parties and Elections.* Homewood, Ill.: Dorsey.

Kennedy, Mary M., Richard K. Jung, and Martin E. Orland. 1986. *Poverty, Achievement and the Distribution of Compensatory Education Services.* Washington, D.C.: U.S. Department of Education.

Kettl, Donald F. 1983. *The Regulation of American Federalism.* Baton Rouge: Louisiana State University Press.

Ladd, Helen F., and Fred C. Doolittle. 1982. "Which Level of Government Should Assist the Poor?" *National Tax Journal* 35:323–36.

March, James G., and Johan P. Olsen. 1984. "The New Institutionalism: Organizational Factors in Political Life." *American Political Science Review* 78:734–49.

Mayhew, David. 1974. *Congress: The Electoral Connection.* New Haven, Conn.: Yale University Press.

Nathan, Richard P., and Fred C. Doolittle. 1987. *Reagan and the States.* Princeton, N.J.: Princeton University Press.

National League of Cities v. Usery. 1976. 426 U.S. 833.

Oates, Wallace E. 1972. *Fiscal Federalism.* New York: Harcourt Brace Jovanovich.

Palmer, John L., and Isabell V. Sawhill, eds. 1982. *The Reagan Experiment.* Washington, D.C.: Urban Institute.

Peterson, George E., and Carol W. Lewis, eds. 1986. *Reagan and the Cities.* Washington, D.C.: Urban Institute.

Peterson, Paul E. 1981. *City Limits.* Chicago: University of Chicago Press.

Peterson, Paul E., Barry G. Rabe, and Kenneth K. Wong. 1986. *When Federalism Works.* Washington, D.C.: Brookings Institution.

Polsby, Nelson W. 1968. "The Institutionalization of the United States House of Representatives." *American Political Science Review* 62:144–68.

Shepsle, Kenneth A. 1986. "Institutional Equilibrium and Equilibrium Institutions." In *Political Science: The Science of Politics,* edited by Herbert F. Weisberg. New York: Agathon.

Shepsle, Kenneth A., and Barry R. Weingast. 1981. "Political Preferences for the Pork Barrel: A Generalization." *American Journal of Political Science* 25:96–111.

Stein, Robert M. 1984. "Municipal Public Employment: An Examination of Intergovernmental Influences." *American Journal of Political Science.* 28:636–53.

Sundquist, James L. 1986a. *Constitutional Reform and Effective Government.* Washington, D.C.: Brookings Institution.

———. 1986b. "American Federalism: Evolution, Status and Prospects." Brookings Discussion Paper in Governmental Studies.

Tiebout, Charles M. 1956. "A Pure Theory of Local Expenditures." *Journal of Political Economy* 6:413–24.

Tribe, Lawrence H. 1978. *American Constitutional Law.* Mineola, N.Y.: Foundation Press.

Wahlke, John, Heinz Eulau, William Buchanan, and Leroy C. Ferguson. 1962. *The Legislative System.* New York: John Wiley and Sons.

Walker, David B. 1981. *Toward a Functioning Federalism.* Cambridge: Winthrop.

Wright, Deil S. 1979. *Understanding Intergovernmental Relations.* Belmont, Calif.: Duxburg.

PART

★ V ★

Conclusion

⋆ 11 ⋆

The Empowering and Protective Concerns of American Constitutionalism

FREDERICK M. WIRT

The contributors to this volume have examined the effects of the U.S. Constitution on the development of American political institutions. This concluding chapter incorporates their insights and observations into a larger schema of understanding. The overview focuses on two basic concerns lying at the heart of American constitutionalism—the desire to make governmental power effective and the desire to protect citizens against its abuse.

These twin concerns—empowerment and protection—are so fundamental to any system of government attuned to the necessity of limiting coercive power that they are easily overlooked in efforts to explain how systems of government operate and evolve. At the same time, they were at the heart of the founders' struggle to devise a workable, responsive framework for government; the effects of their labors are still visible in the American political arena, as the authors have so forcefully demonstrated. The role of these twin concerns in the development of constitutionalism is first described, and then their ongoing importance is illustrated by the contributor's analyses. Concluding observations suggest the future course of empowerment and protection in the ever-evolving American political system.

Protection and Empowerment

Before the founders met at Philadelphia in 1787, they were familiar with a stream of ideas that can be traced to at least ancient Greece.

We need to understand these origins to appreciate the founders' contributions to the concept of contitutionalism and to apprehend more fully a fundamental tension in politics. From Aristotle's "polity" and Hellenic city constitutions through the Roman Republic and on to the medieval institutions, there has been a concern with protecting society—or some elements in it—from unrestrained authority in the hands of those who ran the state (Freidrich, 1968:chaps. 1, 7; McIlwain, 1947). This element of constitutionalism we term the *protective concern*.

In the beginning, Aristotle and other Hellenes sought restraints against tyranny to provide a society with internal stability and strength. The society was an all-encompassing *politeia*, variously defined in Aristotle's *Politics* as "an imitation of the best and noblest life," "the soul of the *polis*," and "the life of the city." The all-inclusive nature of *politeia* was captured by Charles McIlwain: "It means above all the state as it actually is. It is a term which comprises all the innumerable characteristics which determine that state's peculiar nature, and these include its whole economic and social texture as well as matters governmental in our narrower modern sense" (1947:26). As Aristotle noted, constitutions were to embody these qualities primarily because they shaped citizens' virtue. It was inconceivable that the reverse could occur, since no notion of empowerment of government by citizens existed then. As for dealing with abuse of power, what they termed "tyranny," there was no recourse but revolution.

Later, Roman constitutionalism evolved to define restraints on all public offices to secure not only Aristotle's goals—stability and strength—but also protection for the individual. The Romans advanced the idea, no matter how corrupted in practice, that the people were the source of all law. Some medieval political theorists built on this idea to argue that governmental acts were not legitimate unless they conformed to law. One medieval version of constitutionalism sought to restrain autocrats to protect certain groups in society, in this case the Roman Catholic church. This protective concern is also evident in another constitutional stream, the Magna Carta's limits on a monarch; other European nations later developed such charters to restrain their princes. This stream, however, did not apply to the Roman Catholic church; indeed, Pope Innocent III voided the Great Charter.

In later centuries, recognition of the people as the ultimate sovereign eventually led to the distinction between public and private law, which limited (in principle) what government could do within certain spheres. Judge Bracton argued that when government acted outside public law, it was bounded by legal principles of the common law. Over time, as the individual emerged as the central focus of the political order, constitutionalism was linked to democracy. Two separate strains of political theory became meshed. Indeed, in this view citizens made government and their charters, a most unhellenic concept. As Thomas Paine wrote succinctly in *The Rights of Man*, "A constitution is not the act of government but of a people constituting a government." Thereafter, as democracies sought their roots in constitutionalism, an explicitly political orientation emerged. Carl Freidrich noted that "if we ask what is the political function of a constitution, we find that the core objective is that of safeguarding each member of the political community as a person. Each man is supposed to possess a sphere of genuine autonomy. The constitution is meant to protect the *self*; for the self is believed to be the primary and ultimate value. This preoccupation with the self, rooted in Christian beliefs, eventually gave rise to the notion of rights which were thought to be natural" (1968:8).

The protective concern of constitutionalism also deals with a self that has a dark side—its self-destructive capacities. Politics in any society can open up those capacities with dreadful consequences for citizens. Constitutions, then, become protections against that dark side of the self. Murray Edelman encompassed these fears of the unrestrained self when observing that the Constitution "becomes the concise and hallowed expression of man's complex and ambivalent attitude toward others: his wish to aggrandize his goods and powers at the expense of others; his fears that he may suffer from powerful positions of others and from their predations; his seeking for an encompassing principle that will introduce stability and predicability into this explosive clash of interests" (1967:19).

The U.S. Constitution is clearly imbued with this protective concern. Its preoccupation with the division of powers, with what later was termed judicial review and federalism, and with civil rights and liberties speaks to that concern. These elements were not totally new, as the authors of *The Federalist Papers* point out. They did, however, speak directly to concerns for individual liberties, and they did so in a way that was balanced and innovative.

The history of constitutional struggles in Europe involved limiting governmental power, but the founders had to balance this historic concern with another. The failure of the Articles of Confederation had sensitized them to the necessity of investing their new government with powers that would make it effective in dealing with national problems. This necessity gave rise to what we term an *empowering concern*. That provision carried a problem with it, for there is an inherent tension between protection and empowerment. This tension could be resolved only by an ambiguous, formal separation of powers among a set of institutions that then had to cooperate in a structured policy-making process to operate effectively on the nation's problems. The tension required ambiguity of expression in the document and collaboration in the policy process.

The extent to which the balancing of protective and empowering concerns preoccupied the framers is suggested by the space given to allocating powers, as seen most clearly in Article I, Section 8. That section encompassed their efforts to deal with the substantive problems of war and peace, commerce among nations and their own states, and taxing and spending. In their judgment, these were real problems of national survival and social order with which the Articles of Confederation simply could not cope. Facing equivalent problems, later generations of Americans would greatly expand the meaning of these substantive powers. This adaptability in the face of new problems has often been cited as the major advantage of the U.S. Constitution. That the Supreme Court would permit the central government to regulate production on a small farm wholly outside the flow of interstate commerce (*Wickard v. Filburn*, 1942) vividly symbolizes how changes in society can bring the adaptive qualities of the Constitution into play.

A key to understanding how this adaptability has evolved can be found in the interaction between protective and empowering concerns as they have been institutionalized in the Constitution. That document's architecture of power contained internal design features that subsequently generated elaborate rituals of interaction among the branches. Although separated in the Constitution, the presidency, Congress, and courts are united in the policy-making process. The intensity and complexity of their interactions increased dramatically as social and economic changes led to demands for greater government involvement in more facets of life. Increased government activity led to more interaction between the levels of government, whose powers are both specific and ambiguous in the Constitution. This heightened government activity also stimulated an expansion of the rights guaranteed to individuals, which in turn affected how well governments could exercise their newfound empowerments. The individual's right to engage in electoral, party, and interest group activities ensured the effective representation of citizen concerns.

The founders' contribution to the evolution of constitutionalism is a written social compact that strikes a workable balance between these two fundamental concerns. It blends them in such a way that its institutions subsequently were able to respond to change by expanding on the Constitution. While specifying the powers and structure of government, the expanded Constitution acknowledges that the people are sovereign and enjoy certain inalienable rights, concepts transferred into our political culture through the Declaration of Independence. Given the ancient history of tyranny they knew so well, the insults of contemporary regal power they had endured, the failure of their initial efforts to establish a government, and the fears of unrestrained ambition in their own people, the founders were acutely aware of the need for a balance between protection and empowerment. It was this combination of political needs that stimulated their ingenious blend of structures and procedures in the original document. Similar needs would cause later generations to expand the Constitution through judicial review, intergovernmental accommodations, and constitutional amendments.

Understanding the Development of the Original Branches

The founders conceived legislative, executive, and judicial branches as instruments for addressing matters of national importance and as reciprocal checks that would limit the abuse of governmental power. These empowering and protective concerns necessarily underlie any discussion of these branches. Empowering the national government in any era has triggered protective concerns among those who fear their interests would be injured by that empowerment; the strengthening of any single branch has also generated similar fears of governmental encroachment on freedom. This situation was anticipated—even desired—by the authors of *The Federalist Papers*. They could not see how any permanent protection of freedom could develop except in the context of a division of power, thus setting "ambition against ambition." The major branches would incorporate the tension and uncertainty attendant in all policy-making. Better to live with ambiguity, the Constitution makers presumed, than to live with unrestrained power. History told them clearly what to expect with a lack of restraints, so ambiguity seemed a reasonable price to pay to achieve the requisite empowerment. The contributions in this section nicely illustrate the ongoing struggle to deal with this ambiguity within the framework of government structured in the Constitution.

Congress and Empowerment

The central, indeed almost dominant, role in policy-making the founders ascribed to the national legislature is evident even at first glance. It is the *first* article that deals with the Congress, and it is also in this article that the major powers of the new national government were placed. Clearly intending to build an institution to reflect their empowerment and protective concerns, the founders established two houses, whose subsequent history demonstrates how purposes can be thwarted—but also fulfilled—by intervening events.

Those events were particularly dramatic in the case of the House of Representatives, as David Brady's essay soundly demonstrates. The founders' protective design of a system of single-member districts underlay, even helped create, a later decentralization in the party system and an incrementalism in national policy-making. Those latter developments actually protected the interests of localized society, since each local unit wanted to protect itself from other interests that might use the policy powers of Congress to thwart it. However, the party system could dampen, if not contain, this threat by giving the "home folks" control of nomination, election, and legislative voting.

National policy-making consequently required no major changes, except in emergencies; the threat of change to this localized system created an interest on both the national and subnational levels to protect it. Such protection fitted quite well with the founders' views; one could thus guess they would have approved the structural and electoral fragmentation affecting national policy-making that Brady's historical analysis demonstrates. Understanding the protection of localism to be a driving force in the politics of their time, the founders would have understood why that force drove subsequent history.

While the founders (with the exception of Alexander Hamilton) did not want an all-powerful national government and so did not seek it, they did want one that was able to deal with issues of national importance. They did not construct a government that could not work at all (the Articles of Confederation was example enough for them); rather, they created a government that could work when a widespread need for action arose. That empowerment concern was evident in the early nationalist programs of a Hamilton or Marshall. Brady's analysis of three later periods of critical elections demonstrates exactly what resulted in the House when such national needs arose. In all three periods, plagued by problems of abolition, industrialization, and social welfare, the national government took on more power, which was never subsequently relinquished. National power was further enhanced by the need to wage war, a need that overcame sectionalism and united Congress in every war of the last hundred years.

Limitations on national power were also intended when the founders devised the U.S. Senate. As Charles Stewart III demonstrates, although they intended this body to be a conservative influence in policy-making, their provisions were overcome by events in one case but effective in another. The electoral provisions to provide checks on popular influences in the Senate were overcome by the rise of parties and the expansion of the electorate. Both developments enabled Senate candidates to reach over the head of state legislatures to parties and voters—even before adoption of the Seventeenth Amendment. As a result, popular concerns began to influence the Senate, whose membership became even less stable than the House's during this century. Ironically, that change also enabled it to remain an important part of national democratic policy-making, unlike upper houses in other democracies.

The founders' provisions for the Senate's internal structure produced a different result, for they actually did conservatize that body, as Stewart shows. Its small size, federal role, and informality enabled the Senate to develop with few limits on individual members and with a power structure that could not firmly control the legislative process, unlike the conditions in the House. The historical record Stewart presents clearly demonstrates the Senate has had periods of even greater conservatizing influence than exists today. But even now, it looks like a body the Constitution makers would have hoped for.

The implications for the founders' twin concerns are clear in these analyses of the Congress. Incrementalism was expected, and it became the norm. Increasingly, that norm has been reinforced by ever-decreasing party control and by ever-increasing institutionalization in the two houses. That result would accord with the intent of the Constitutional Convention. Crises that are perceived among elites or citizens can, however, influence the work of Congress; the results were not always immediate because a fragmented localism did not always perceive a crisis in the same way. In most eras, this body, rooted in neither monarchy nor confederation, could satisfy localism by resisting policy innovation. Empowerment and protection thus kept an uneasy balance throughout our history, their tensions muted by the decentralized nation. That is why there was great insight in Speaker of the House "Tip" O'Neill's aphorism, "All politics is local."

The Presidency: Protection and Empowerment Fused

Scholars of the presidency constantly seek metaphors to enhance understanding of its operations and political role. In this volume, Bert A. Rockman uses market theory to add an insightful corrective to the simplistic notion of the "imperial" presidency. The primacy of concerns for both protection and empowerment underlie much of his analysis. In Rockman's view the president is in competition for control of a policy market. The role of profit is parallel to that of "ambition" exemplified in *Federalist No. 51*, for it is a force driving humans to be channelled creatively and carefully. Competition across branches of government can protect citizens and their interests from a presidential monopoly of power, with all the inherent dangers of any monopoly. When Congress will not cooperate with the president, the costs of policy action become too high and a decision cannot be supplied. This constraint accounts for the policy system's traditional adherence to the status quo rather than to nonincremental leaps. Major policy innovations occur only when demands for governmental services arise that are strongly felt and widely expressed. Only then are the mutual interests across branches strong enough to bring about the level of cooperation necessary for fundamental, nonincremental change.

Rockman's historical analysis is instructive about the interplay between protective and empowerment concerns as the presidency evolved. During the Republic's first century, the national government focused on economic development policy. Strongly supported by the public, such policy depended more on Congress and political parties than on the president. When consensus was absent, however—as with slavery—the national policy system could not act, except to go to war. The presidency dominated the conduct of that war and reunification, albeit with competition from Congress. Then, as now, the protective concern produced a system "in which state sovereignty was a powerful norm and through which institutions of representation in Congress were organized to reinforce this norm." In light of these factors, the Constitution normally operated with the presidency outbalanced by other institutions in the control of the policy supply.

The first third of the twentieth century opened with stirrings of presidential power that had always been latent in that office. Theodore Roosevelt and Woodrow Wilson expressed the need for national leadership to serve national goals, and they acted on this idea. The Progressive movement's goals of efficiency, effectiveness, and direction in the political system were realized in state and local policy and structural reforms. These values were also echoed by some presidents, especially Theodore Roosevelt with his "stewardship" theory. He wanted to identify national goals that could best be realized by a newly empowered leader. His perspective foreshadowed the much stronger presidents of the last half-century, the era of the modern presidency.

In Rockman's words, "The defining characteristic of the modern presidency is the assumption that presidents are at the center of the political system; that if they fail, the system fails." Traumatic events of the depression and wars greatly weakened the controls of the past (e.g., the local party system and congressional leadership) as popular demands obliged presidents to supply policy. In nontraumatic periods, however, presidents still struggled (often unsuccessfully) with Congress over supplying policy. The Supreme Court also imposed constraints on the president in domestic matters. These constraints help explain why recent presidents, especially Richard Nixon and Ronald Reagan, have turned to using executive authority and politicizing the bureaucracy. Competition drives the president to enlist other powers to control—if not monopolize—the policy supply. Even then, as presidents have discovered, the federal courts can block some policy actions on constitutional grounds. As it is now, Rockman concludes that "presidents have not been bashful about asserting their prerogatives, and Congress has not been timid about seeking to constrict these. . . . Uncertainty reigns because we are in exactly the situation Madison foresaw—a clash of ambitions with no definite resolution."

Bureaucracy: Administration as Governance

The general lack of specific references to administration in the Constitution bespeaks an era when the bureaucracy was tiny and its important role not yet understood. The founders, however, had a broad notion of administration. As Hamilton noted in *Federalist No. 72*, "The administration of government, in its largest sense,comprehends all the operations of the body politic, whether legislative, executive, or judiciary. . . . " Aspects of the Constitution, especially its concern for protection and empowerment, also influenced the growth of the "fourth branch of government."

That development has been shaped by changing notions of what administration was supposed to do and how it would affect citizens. David Rosenbloom's contribution to this volume admirably synthesizes these different views of administration, providing a coherent statement of diverse trends. His contribution emphasizes the way in which constitutional values drive the political process, specifically, the way in which administration is increasingly viewed as a process of governing within a "democratic constitutional" system.

Rosenbloom contends there have been continual tensions between the administrative state and democratic constitutionalism over structures, procedures, legitimacy, and especially civil rights. Each of the three branches has sought to control administrative agencies. The presidency has tried to control them through appointments and budgets, the Congress through oversight and the legislative veto, and the judiciary through control of presidential discretion. But these statutory and administrative constraints were insufficient to control fully a growing public administration.

New views of administration thus arose over time, centered on guardianship, spoils, or business efficiency. The newest perspective considers administration as governance that has been "constitutionalized through the declaration of new rights for individuals as they come into contact with government agencies and officials." This perspective has brought in its wake many changes in how the federal bureaucracy operates. These changes include new rights for clientele and public employees, more representation of the diverse public, more openness and citizen participation, more checks and balances within the administrative system, and administrators' greater personal responsibility to bodies outside the bureaucracy. As Rosenbloom explains these changes, all are attributes of administration conceived as democratic governance.

These changes are constraints, and they match the Constitution's protective and empowering concerns. Each new constraint protects citizens against bureaucratic abuse of power, either by opening up decision making or by ensuring that authority is exercised only in accordance with law. Each new constraint also ensures that government is empowered to take into account views other than just the professional administrators'. It is not surprising, then, that these dual concerns have caused public administration to become, to use Rosenbloom's term, "constitutionalized."

The Supreme Court: Keeper of the Constitution

Popular support for the special role the Supreme Court plays in interpreting the Constitution, a role unmentioned in its text, is understandable in light of that body's deeply held protective concerns. Judicial review has also been useful in delineating and clarifying the powers of government under the Constitution. The role of the Court in these matters is clear in Lawrence Baum's analysis, which focuses on the area of civil rights. The Court's protective concerns were evident in this area before 1937, when it was primarily protecting business and property rights; a similar concern is evident when later it expanded civil rights. Earlier courts had their own policy interests—John Marshall's nation-building programs, Roger B. Taney's slavery and Civil War issues, and economic regulation after that war. None, however, has played as active a role as has the modern Court, which echoed the more active policy of the other branches. Baum notes, for example, that nearly half of the Court's decisions to overturn federal, state, and local laws have been made since 1950.

Such activism, Baum notes, is driven by the Constitution itself, with its vague terms of empowerment and its imposition of limits across branches. Vagueness invites definitions, and limitations require an umpire when the play of the policy game crosses the foul lines. Popular acceptance of the Court's role as keeper of the Constitution's terms has legitimized the Court's pronouncements on the boundaries of governmental action. At the same time, the Constitution imposes severe constraints on what the Supreme Court can do to limit the activities of the other branches, especially certain policy domains (economic policy and national security). Thus, although the Court has voided parts of many federal laws in recent decades, only a few have been of major importance. When confronted by a federal branch determined to pursue a particular course of policy, the Court normally recedes, at least in time. This judicial deference has done much to strengthen the power of the other branches to address pressing and ever-changing societal needs. At the same time, those branches exercise their powers ever mindful that their actions can be reviewed by the keeper of the Constitution. That Banquo's ghost sits in at every decision-making council within the other branches.

Growth in the Supreme Court's activism, Baum notes, has had another important consequence for the political process. If the nature of the Constitution drives the judiciary to play a role in the formation of public policy, there then exist more arenas in which political conflicts can be resolved. The major example may be the search by blacks for a favorable arena in the civil rights movement. They focused on the Supreme Court because access to the other branches was either blocked or problematic. The emergence of the Court as an alternative policy arena has meant an increase in the number of groups participating in the judicial arena; their success in it reinforces the Court's stature and legitimacy as a policy actor.

Understanding Extraconstitutional Institutions

That the U.S. Constitution exists beyond a framework of governing institutions can be seen clearly in the political institutions that developed around the framework subsequently. The framers knew that future needs and developments would give rise to new demands on governmental institutions and stimulate the growth of extraconstitutional bodies that would play a crucial role in the political process. The most important of these are political parties and interest groups. Their development gave meaning to the notion of popular sovereignty on which the Great Convention founded the Constitution. Traditional American concerns with empowerment and protection have stimulated citizens to create political parties and pressure groups for political action that led, in time, to "big government" at all levels. The development of these institutions nicely demonstrates the interactive nature of these dual concerns.

The Three Faces of Party and Citizen Empowerment

The party system that emerged in the 1790s has moved from domination by a national elite to extreme decentralization and mass membership. Despite the fact that the Constitution did not mention political parties, it has had a marked impact on their development. Their evolution furthers our understanding of how the

Constitution's concerns with protection and empowerment shaped the U.S. political process.

To discuss the role of the Constitution in the formation of U.S. political parties, it is necessary to differentiate their three basic components—party-in-the-electorate, party-in-the-organization, and party-in-the-government. The Constitution's role in the development of the party-in-the-government was quite direct. Fragmentation of powers gave rise to a need for coordination across and within branches of government, and parties emerged to fill that need. Although competition within and between parties remains the norm except during periods of crisis, political parties are one of the few cohering agents in the U.S. political process. Even though party loyalty may fail at any point in the policy process, parties still remain a key factor in congressional voting, judicial selections, and administrative appointments. It may be unrealistic to expect more regimentation from parties, given that they must operate within an intentionally fragmented and decentralized governmental structure.

The Constitution's role in shaping the party-in-the-electorate was much more indirect. The electorate has been gradually expanded by enfranchising discrete groups. These expansions have invariably been sought by one party or another, always with an eye toward enlarging its popular base. But the continual broadening of the electorate is not unrelated to constitutional values and concerns. Perhaps the most important of these is the sentiment expressed in Thomas Jefferson's assertion in the Declaration of Independence that "all governments derive their just authority from the consent of the people." The Constitutional Convention's notes and *The Federalist Papers* constantly referred to "the people" because "just consent" had provided a legitimate alternative to royal absolutism. Although founders thought of "the people" as *their* kind of people (see their reflections on property-holding as a condition for voting), they advanced a justification that could be extended to *other* kinds. From an era of limited suffrage to our own era of full suffrage, party-in-the-electorate has always been rooted in the most fundamental principle of the Constitution—popular sovereignty.

The shape of the party-in-the-organization was fundamentally affected by another constitutional principle, federalism. The Tenth Amendment, which reserved to the states and people all but the delegated powers of the national government, meant in time that states had the power to build party organizations. Across the noncentralized system of federalism, party organization became a matter for the states to decide. More important, this meant that power in the party organization would be localized, consonant with that same localism that drove the actions (and inactions) of the Congress, as noted earlier. Consequently, from the Jacksonian to the modern era, national political parties have been only loose confederations that assemble quadrennially to nominate a presidential candidate. Recent efforts by their national committees to provide funding and expertise demonstrate a thrust that is still only supplementary, not supplanting.

Are these constitutional influences on political parties special to the United States? Kenneth Janda's contribution to this volume is an exploration of that question. He seeks the causal connection between separation of powers and federalism on the one hand, and party decentralization on the other. Among twenty-two democratic nations Janda examines, the United States is the only country that has a functioning federalism and separation of powers and whose constitution does not have explicit provisions for political parties. Janda concludes that U.S. parties are much more decentralized than others because of constitutional provisions for federalism and the fragmentation of powers. Party ideology and institutionalization also help explain decentralization in political parties, as do a nations' physical characteristics, socioeconomic qualities, and statutory requirements for parties.

These findings have important implications for party reform, as Janda points out. It may be necessary to remold the U.S. system of government before meaningful party reform is possible. The party system, after all, was developed out of the structural and ideological interstices of the U.S. Constitution. A decentralized party system emerged because the founders had to accept the vitality of localism in national politics and policy. Control of national government became undisciplined and inefficient because the framers believed this condition preferable to the dangers of a strong central government; virtually every subsequent generation has assented to that belief. Finally, an expanded electorate developed because of the founders' passion for the idea that only the people should legitimate a constitution and its exercise of authority. The result was a political arrangement in which electoral participation guarded against many abuses of federal power and an empowered federal government was responsive, in the main, to broadly based policy demands.

Pressure Groups: Federalist No. 10 *Writ Large*

The framers were keenly aware of the presence of diverse interests or "factions," and, indeed, pressure groups were to become a legitimate extension of the First Amendment's protection of the right of assembly. While the founders worried about these groups' potential for shaping government for their exclusive benefit, they recognized the vital role these groups played in a healthy political system. The framers wanted to ensure that these groups could mobilize and articulate their interests, but they felt a need for some arrangements to protect against their potential abuse. Pressure groups thus fell under both the protective and empowering concerns of the Constitution.

The few pressure groups Madison described in *Federalist No. 10* were but a fraction of those that later emerged. This growth has been unparalleled over the last few decades in Washington, in the states, and in the fifty state capitals. Even policy-advocacy networks, which originated in the abolition and temperance movements of the last century, exist today. This recent growth has developed in large part because of new and broad issues now engaging many citizens—environment, consumer safety, education, welfare, and rights for women and minorities. Indeed, interest group activity has even worn the cloak of "public interest." A factor underlying this growth was a more educated citizenry that learned to play the game of pressure politics. This area of growth notwithstanding, the largest increase in pressure groups has come from elsewhere—the business sector. Because of heightened governmental involvement in contemporary society, the business community has learned more sophisticated ways of affecting public policy.

In his contribution to this volume, Graham K. Wilson traces the Constitution's effects on the role played by interest groups in the American political process. Fragmentation of powers facilitated group activity by providing multiple access points to decision making, buffering major threats to the interests of large groups, making difficult the unification of groups in a corporate style, blocking secrecy about government action, fostering policy-making power in iron triangles, and using the judiciary's requirements to limit some legislative options. In addition, due process requirements strengthened these groups vis-à-vis bureaucracies, and federalism weakened political parties that otherwise could have taken over the functions of pressure groups. One strength of Wilson's analysis is the comparisonison of U.S. and European pressure groups. Especially instructive are the ways in which the latter cohere, interact privately with unified party leadership, and arrive at policy decisions in a less fragmented manner. Much of the difference in group behavior may be traceable to different governmental arrangements in the Europe and the United States. Wilson's discussion of neo-institutionalism further stresses the importance of those differences.

His analysis can be extended to our protective and empowering concerns by noting the founders' views about the necessity of such groups as a condition of freedom. They saw pressure groups not in corporatist terms but rather as a reflection of a pluralistic society, providing a vital connection between citizens and government. They were the only effective way, other than elections, by which the people could influence government to support their interests. The founders also exhibited a protective concern for pressure groups in the First and Fourteenth amendments, which prevent the government from constraining the formation or activities of such groups. That protective concern has been maintained by Supreme Court decisions in the modern era.

The Constitution and the Extended Republic

Although the framers were conscious of their state loyalties to a degree almost unfathomable to modern Americans outside the South, they also believed that the passion for state authority was destroying the Articles of Confederation (a view that some modern analysts dispute). They knew their proposal would require a large majority of the states to adopt it. A political awareness of state sensitivities thus permeated their deliberations on most aspects of the new government. That awareness forced them to seek balances between state guarantees (e.g., extending full faith and credit to the states) and state limits (e.g., supremacy of the national law). This balancing was the basis of the famous compromise between the large and small states.

Most of the founders expressed an elaborate defense of the necessary role of states. States would not be abolished but would be made "constituent parts of the national sovereignty [by various provisions]" (Hamilton, *Federalist No. 9*, a view he might not have believed privately). A more explicit defense was set out by James Madison's classic design in *Federalist No. 51* for an "extended republic" operating under federal principles. By dividing power between two levels of government and subdividing it within each, "a double security arises to the rights of the people." Moreover, Madison asserted that giving the states an independent power would "render an unjust combination of a majority of the whole very improbable, if not impracticable [because] the society itself will be broken into so many parts, interests and classes of citizens [that] a majority . . . could seldom take place on any other principles than those of justice and the general good. . . . "

Two essays in this volume, reflecting the diverse topics and methods in the current study of federalism, examine how this institution has evolved and operated within a changing constitutional framework. They demonstrate the great variety of responses the fifty states have provided to basic questions of governance. They also illustrate another important theme implicit in this book. Much standardization has occurred among state governments, a development directly related to the preeminent empowering document, the U.S. Constitution. The national Constitution has had a standardizing influence on state constitutions, originally the prime protector of rights. Also, the recent development of intergovernmental coalitions working through all levels and all branches has standardized the way in which the needs of the American people are served.

None of this is to contend that the standardization among the American states is either pervasive or inevitable in all matters. Indeed, federalism has always permitted diversity to flourish. The framers saw such diversity as a healthy sign in the political system; today its influence still limits any centralizing thrust. This diversity, however, always lives in uneasy balance with the forces of standardization. Together these two factors exert an important influence on policy-making at the state level. In major respects, standardization and diversity have worked to enhance the ability of state governments to meet citizen needs, while also furthering the protective concerns that so preoccupied the framers.

The Garden of State Constitutions

No better example of the joint effects of diversity and standardization exists than the evolution of state constitutions. In this garden of governance, both ivy and wildflowers bloom. Each has deep roots in differing attitudes of localism and in a common American suspicion of government. These documents emerged early in colonial life, even though they were not drawn from the British tradition.

Judaic, Catholic, and Protestant beliefs have helped foster their development by conceiving individuals in a "covenant," or contractual arrangement, with God, with all the attendant duties and responsibilities that a contract entails. In a parallel tradition, colonial entrepreneurs customarily worked through the instrument of a company charter, with its consequent obligations. And, of course, British theorists like John Locke laid a philosophical basis for the political compact. Out of this context, starting with Massachusetts in 1780, each state produced a constitution that defined and limited the authority of both government and citizens.

As Kermit L. Hall's contribution points out, these constitutions had much in common, acknowledging legitimacy in the people, vesting fragmented authority among branches, and protecting citizens with judicial review and civil rights. It is as if the states gave the same answer to a universal question: what should government look like? But the states evidenced much diversity in answering another question: how do we fit government to our own distinctive culture? The mechanisms of operating similar types of government have varied because different historical roots have shaped citizens' expectations of the political system. While the basic structures of these constitutions remained constant over two hundred years, their details have altered—and proliferated—so much that, as Hall concludes, "they have increasingly become codes rather than fundamental frames of government."

The national Constitution has had a significant impact on state constitutions, not merely because of the supremacy clause. Far more important was its imitative influence. Article IV, Section 4, orders the federal government to guarantee "a republican form of government" for new states, and Hall suggests that leaders in would-be states thought it politically prudent to define that phrase by mimicking the constitutions of the federal government and existing states. Much the same dynamic shaped prospective states' responses to congressional requirements. Nevertheless, state constitutions came to reflect much diversity. As Hall concludes, what followed for the states "can be understood as a working out of the implications of the incomplete nature of the federal document. Succeeding generations of Americans have adapted their organic laws to changing social and economic circumstances." Incidentally, that result also includes state policy innovations that were later adopted in the federal Constitution.

While state constitutions yielded to the national document, they have evolved in several traditions, as Hall aptly points out. States in the nineteenth century wrestled with issues special to each era, such as the role of political parties, race, and economic development. In addressing those issues, they increasingly wrote their policy decisions into new versions of their constitutions, thereby insulating policy from legislative interference. It is a picture of shifting constitutional provisions in response to changing ideas. But underlying these evolving state constitutions were concerns for both empowerment (e.g., public services that legislatures would provide) and protection (e.g., safeguards against abuses by party government). The emphasis, however, was on the latter, since "antigovernmentalism" pervaded all states. In the twentieth century, the Progressive movement attempted to supplant this earlier negativism by making government a mix of rational administration, democratic procedures, and antiparty constraints. Also important in this century have been changes in state constitutions introduced from above by the U.S. Supreme Court. Their force extended the protective concerns of the founders to recognize the rights of minorities against encroachment by state governments. The wildflowers of differences and the ivy of national influence thus combine to produce a garden of state constitutions. The U.S. Constitution's influence has been pervasive and durable in yet another aspect of our political system.

Intergovernmental Coalitions in American Federalism

The framers believed that coalitions of the states might grow so great as to imperil the national government's functions. Except for the Civil War, they were wrong in this prediction, but they were sensitive to the possibility that intergovernmental arrangements might arise, and here they hit the mark. In the last third of the twentieth century, mighty institutions of empowerment were created to link all governmental levels. Indeed, so prevalent have such practices become that federalism is today most often studied as "intergovernmental relations," frequently involving private groups seeking public resources from all levels to promote their policy services. Obviously, the Constitution's empowering concern is not simply just a national matter.

John Chubb's chapter documents some recent changes in the underpinnings of intergovernmental institutions. These institutions are increasingly supported by elected and administrative personnel in the states who find strong inducements to continue the federal programs of recent decades. These recent developments stand in sharp contrast to the longer, earlier history of federalism, the foundation of which was "long unsettled and almost constantly shifting." Ambiguities in the Constitution's very terms invited conflict and uncertainty when different levels of government sought to act. From the New Deal era onward, however, more agreement was achieved. A centralized set of institutionalized practices arose providing a more settled foundation to federalism.

Dramatic evidence of this expansion is seen in the post-1950 growth of federal grants-in-aid to help state and local governments in their policy services, particularly in nonredistributive areas. This process was stimulated in part by congressional members' desire to be reelected; that goal could be furthered by claiming credit for federal grant benefits or assisting constituents with red-tape problems over these services. Decentralization within Congress after 1970, giving more members more influence over such policies—and hence over their reelection—also fostered a supportive environment for more generous federal grants.

In the face of this growth, Chubb observes, the Reagan administration very energetically sought to cut back program authority and funding. This attempt to retrench was only modestly successful, however. Most of the cuts came in the 1981 budget reconciliation and tax reduction laws, and later efforts to institute major cuts were unsuccessful. Grant assistance remains popular in the Congress as this century draws to a close. Categorical grants take up a larger share of all grant expenditures, Congress now ties strings on block grants, and President Ronald Reagan's dramatic offer to states and cities to swap federal programs died aborning. In sum, pressure from below to retain the programs remains strong and persistent, despite recent and continuing federal deficit problems.

Meanwhile, the federal thrust that began in the early part of the twentieth century has built cooperative and supportive institutions among the states and their policy agencies. Earlier conflict among levels diminished as intergovernmental bureaucracies developed to implement programs effectively. Federal programs have had built-in incentives for subnational bureaucracies to cooperate in policy implementation, reflected in the latter's growth in numbers under the stimulus of federal aid, regardless of which party controls the state house. As a result, bureaucracies have developed the ability to administer these programs despite cutbacks from Washington. In turn, they have become the most powerful local advocates for subnational policy action. Moreover, Chubb reports, they connect with their state legislators and client interest groups to form classic "iron triangles." All three segments thereby become part of this intergovernmental institution and—above all—become lobbyists for the status quo to maintain federal programs.

Conventionally held beliefs about the fate of elected officials do not hold in such an institution. Chubb found that state elections since 1940 were affected less by state than by national matters, such as the success of national candidates. Further, little evidence emerges to attribute state electoral outcomes to the condition of the state economy. If officials have less to fear from voters on state economic matters, over which they have little control, they may pay more attention to matters they do control, such as federal grant programs. This logic contributes to their continuing commitment to intergovernmental programs.

Chubb's analysis crystallizes, as well as adds to, a developing understanding of a new breed of federalism. The growth of grant programs, which created clients and attracted officials' support from outside Washington, was once thought to be vulnerable to reduction. The Reagan administration, however, tested that possibility and found it wanting. Everywhere there is evidence of the potential for growth at all levels of government. There has always been a latent potential in the Constitution for the expansion of government at any level. What the national government might do under the vaguely worded Article I, Section 8, was never really known, and the same applies to states under the Tenth Amendment. Furthermore, these ambiguous terms of empowerment could be expanded by the principle of popular sovereignty, which implies that popular will can redefine what government should do.

These potentialities became realities in the last few decades. Moreover, this growth has an air of permanency about it, reflected in two facts: federal and state governments clashed less frequently over program administration during the 1970s, and they successfully resisted the retrenchment efforts of a very popular president in the 1980s. In sum, the Constitution permitted standardization of policy action across the states, and the localism of American politics stimulated this new kind of federalism.

Historical Change and the Dilemma of Empowerment and Protection

Our review of these various contributions to understanding the dual concerns of protection and empowerment suggests an enormous growth in both. The rains of historical change have nurtured the seeds planted by the founders. On the one hand, as government at all levels does more, it provides more rewards for more beneficiaries. The catalogue of beneficiaries is at least as long as the list of pressure groups in the Washington phone directory. Add to these beneficiaries the officials in the family of American governments, and we see how vastly different our political world is from that of two centuries ago. Whether these benefits come as subsidies of one's interests or as regulations of opponent's interests, and whether the instrument is persuasion, inducement, or coercion, the scope of empowerment is unprecedented. Always the legitimation of this empowerment lies in a Constitution that shaped much of it directly and indirectly.

On the other hand, the potential for abusing governmental power, far harder to catalogue, is much greater now than in earlier eras. But we have also constructed new safeguards and expanded old ones to ward against that potential. These safeguards include Supreme Court decisions on the three branches' relations and on civil liberties; congressional committee oversight and members' casework staff; executive coalition constraints; bureaucratic controls; and the spread of political action committees and legislative lobbies. There are also over 50,000 annual elections, with their potential to correct abuses of power. Although that opportunity has decreased as incumbency has increased (96 percent in the House elections of 1990), the possibility of defeat—no matter how faint—still moves legislators to be cautious about abusing power. To all this, add the increasing education of the public, which motivates more people to challenge abuses. There is also the blanketing effect of the media, always eager to ferret out abuses that will bring journalistic distinction.

This enlargement of both empowerment and protection—much of it in the last half-century—is but a new variant of the older concerns. Such changes are always inherent in the practice of constitutionalism, as Carl Freidrich's magisterial analysis of world constitutions has noted: "Constitutionalism is an achievement of the modern world. . . . Indeed, it is a very complex system of providing for orderly change, and there is no reason for assuming that the need for change will come to an end in the immediate future" (1968:4). Change is not beneficial to all involved, however. Growth in both empowerment and protection raises the inherent conflict that exists between them. Can protective mechanisms continue to be generated to counter new abuses that attend the growth of empowerment? American history shows frequent occasions when new policies created new abuses, often unintended, that took time to counter with new protective mechanisms. Equally worrisome are imbalances in empowering and protective concerns that arise when change stimulates the perennial majority-minority problem.

Clearly, social change has been the driving force for constitutional developments throughout U.S. history. Empowerment and protection can be reinforcing—as can be seen with the growth of bureaucracy and of litigation to expand civil rights and liberties—but these concerns can also be in conflict. It is along these lines of political response to systemic change that constitutional theory and practice evolve. It is in this evolving sense that we can see how change can be a creative force for society and its governance—a notion alien to ancient Hellenes and also painful to modern citizens undergoing it. If change is looked upon as intrinsically necessary and unavoidable, then, as Freidrich notes, "The question is . . . how to turn such change to good account, how to adapt political life to the changing social context in order to secure the greatest satisfaction for the people" (1968:6). In answering that basic question, this volume is a testament to the role played by the Constitution in modifying the forces of change to meet its concerns about empowerment and protection, both of which will continue to shape the future of our political system.

REFERENCES

Edelman, Murray. 1967. *The Symbolic Uses of Politics.* Urbana: University of Illinois Press.

Fairfield, Roy P., ed. 1981. *The Federalist Papers.* Baltimore: Johns Hopkins University Press.

Friedrich, Carl J. 1968. *Constitutional Government and Democracy: Theory and Practice in Europe and America.* Waltham, Mass.: Blaisdell.

McIlwain, Charles H. 1947. *Constitutionalism, Ancient and Modern.* Ithaca, N.Y.: Cornell University Press.

Wickard v. Filburn. 1942. 317 U.S. 111.

Notes on Contributors

DAVID BRADY is a professor of political science and of business and politics at Stanford University. He is the author of *Critical Elections and Congressional Policy Making* and *Congressional Voting in a Partisan Era.*

LAWRENCE BAUM teaches political science at Ohio State University. His research interests include judicial decision making, the behavior of specialized courts, and voting behavior in elections to state office. He is the author of *The Supreme Court* and *American Courts.*

JOHN E. CHUBB, a senior fellow at the Brookings Institution in Washington, D.C., since 1984, specializes in issues of education, federalism, and political institutions. His most recent book is *Politics, Markets, and America's Schools,* coauthored with Terry M. Moe.

KERMIT L. HALL is a professor of history and law at the University of Florida, where he teaches courses in American constitutional and legal history. His publications include *The Politics of Justice; A Comprehensive Bibliography of American Constitutional and Legal History;* and *The Magic Mirror: Law in American History.* He has been a Fulbright scholar in Finland and a visiting scholar at the American Bar Foundation.

KENNETH JANDA is Payson S. Wilde Professor of Political Science at Northwestern University, where he has taught since 1961. He is the author of *Political Parties: A Cross-National Survey* and coauthor of *Challenge of Democracy.* He is currently studying the factors that induce change in political parties across nations.

PETER F. NARDULLI is a professor of political science at the University of Illinois at Urbana-Champaign and holds a joint appointment in the Institute of Government and Public Affairs. He is author of

The Tenor of Justice and is currently working on a study of the structure of electoral change in the United States from 1828 to 1984.

BERT A. ROCKMAN is a senior fellow in the Governmental Studies Program at Brookings Institution and a professor of political science and a research professor in the University Center for International Studies at the University of Pittsburgh. He is currently working on a twenty-year time series study of senior executives in the U.S. federal government.

DAVID H. ROSENBLOOM is Distinguished Professor of Public Administration at the American University, Washington, D.C. He also serves as editor in chief of the *Public Administration Review.* Among his books are *Federal Service and the Constitution; Bureaucratic Government, USA* (with D. Nachmias); *Representative Bureaucracy and the American Political System* (with S. Krislov); *Public Administration and Law; Public Administration: Understanding Management, Politics, and Law in the Public Sector;* and *Toward Constitutional Competence: A Casebook for Public Administrators* (with J. Carroll).

CHARLES STEWART III is Cecil and Ida Green Career Development Associate Professor of Political Science at MIT. He is the author of *Budget Reform Politics* and several articles on budgetary politics, the history of Congress, divided government, tax reform, and Senate elections.

GRAHAM K. WILSON is a professor of political science at the University of Wisconsin–Madison. He has written numerous books on interest groups, including *Interest Groups; Business and Politics;* and *Interest Groups in the United States.* He is currently involved in a comparative study of politics and senior bureaucrats.

FREDERICK M. WIRT is a professor of political science at the University of Illinois at Urbana-Champaign. He is the coauthor of *Schools in Conflict* and *Culture and Education Policy in the American States* and the editor or author of several collections and articles on local and state policy-making. He also writes on urban politics and American federalism.

Index

Bowsher v. Synar, 170n.13
Bracton, Henry de, 295
Brady, David, 22, 180, 298-99
Brant v. Finkel, 126
Brennan, William, 164
British Medical Association, 222
Brownlow Committee, 126, 128
Brown v. Board of Education, 153,
172n.19, 239, 253
Bruce, Harold, 181
Bryan, William Jennings, 46
Bryce, James, 180, 248-49
Buckley v. Valeo, 124, 170n.13, 218
Bureaucratization, 122. See also Administrative state, development of
Bureau of Land Management
(BLM), 215
Burger, Warren, 126, 144, 161
Burnham, Walter Dean, 44
Bush, George, 117, 272
Business Roundtable, 223
Butler, David, 47

Calhoun, John, 29n.1, 81
California Constitution, 250-51, 255
Canada, 169n.9, 184-85
Cannon, Joseph, 110, 111
Cardozo, Benjamin, 6
Carter, Jimmy, 112, 128, 170-71n.15,
262
Ceaser, James, 106
Central Hudson Gas and Electric Corporation v. Public Service Commission of New York, 211
Central Intelligence Agency (CIA), 212
Chamber of Commerce, 223
Charter of Rights and Freedoms (Canada), 169n.9
Checks and balances: in House, 35;
and interinstitutional checks, 19, 21,
25, 28, 38, 39, 181; and political parties, 40; on presidency, 97; presidential evasion of, 128-29; in public administration, 140-42, 144, 145; in Senate, 85
Cheney, Richard, 128
Chile, 211
Chisolm v. Georgia, 29n.1
Chubb, John, 26, 311-13
Citizen participation. See Participation

City of Mobile v. Bolden, 170-71n.15
Civil liberties, 150, 158, 159-64, 211,
249, 255, 295, 303, 314
Civil Rights Bill of 1960, 90
Civil rights movement, 16, 87; and discrimination in federal bureaucracy,
138; and legislation, 89-90; and New
Deal, 40; public employees' participation in, 136; and Supreme Court rulings, 219, 238-39
Civil service, 108, 112, 133. See also
Administrative state
Civil Service Commission, 141
Civil Service Reform Act of 1978,
138, 141
Civil War: administrative battles
following, 29n.2; decline of state
constitutions following, 249; industrialization following, 16, 45, 266-67;
and partisan realignment, 45, 46,
48-49, 50, 52-53; reconstruction
following, 41, 156, 157, 237; and sectionalism, 38; and Southern secession, 29n.1, 45, 52, 58n.9, 58-59n.10,
235, 266; and state sovereignty, 106;
strengthening of federal government
following, 13; suspension of habeas
corpus during, 83
Clay, Henry, 81, 85
Cleveland Board of Education v. Loudermill, 136
Cloture, 88, 90, 91
Colorado Constitution, 250
Community Action Program, 140
Compromise of 1850, 45
Confederation of British Industries
(CBI), 227
Congress. See U.S. Congress
Congressional Budget Office, 129
Congressional Government
(Wilson), 108
Connecticut Constitution, 257n.11
Consolidated Edison Co. v. Public Service Commission of New York, 218
Constitutionalism: and American values, 14-16, 21, 27; ancient, 293-94;
and commercial republicanism, 245;
commonwealth tradition of, 244-45;
contractual tradition for, 245-46, 249,
251; federalist tradition of, 243-44;

Index